PRAISE FOR

# WE STARTED WITH RESPECT

"You'll be drawn in by the compelling story that unfolds and energized by the lessons it reveals. If you're serious about transforming your team, your department, your organization, let *We Started with Respect* be your guidebook to improving your leadership and the precious lives in your span of care!"

—Bob Chapman, CEO of Barry-Wehmiller, Author of *Everybody Matters: The Extraordinary Power of Caring for Your People Like Family,* named no. 3 CEO in *Inc.* magazine

"In *We Started with Respect,* George Saiz shows what it really takes to lead with respect and how to create a high-functioning people-learning organization that delivers results through engaging its people. Through an engaging story of leadership and organizational transformation, readers follow the journey from a struggling to flourishing organization and can draw lessons to apply to their own practice. Let *We Started with Respect* be your blueprint for how to create the alignment, processes, and skills you need to create meaningful impact for yourself, your team, and your organization."

—Katie Anderson, Leadership and Learning Coach, Keynote Speaker, Lean Consultant, Japan Study Trip Leader, Author of *Learning to Lead, Leading to Learn: Lessons from Toyota Leader Isao Yoshino on a Lifetime of Continuous Learning*

"Timing is everything! *We Started with Respect* delivers a front-row-seat journey to the best thinking on culture and leadership both team members and firms are starving for. The world has changed. Fulfillment, engagement, and creating value have become essentials for success. This book is a must-read to unlock the potential in any organization."

—Paul Eidenschink, Co-President and COO, Steffes LLC

"I have visited and benchmarked more than 100 exceptional companies representing a wide variety of industries over the past twenty years. Most of these companies are recipients of very prestigious awards and have been written about in many books and publications. Even these companies struggle to connect all the dots—they excel in many areas but still have gaps in others. In *We Started with Respect*, George Saiz connects the dots in a realistic and captivating story of a company—maybe much like yours—that goes on the journey, fights the inevitable battles, and produces extraordinary results."

—Greg L. Williams, Former Lean Director, Aera Energy LLC; President, Western Sensei Consulting

"George Saiz has done the impossible: he has written a business-based book with the right balance of leadership principles and great storytelling that captures your attention. While the storytelling is excellent, the learning is even better. By following the company's journey from a struggling team to a successful company-saving product launch, George walks us through the steps of managing change and building an enduring team. I found myself relating to the characters and the challenges they faced along the way. Well done."

—Darril Wilburn, Senior Partner, Honsha.org

"This is 'transformational leadership' at its finest and a must-read from both an educational and practical-application perspective. The future of successful leadership is dependent on specific critical elements—as you will learn from author George Saiz's real-life experience—in this descriptive and well-written book.

"From the boardroom to the shop floor, communication, building relationships, and respect are just a few of those key elements addressed. If you have the desire of becoming a successful growth leader, this is an important tool for you, whether you're a new or an experienced leader in business."

—Diane Michelucci, MBA, Executive, General Electric Company

"In *We Started with Respect*, George Saiz provides the answer to the most vexing business challenge of our times—how to lead organizations to success through uncertainty. Through the narrative of the book, the required leadership disciplines unfold such that veteran and aspiring leaders alike can unlock the value in their own leadership approach. I will be using George's work with my team, and I encourage others to do the same."

—Brian Wellinghoff, Director of Strategy Improvement Culture, Barry-Wehmiller

"My first reaction to reading *We Started with Respect* was that George Saiz had retold our transformation story at Wiremold, save for the order of a couple of elements. This book reflects a true picture of what a lean journey looks like by a *leader* who has implemented the *journey*. It emphasizes that respect is fundamental, leadership engagement is essential, and running the business in parallel is both challenging and necessary.

"*We Started with Respect* establishes a road map for any leader to follow when launching their lean journey and developing a winning culture, aimed at establishing a successful and growth-oriented business."

> —Dick Ryan, Former President, Shape Electronics; Former Lean Journey Leader, Barry-Wehmiller

"George Saiz's *We Started with Respect* presents a practical road map for developing a healthy and effective culture that fosters employee engagement and continuous improvement. In our rapidly changing and competitive business environment, creating a culture where all employees contribute is no longer a 'nice-to-have' but a 'must-have' to thrive.

"Saiz's guide will make your company journey easier to navigate, with real-world examples of pitfalls and workarounds. Saiz draws upon his years of experience in business leadership to provide an easily digestible handbook, filled with practical insights that will provide wisdom as you chart your course forward and inspiration for when you hit the inevitable bumps in the road."

> —Allan R. Coletta, Senior Director of Engineering and Facilities, Siemens Healthineers

"After working with George through three company transformations, he has shown that his clear observations and implemented changes make a difference. He not only attacks the operational weaknesses, but like the company in *We Started with Respect*, he deals with the people issues that make up the basis for those difficult changes."

> —Tom Weisel, President, Arch Day Design

"George knocked it out of the park. This book is a breath of fresh air and puts the whole package together. Many times, I've seen groups trying to implement improvement plans, yet they're only marginally effective.

"The good news is this book lays out a road map of the key elements to success. It shows you how to successfully build an environment where the group truly is a team, which differs significantly from situations where the word 'team' is just the newest fad. There's also enough guidance to let the reader know and celebrate the differences within their respective organizations. Well done."

—Bill Coy, President, Velocity Orthopedics

*We Started with Respect*
by George Saiz
© Copyright 2023 George Saiz

ISBN 979-8-88824-035-9

All rights reserved. No part of this publication may be reproduced, stored in a retrieval system, or transmitted in any form or by any means—electronic, mechanical, photocopy, recording, or any other—except for brief quotations in printed reviews, without the prior written permission of the author.

This is a work of fiction. All the characters in this book are fictitious, and any resemblance to actual persons, living or dead, is purely coincidental. The names, incidents, dialogue, and opinions expressed are products of the author's imagination and are not to be construed as real.

Illustrations and infographics: Meghna Kamboj

Published by

**köehlerbooks**™

3705 Shore Drive
Virginia Beach, VA 23455
800-435-4811
www.koehlerbooks.com

# WE STARTED WITH RESPECT

A N~~OVE~~L **BLUEPRINT**

# GEORGE SAIZ

VIRGINIA BEACH
CAPE CHARLES

# TABLE OF CONTENTS

Preface ............................................................................. 1

Organization Chart ........................................................ 4

Character Biographies ................................................... 5

Prologue ........................................................................ 11

Chapter 1: Careful What You Wish For ....................... 16

Chapter 2: All Aboard the Burning Platform .............. 21

Chapter 3: A Weekend at the Beach: If I Were in Charge ... 31

Chapter 4: Laying the Foundation: Part One .............. 38

Chapter 5: Laying the Foundation: Part Two .............. 62

Chapter 6: Laying the Foundation: Part Three ........... 81

Chapter 7: Let's Hear from Everyone ......................... 101

Chapter 8: Spreading the Word .................................. 122

Chapter 9: The Meeting at Corporate ........................ 132

Chapter 10: The Work Begins ..................................... 139

Chapter 11: A Framework Takes Shape: Part One .... 143

Chapter 12: A Framework Takes Shape: Part Two — 155

Chapter 13: A Framework Takes Shape: Part Three — 173

Chapter 14: Timing Is Everything — 186

Chapter 15: "The Only Person Who Likes Change Is a Wet Baby"—Price Pritchett — 205

Chapter 16: Time Flies By Fast: Part One — 219

Chapter 17: Time Flies By Fast: Part Two — 237

Epilogue — 253

Acknowledgments — 254

Reflections — 255

Appendix — 265

References — 283

About the Author — 285

# PREFACE

Many years ago, for the first time, I read a business book written as a novel. It was *The Goal* by Eliyahu M. Goldratt.

The format was revolutionary to me and kept my interest from beginning to end. It also provided me with the opportunity to share the book with my wife without her being overwhelmed by a lot of complex business concepts. She could follow the story while learning more about what I was going through in my first business transformation experience. I have likewise structured this book as a novel, allowing the story and its characters to be a vehicle for bringing the ideas and methods to life.

I've read business books that have been insightful but left me wondering how to apply the concepts practically. My goal here is to share ideas on how to transform your team, your department, or your organization while also providing a blueprint of what that might look like. However, my intent is to be descriptive, not prescriptive, so I encourage you to take what you learn here and design a plan tailored to the needs of your business. There's also a section at the end of the book titled "Reflections," which provides questions for each chapter that you, or your team or book club, can review in order to take that first step in evaluating your current state—much as the company in this story does.

Finally, I wrote this book through the eyes of one main character, Jason Bailey, as company president, and two other characters: Bryan O'Conner, the supply chain manager; and Jimmy Marino, a distribution associate—three roles I've held in the past. I've taken the liberty of sharing my experiences and perspectives while in those positions and from throughout my career.

Enjoy the book.

George Saiz

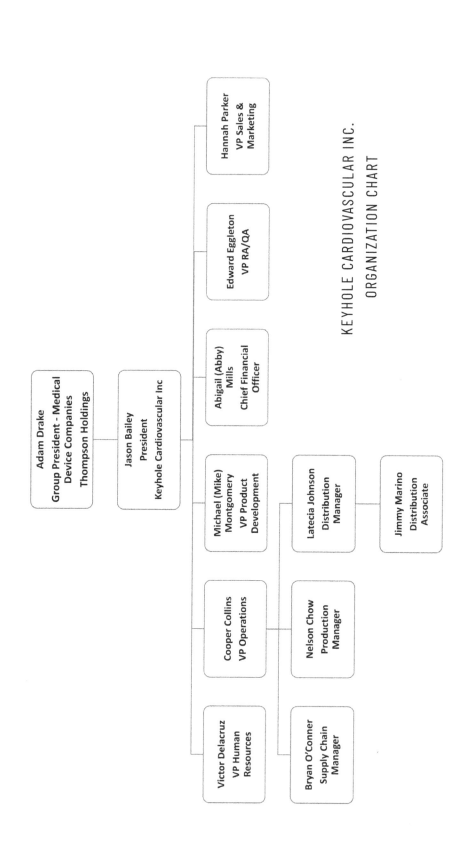

# CHARACTER BIOGRAPHIES

## ADAM DRAKE:

*Group President, Medical Device Companies, Thompson Holdings*

Adam Drake, a Stanford graduate, comes from the farming town of Fresno in Central California. He's a balanced leader with good listening skills and is a lifelong learner. His business philosophy is based on three tenets: take care of the people part of the business; do everything with the highest of integrity; and always consider the long-term health of the organization in any decisions.

## JASON BAILEY:

*President, Keyhole Cardiovascular, Inc. (KCI)*

Jason Bailey, a UCLA graduate, attended the school on a basketball scholarship, which resulted in him having the best seat in the house for some great NCAA clashes. Jason and Adam enjoy ribbing each other based on the results of the latest UCLA–Stanford games, especially during football and basketball seasons. Jason's sports background helped shape his competitive nature. He's extremely optimistic—perhaps to a fault—and an outgoing person who communicates well. He has good business instincts and aspires to, as he says, "grow people who grow businesses." Jason has been married for sixteen years and has two daughters entering their teens.

## SENIOR LEADERSHIP TEAM: KEYHOLE CARDIOVASCULAR, INC.

### VICTOR DELACRUZ:
#### VP Human Resources

Growing up in East Los Angeles, Victor Delacruz has overcome several challenges. He lost an older brother through gang activities and vowed not to follow the same path. He worked his way through college, earning a business degree at Cal State University, Dominguez Hills. He's a committed family man with five kids and promotes a family environment at the company. Victor joined KCI two years ago.

### COOPER COLLINS:
#### VP Operations

Over the past twelve years, Cooper Collins has worked his way up through almost every operations position there is until being promoted to vice president two years ago. Although he never completed his business degree, he's a "get it done" kind of guy who always says, "Get me the parts, and I'll put it together."

Employees like working for Cooper and appreciate his balanced approach to business. He spends many of his weekends out on his fishing boat. He's been married for thirty-five years and has two grown sons.

### MICHAEL (MIKE) MONTGOMERY:
#### VP Product Development

The company is living on the strength of an innovative technology Mike Montgomery helped develop twelve years ago when he was an entry-level product development engineer fresh out of the University of California, Irvine, Engineering School. Mike was recently promoted to the position of VP of product development and has been challenged to revive the new product pipeline. He has built excellent relationships throughout the company and has a strong internal motor while presenting an even-keeled approach. On weekends, Mike helps his wife with her fast-growing home-based craft business.

## ABIGAIL (ABBY) MILLS:
### Chief Financial Officer (CFO)

Upon graduation from the University of California, Berkeley, Abby Mills joined the PwC audit team and, over a ten-year span, progressed into a management position with the firm. KCI had been a client of hers for three years when the incumbent CFO retired, and Abby pitched herself for the role. With a good feel for the business, she had already developed solid relationships with members of the senior leadership team. Once in place, new president Jason Bailey agreed Abby would be a great fit at KCI and completed the hiring process. Abby believes the senior financial role is much more than being a high-level scorekeeper and uses leading indicators (predictive measurements) instead of lagging indicators (making decisions based on history) to provide a set of eyes and ears for the company. Abby is single and spends her spare time volunteering with inner-city kids.

## EDWARD EGGLETON:
### VP Regulatory Affairs & Quality Assurance (RA/QA)

Edward Eggleton, a software engineering graduate of DePaul University in Chicago, made his way out west as an intern for a major manufacturing software development company. While working with manufacturing teams, he developed a strong interest in the quality and regulatory aspects of the medical device companies for which he consulted. Once an opportunity came up for a mid-management role in quality assurance at a medical device company, he applied and got the job.

He progressed through numerous roles and, just over a year ago, was found by the recruiter conducting the search for the VP position at KCI. Edward is single and still dabbles in software development with hopes of one day developing his own app.

## HANNAH PARKER:
### VP Sales & Marketing

Hannah Parker joined KCI as a sales rep upon completing her business degree at San Diego State University. After six years in the field—and dominating the individual national sales awards for the latter three of those years—Hannah was promoted to sales manager for the western region. Her region went on to set the pace for the next four years, and when the VP role opened, she applied and was a consensus selection. The recruiting team hoped she could replicate her regional success at the national/international level. Hannah is still learning the marketing side of the business but is aggressive and has a good business head. She's been married for four years, and she and her husband are discussing the possibility of starting a family.

# OTHER KEY EMPLOYEES

## BRYAN O'CONNER:
### Supply Chain Manager

Bryan O'Conner joined KCI as a distribution associate right out of high school. Early on, he became interested in the supply chain area and started working on his college degree at night. He caught a break when there was a need for an entry-level buyer and was selected by the hiring manager.

Bryan went on to complete his bachelor's degree in business at night and through hard work progressed up to the managerial level. He has built excellent relationships throughout the organization and across the supplier base. He is a continuous learner and aspires to the VP of operations role in the future. Bryan is a newlywed (one year) and enjoys camping with his wife and hitting the Southern California beaches when they can.

### NELSON CHOW:
#### Production Manager

Like Bryan, Nelson Chow joined the company out of high school, as a production associate in the mechanical assembly department. Nelson is a hard worker and can put almost anything together—probably because he and his dad spent a lot of time together restoring 1960s and 1970s muscle cars. Nelson is a highly respected leader throughout the production areas. He's single but is interested in finding the right person to settle down with.

### LATECIA JOHNSON:
#### Distribution Manager

Growing up in a family of seven kids in Chula Vista, California, Latecia Johnson is a mom to four of her own. She expects her employees to work hard, make minimal errors, and get along. Although not into the relational side of leadership, she's fair minded. Latecia's done an excellent job of preparing young talent to go on to roles of additional responsibility within KCI—something she's proud of.

### JIMMY MARINO:
#### Distribution Associate

Jimmy Marino is a young man who's trying to figure out where he's going in life. He applied for the job at KCI based on the recommendation of a friend who also works there in distribution. Having taken a few college courses, Jimmy still has no real direction. Right now, he just needs a job so he can pay his living expenses and take his girlfriend out on fun dates. He's always been smart enough to get by and has some natural leadership abilities. Jimmy dreams big but has no idea how to achieve those dreams. Maybe he will find his future at KCI.

## PROLOGUE

Jason Bailey wore his favorite olive-green suit with a blue shirt for the interview—something he hoped might distinguish him from the other candidates, even in a small way.

He'd already been through two phone interviews and an in-person lunch meeting with the recruiting firm, as well as a third phone interview with Adam Drake—for whom he'd be working if he got the position.

The recruiter had let Jason know that he was one of three final candidates for the job of president of Keyhole Cardiovascular, Inc. He wasn't so much nervous as he was anxious to meet Adam and discuss the opportunity face-to-face. They seemed to have good chemistry on the phone, but it was hard to tell for sure in a thirty-minute call.

The opportunity was in Carlsbad, California, north of San Diego, but Jason had flown up the coast for this interview at the Thompson Holdings headquarters in Palo Alto, just outside San Francisco. He'd be meeting with Adam first, then the key executives of Thompson Holdings, followed by a wrap-up with Adam at the end of the day.

Upon arrival, Jason was escorted into Adam's office, where he was shown a seat at a small conference table. Apparently, Adam was on his way back from another meeting and would be in "momentarily." Jason looked around the neatly furnished office, which showed signs of a Stanford graduate and a person who enjoyed the outdoors.

A moment later, Adam walked in and introduced himself.

"Jason, I know you've probably heard most of this or have been able to piece it together, but let me briefly set the table for what this opportunity is about. Then we'll get into the interview, and finally we can discuss any questions you've prepared for me. Feel free, though, to ask if something comes to mind along the way."

"Will do," said Jason.

"We'll begin at the top. Thompson Holdings started thirty years ago with its first acquisition of a struggling industrial electronics manufacturing firm," said Adam. "Its focus remained on industrial electronics until fifteen years ago when it was the highest bidder for an electronics company, this time based in medical devices. Today, the Thompson Holdings portfolio consists of sixty-five companies, of which ten are based in medical devices."

Adam continued, "I joined Thompson Holdings nine months ago as group president for the medical device companies. A priority for me was to assess Keyhole Cardiovascular, or KCI, and determine how to get it back on track.

"As a startup, KCI helped pioneer minimally invasive cardiovascular surgery in which procedures are completed through small portals or 'keyholes,' hence the company name. The keyhole approach is less traumatic to the patient, and, in many cases, the surgery can be completed without taking the heart to a full stop.

"Through the innovative products KCI developed in its early days, it was able to pull many of the world's leading cardiovascular surgeons into its camp. However, most of the folks who developed and marketed those products left at the end of their buyout contracts, taking with them some hefty payouts. The company lost its competitive edge and now hosts a portfolio of outdated technology products. As a result, its financials have shown lower than average market rate growth in sales and earnings.

"To better understand those results, I spent time on-site and talked to as many people as I could. What I found was a disconnected company. There was a lack of leadership and alignment—a lack of direction—and no signs of teamwork.

"Product development was underfunded and had become stagnant. The operating systems were described as 'homegrown.'

Also, there had never been an internal investment made in culture or leadership, which left employees feeling disengaged. It appeared that many were just going through the motions. They said it was a decent place to work—not great, but they could do a lot worse."

Adam paused.

"You've painted a pretty bleak picture so far," thought Jason, before realizing he'd said it out loud.

"Yeah," said Adam. "And I'm sure there's even more once someone spends time digging in there. Still sound like something you're interested in?"

"Yes, absolutely," Jason responded immediately. "Early in my career, I was hired into a similar situation and was also told I'd probably need to replace several staff members. However, by providing direction and developing a team approach, we were able to turn the business around without any personnel changes.

"Since then, every job I've taken has required some type of transformation. Honestly, I enjoy the challenge and seeing the change that occurs in people as we go through it. Once you solve that part of the puzzle, you're able to go after the business issues with a coordinated attack. My personal mission statement is to 'grow people who grow businesses.'"

Jason continued, "I'm just one person, or one piece of that puzzle, so I like to envision what three hundred, one thousand, or ten thousand employees committed to working together can do to improve and grow a business. From what you shared, KCI could benefit from that."

Adam beamed. "They sure could! I appreciate your mission statement and vision—both simple and straightforward. And yes, I was pleased to see the turnaround experience in your resume and in the recruiter's comments. It appears you have a lot of expertise in this area; although, has it been on this scale?"

Jason thought for a moment before he replied. "Hmm. Scale could apply to either the size of the company or the scope of the turnaround. My current company is smaller in size, but much like KCI, it also needed a complete transformation, and it's been a fantastic growth opportunity for all of us who've been involved."

He continued, "I was surprised to hear from your recruiter as I wasn't looking for a new opportunity, but I was intrigued with this one. Being in the cardiovascular market myself for the past twenty years, I was aware of the splash KCI made with its revolutionary approach. When you hear something like that, you find yourself wondering what happened at this company for it to get into the position it's in today. Once the recruiter explained your commitment to rebuild it, well, it sounded like a great challenge, and I thrive on those."

"I'm glad you're interested; I didn't expect a different response," said Adam. "It looks like this is a good fit with what you've done previously. I'll want to hear more about those transformations and your role in them. By the way, I've worked through several turnarounds myself, so whoever is selected can count on me as a sounding board when they develop their strategies and/or make key decisions. My management style is more hands off: I believe my role is to provide resources, integrate you into Thompson Holdings, and then help remove any unnecessary corporate roadblocks and generally provide support when you get stuck.

"I'll be there to help—not to dictate."

Jason nodded. "That's reassuring, Adam, and makes the job even more appealing. How do you lead the medical device group? Are there any tenets by which you like to manage?"

"Good question," said Adam. "Yes, I work with the company presidents to jointly establish three principles: First and foremost, take care of the people. Second, abide by the most ethical standards—which includes staying out of the gray. Third, in all decisions, do everything for the long-term health of the company."

Jason smiled. "All three resonate with me."

He felt their chemistry growing as the interview continued and thought about how good it would be to take on a challenge of this magnitude with a leader like Adam supporting him.

As the day went on, Jason thought the interviews with the Thompson Holdings executives went equally well. The wrap-up meeting with Adam seemed comfortable, and he advised Jason that they would be deciding soon and would be back in contact with him.

On the plane home, Jason reflected on the day's discussions. It would be a fantastic opportunity for whoever got the job. He recalled that in his first turnaround situation, he hadn't had any real experience and went into it blindly. As they say, "Ignorance is bliss." Jason had worked his way through every new problem that arose, but the challenges had seemed endless. He didn't know back when he started that it would be such a long and sometimes lonely road.

The difference this time was that he had a pretty good idea how much work it would take to get the company going in the right direction. If he got the job, he knew exactly where he would start.

# 1
## CAREFUL WHAT YOU WISH FOR

It had been almost five months to the day since Jason Bailey had been offered the role as president of Keyhole Cardiovascular, Inc., (KCI) with the challenge to "breathe new life" into this stagnant company. When he joined, KCI was in full survival mode, living off a legacy of products that no longer competed. But he'd already taken steps to get those wheels turning.

Jason had just arrived back to his office after lunch and was going through email when he heard a quick knock on the doorframe. Before he had a chance to look up, Mike Montgomery burst into Jason Bailey's office, beaming from ear to ear.

"It works, Jason. I think we nailed it!" he almost shouted. "We've been in the lab since early this morning working on our latest idea for a safe pathway to the surgical site, and we got there! We had to make a few adjustments to the procedural tools, and it's still a little rough, but we can focus on optimization and complete everything that will be needed from here."

Seeing Mike's face light up, Jason knew a breakthrough was in the making. Perhaps the doorway to the future had been cracked open.

More than a decade ago, KCI had released its initial breakthrough product in part due to a novel idea of Mike's, then a young engineer who was fresh out of college. That product paved the way for an innovative approach to open-heart surgery, which propelled the company into national prominence.

After Jason had been on the job for two months, he'd recognized the passion, the connection, and the talent Mike had for product development and promoted him into the vacant VP role. He immediately tasked Mike to take his engineers back into the operating room to observe surgery and to look for opportunities for product innovation. While attending a procedure still being performed via open-heart surgery, one that—according to most surgeons and the other medical device firms in this arena—did not lend itself to the minimally invasive approach, Mike had a radical idea.

He shared with Jason that if he could figure out a safe pathway to the surgical site, he was confident his team could develop the tools for surgeons to complete this unique approach. Jason listened and approved the formation of a "skunkworks" team—in that it was an unbudgeted and unapproved project but certainly an idea worth digging into.

KCI was now sitting on a concept that could potentially propel the company back into a market leadership position.

"That's huge, Mike! You and your team have got to be excited. OK, given a methodology and the supporting products, what's your best guess at the timeline to get this to market?" Jason asked, trying to curb his own excitement.

Mike responded, "I won't bore you with the details, but it's likely an eighteen-to-twenty-four-month project. Let me sketch out what that might look like for you."

He proceeded to outline the steps he and the product development team would be going through: from rough prototypes to bench testing, to cadaver trials, to working with key surgeons to optimize the procedure. He explained that, along the way, they would be filing with the FDA for 510k product approval, a three-to-six-month process.

Finally, once the required testing and approvals were completed, he planned to allow an additional six months to scale up manufacturing. Totaling it up for Jason, he landed right in that window between eighteen to twenty-four months for market release.

"I'll get the staff together, and we can share this with everyone. Great job," Jason said as he shook Mike's hand. "This is just what we needed."

A product of this significance was critical to the revitalization of KCI. Without something like it, it would be difficult to reverse the company's downward spiral. But it was also only one step in the overall process. In Jason's mind, the company had survived for too long off its early success and never developed the foundational systems or culture required to support a growing enterprise. From what he understood, a lot of the senior decision makers made a lot of money in those early days, and then complacency crept in.

Future sustainability was never on the agenda in the executive conference room.

The Keyhole Cardiovascular name still carried weight in the market, and Jason intended to do everything he could to move it back to the forefront. Mike had experienced a breakthrough, and sooner than expected, which caused Jason to reflect on something his mom had always said to him: "Be careful what you wish for because you just may get it!"

He sent a quick note to his assistant and asked him to get the senior leadership team together as soon as possible. He had this very moment in mind when he began crafting the makeup of the team. It was comprised of carryovers from the past, an internal promotion, and one outside hire. He intentionally tried to bring together a mix of wild-eyed dreamers, conservative thinkers ("boat anchors," if you asked the dreamers), and then some in the middle of those mindsets who were open minded but also understood the need for structure. Jason believed his job was to help them become a team—in fact, *the* team—that would lead this company into the future.

There were, however, other questions on Jason's mind, like just how committed Thompson Holdings, the parent company, was to KCI. He'd covered the topic of commitment quite extensively during the interview process but was aware of another medical device company within Thompson Holdings that also competed in the cardiovascular market. KCI catered to the cardiovascular surgeon, while its sister company made products for perfusionists, the professionals who manage the patients' blood and oxygenation circuit while on bypass surgery. Same overall market, but different end users.

With an opportunity of this magnitude, Jason still harbored concerns in the back of his mind.

So far, Jason had seen total support from Adam Drake, the group president of medical device companies for Thompson Holdings. Their professional chemistry had continued to grow since the initial interviews, and they shared a similar vision for the pathway to KCI's revitalization. However, Jason wasn't convinced the rest of the Thompson Holdings' team was of the same mindset.

In Jason's first quarterly corporate review, Adam's line of questioning had been focused on the steps Jason was taking to establish the foundational business elements at KCI, while some of the other leaders—especially the new corporate chief financial officer—appeared more interested in the bottom line and the steps Jason and his team were taking to turn around some of their more glaring deficiencies.

Through Jason's internal assessment, he'd determined there was significant work to do in every functional area to build quality and depth into their systems—especially now, if KCI was to commercialize a new surgical procedure. Moreover, he'd found that KCI never focused on developing a cultural identity or leadership model, which he believed to be two essential building blocks in a successful company's business plan.

He knew from experience that without an intentional plan, culture and leadership had a nasty habit of simply evolving on their own.

A student of culture and leadership models, Jason had taken the opportunity to benchmark some of the best companies in the country. He'd been granted access to these sites for a few years now as a result of joining a group of CEOs who met regularly to share their challenges and the solutions they'd implemented in their companies. Members of the group were noncompetitors and agreed in principle that it was OK to "shamelessly steal"—as they called it—from each other. Their facilitator, an advocate of seeing best-practice sites in person, had organized tours of companies around the country that implemented "best in class" solutions. Jason had gone on each of these go-see trips.

He knew it was the right time to finalize his thoughts and bring everyone together to develop the cultural identity of this organization.

Mike Montgomery's outline of the product development milestones had provided the timeline with which they had to work: a two-year window. Jason thought about all that needed to be accomplished to capitalize on this opportunity successfully while satisfying the watchful eyes of Thompson Holdings. First things first: they'd need to develop their plan and then secure buy-in from Adam Drake and corporate leadership.

# 2

## ALL ABOARD THE BURNING PLATFORM

The next morning, Jason was first to arrive for the hastily called meeting at which Mike would share the product development team's breakthrough. Peeking over the high-back leather chairs of the executive conference room, Jason watched the senior staff filing in, their heads quickly turning towards the bagels, hot coffee, and freshly squeezed orange juice awaiting them. He had always felt that food brought people together in the best way.

The meeting room was outfitted with a round conference table that comfortably seated eight, something Jason had brought in. It was perfect for his team of seven, including himself. He borrowed the concept from Amazon, where one seat was always left empty, representing the customer. However, Jason called their empty seat "the perspective chair."

During meetings, this chair would represent the perspective of anyone who could be impacted by their conversation, whether a patient or surgeon, a supplier, partner, employee, or any other stakeholder. On some occasions, he invited an actual representative of a particular perspective to sit in on their meeting and provide firsthand insight or feedback.

This morning, he was confident that Mike and his team had kept their breakthrough success quiet so far, which was probably difficult, even though it was only for a short time. With both product and surgical method patents to be filed with the US Patent Office, Jason had asked the team to be extra careful in any discussions they might have until the proprietary technology was protected.

Jason had invited his full senior leadership team to the meeting. This consisted of himself, president; Mike Montgomery, VP of product development; Hannah Parker, VP of sales and marketing; Abigail (Abby) Mills, chief financial officer (CFO); Cooper Collins, VP of operations; Edward Eggleton, VP of regulatory affairs and quality assurance (RA/QA); and Victor Delacruz, VP of human resources.

As everyone settled in, Jason opened the conversation.

"OK, let's get right to it," he said. "When Mike was promoted to VP, I challenged him and his team to get back into the operating room and look for opportunities to improve outcomes in cardiovascular surgery for both the surgeons and their patients. Mike ran with that challenge and has exciting news for us. I won't steal his thunder, so take it away, Mike."

Mike started by acknowledging the challenge he'd been given by Jason, then moved on to describe his observations in surgery and closed with the skunkworks he and his team had completed to get to this point.

He unveiled an anatomical diagram on a flip chart and opened a bag filled with prototype instruments, which he used to walk the team through the procedure while carefully pointing out the surgical pathway—beginning at the keyholes and progressing to the surgical site.

From all appearances, the leadership team recognized what this could mean for KCI, quickly launching into discussions about the potential impact to the company, their departments, and to themselves personally.

Jason let all the points sink in around the table and then addressed them.

"This is the breakthrough opportunity we've been hoping for," he said. "There will be a lot of work involved in taking this idea to market. Mike has generated a rough timeline for the development project, and conservatively, we're looking at two years to product release.

"That may sound like a long time, but I can assure you it'll go quickly. We'll run into obstacles along the way. No project of this magnitude is without them. But when we do, I'm confident we'll knock them out—together.

"This is a high-volume procedure, but so far, everyone has thought it too difficult to do via minimally invasive techniques. When we release this product, it must work, really well. Also, since we'll be the first, we need to be sure our proprietary technology is well protected. Mike, how are the patent filings coming along?"

Mike spoke rapidly about what he and his team had completed so far.

"We've filed the provisional patents for both the instruments and the surgical method," he explained. "We think we have the procedure blanketed with protection from every conceivable angle. Our patent attorney is sharp and has a lot of experience in minimally invasive surgery. She shared some excellent insights that we think further strengthened our position. I believe we have it buttoned up and can now make the announcement internally."

He continued, "Although the technology is safe, I wouldn't want to broadcast what we're doing publicly and tip off any of our competitors. The patent application will be published eighteen months from the application date. It'll be hard to keep this under wraps throughout that time, but it'd be good to put as much distance between us and those who'll be following once they understand the surgical pathway."

"Thanks, Mike," Jason said. "So, we have two big tasks in front of us. First, we need to build a project plan around the development and release of this product. It should include a full market analysis; a product-specific profit and loss [P&L] statement going out ten years; the research and development [R&D] plan fully costed out; and a combined commercialization plan from operations, regulatory, marketing, and sales.

"The corporate quarterly business review meeting is exactly four weeks from today, and I'll be presenting the product development plan to Adam Drake and the Thompson Holdings team. Any project of this magnitude in spending—especially with it being unbudgeted—will require their approval before we can launch officially. We'll want our most seasoned project manager to lead this. Let's plan on having weekly check-ins until the quarterly meeting at Thompson Holdings.

"There's a lot of information to pull together in a relatively short time frame. Just know that Adam and the Thompson Holdings team will be scrutinizing everything we submit; that's what they do. Mike, Cooper, Hannah, and Edward, you'll need to clear out your schedule for our initial product development planning meeting tomorrow; count on a two-hour block from 10 a.m. until noon. I plan to be there as well. Abby and Victor, feel free to join if you're available. I apologize for the short notice; however, I'm sure you all realize that there's nothing more important for the future of this company than getting this opportunity up and running."

Jason saw the puzzled looks on their faces and surmised they were probably trying to figure out what was on their schedules for tomorrow morning while contemplating exactly what their role in the planning meeting would be.

"I did say we have two tasks before us," Jason added. "The first is the development of this new product, and the second task is, well, not as clear but desperately needed. It's the *culture* of our company. I define culture as the connector between our beliefs and behaviors. It determines how we interact with each other, and with people outside the organization. It also includes our leadership approach.

"Considering our current state, do you think we're ready for an opportunity of this magnitude?"

Cooper was the first to speak up.

"Our systems are antiquated, and based on the last new products we tried to push through, the handoff between R&D and operations looks more like a game of hot potato," he said. "Great product idea, Mike, but I'm not sure how we'll actually get it to market successfully."

Hannah jumped in next. "I have a lot of confidence in sales

and marketing," she explained. "But I don't have much faith in our organization to work collaboratively to get the product through development and into finished goods, ready to ship to customers. I'm not calling anyone out; it just doesn't work well between departments here."

Jason considered their remarks.

"We've discussed this before, and we're all aware that the products this company was founded on were groundbreaking for their time," he said. "However, as Cooper pointed out, the internal systems that would have sustained and grown this business were never built. Even more critical is the fact that an intentional culture or leadership model was never developed for the company. The overriding strategy was to get products out the door any way possible—in most cases by brute force. All of this adds up to a business model that's neither scalable nor sustainable."

Jason paused for a moment and then continued, "As I said, Thompson Holdings is going to thoroughly examine our plan to develop this new product line, and they'll end up with the same questions you've voiced. Specifically: does KCI have the systems, the structure, and the culture to successfully take this concept to market and not only keep it going but build out a platform of products based on the technology?

"This is a significant market opportunity, and it'll require a sizable investment. Corporate is going to be cautious, and the leadership team will need to be satisfied that this project—and its future potential success—will not be fumbled along the way. We must be able to show them we're ready on all fronts."

Hannah asked the question that others were likely thinking: "What other options does Thompson Holdings have?"

"Hannah, I've been asking myself that ever since Mike showed me this idea," Jason replied calmly. "Let's take a moment and, figuratively speaking, place the Thompson Holdings leadership team right here in our perspective chair.

"Remember, they've seen KCI hit it out of the park, then sit back and essentially live off the technology. Meanwhile, their other medical device companies are all steadily growing in sales and earnings. Based on that, I think they have three plausible options. First, they can give us the green light on this project, which will come with a lot of scrutiny. Second, they could consider moving it to our sister company in the cardiovascular market—its president having made clear he's looking for new opportunities, both internally and through acquisition. Or, third, perhaps they could establish a startup company around this technology."

Jason's statement incited the entire group into grumbling about the role of Thompson Holdings. Mike winced and expressed concern about what these options could mean to his team and his new project.

Jason was relieved that no one from Thompson Holdings was there. Sensing the angst in the room, he moved to head it off.

"Listen," he said, "I shared those thoughts with you because I believe in being transparent about everything. It's the only way we'll become a great team. We all deserve to know what we're up against. That being said, we have a strong advocate in Adam Drake at Thompson Holdings. He's fully supported each move we've made in putting this team together with the express intent of seeing us turn this around. Thompson Holdings knows we're in the best position to support this product, and I know its preference is for KCI to join the other medical device companies that are growing consistently. So, right now, this is on us."

Motioning to the flip chart and the instruments, he added, "We're incredibly fortunate to have this product opportunity. However, in addition to constructing the product development plan, we're going to create another plan—*our* plan—of how we'll transform our culture and operate our business in the future. When I say we, I don't just mean the people in this room. Every member of the KCI team will have input into creating a winning culture here.

"We have a deadline for putting together the product

development plan, with the Thompson Holdings quarterly meeting coming up one month from today. I'm also expecting the leadership team there will want to hear our plans to support the growth of the business internally when this product is released. We don't have a lot of credibility right now. It's not just our ability to develop or manufacture and distribute a product. They're aware of the disconnected way we've been operating for the past several years.

"I plan to be prepared when I go in, and to that end, I've been benchmarking companies and researching how others have approached their cultural transformations. I also have thoughts based on my experience. I'm going to take the next couple of days and pull it all together. Then we can sit down as a team and begin working on our path forward. I'll set up a meeting for Monday, so you'll have tomorrow and Friday to gather your thoughts on this."

"Part of tomorrow, now, for those of us in the product development project meeting," Hannah interjected.

Jason acknowledged her comment. "OK, part of tomorrow and Friday," he said with a half grin. "In the meantime, I am challenging each of you to consider your preferences for the culture and leadership model here. What do you think should be at the top of our list?"

"Maybe our independence," Cooper quipped.

"Well, let's focus on what we can control—like determining how we'll operate as a team and as a company. We'll discuss that on Monday. In addition, I also want you to think about our current systems and our most vital needs. A second meeting will be set up to go through those thoughts as they're critical to our success as well. Again, this first meeting to discuss our culture will be on Monday from 8 a.m. to 4 p.m., and as if you'd need a further bribe, we'll be bringing in lunch from that great little taco shop down by the beach."

Everyone looked a bit overwhelmed as Jason paused to consider how to close the meeting.

"So, are there any other thoughts, comments, or questions in the whole world?" he said.

Blank faces.

"Well then, let me be the first to welcome you aboard the KCI burning platform! Most or all of us will be together tomorrow for the product development project meeting. Then, we'll all be back in this conference room on Monday at 8 a.m. sharp to begin work on the cultural transformation. Bring your A game to both meetings.

"This is our future, and we're in this together. As we dig in, I want you to remember this thought: 'Without a great challenge, you cannot have a great success.'"

Next on Jason's agenda was an update call to Adam Drake. He looked forward to calls with Adam, but now he was about to make the call about which he'd been anxious since joining the company. And not only that, but last night, Jason's alma mater, UCLA, had stolen a prized five-star basketball recruit from the clutches of Stanford.

Jason had gone to UCLA on a basketball scholarship, and though he was a top-level player in high school, he was a second-tier bench player there. But that didn't quell the competitive spirit motoring within him. As Adam was a Stanford graduate and quite a college sports fan as well, they'd already discussed their basketball and football teams. These tête-à-têtes added to the friendly relationship they were developing.

"This is Adam Drake."

"Hi, Adam, Jason Bailey here. You have a minute? I've got news to share."

"Are you calling to gloat over the recruit you guys stole yesterday?"

"Well, that's not the primary reason for the call, but since you brought it up, no harm in gloating a little, is there?"

"I really thought he was coming to Stanford, you know. That's a big score for UCLA basketball." Adam paused. "Anyway, what's the real reason for your call?"

"Remember that skunkworks project we started a few months back?"

"Yes, your team was working on a minimally invasive surgery concept that Mike Montgomery came up with."

"Exactly. They figured out the pathway yesterday, and we're starting on the product development proposal as we speak. I'll have a preliminary package to you before the quarterly meeting, and we can review it in detail there with the rest of the Thompson Holdings executive leadership team."

Jason could almost hear Adam smiling down the line.

"That's amazing. You've got to be excited," said Adam. "That really happened quickly, Jason. But let me ask you a question. Do you think your team is ready to tackle a project of this magnitude?"

Jason cleared his throat.

"Good question," he said. "The initial estimate for the product development project is two years. That's how long we've got to get ourselves into ready mode."

"I know it's early, but how are you feeling about your team? Any concerns?" Adam asked.

"We have a good balance of mindsets, and we're going to find out real soon just how committed they are. In all honesty, this breakthrough happened quicker than I thought it would, but I'll take it. As far as concerns, if any, maybe a *little* with Edward Eggleton."

"Your VP of RA/QA?"

"Yes. You know, I see real talent there, but he can be a bit, um, stiff at times. He participates as a team member but keeps his distance. That's the best way I can describe it. I looked a little deeper, and he has a solid RA/QA background and a good working knowledge of KCI, but it just feels cold when you go into his department or interact with any of his team. I plan to spend more time with him to get a better feel for his approach to leadership. I'll keep you posted."

"Good. Do that," said Adam. "I know he's interacted with the RA/QA execs at our other medical companies, and he's well thought of."

Adam continued, "I look forward to receiving the preliminary project plan. I know you're working on it, but I can't get it soon enough. I need to know it well enough to provide support when you need it. And, hey, no more stealing our recruits."

"Definitely on the project plan and the senior leadership team update," said Jason. "Can't promise you anything on the recruits, though!"

# 3

## A WEEKEND AT THE BEACH: IF I WERE IN CHARGE

*A relaxing day in paradise*, thought Bryan as he and his wife, Lora, sat in their beach chairs, letting the waves lap against their feet.

Bryan O'Conner had joined KCI in its early days as a distribution associate when he was fresh out of high school. He made an immediate impact with his ability to work through chaotic situations, which were an everyday occurrence back then. Making the most of those opportunities to shine, Bryan became known as a fixer. He caught a break when the rapidly expanding company needed an entry-level buyer, and he got the job.

He took to the supply chain role immediately, responding quickly to his internal customers' needs while demonstrating the ability to source hard-to-find items. He had a knack for negotiating and enjoyed the relationship aspect of his role.

Over the next seven years, Bryan was promoted four times until reaching his current position as supply chain manager. Someday he hoped to be considered for the VP of operations role, something towards which Cooper Collins, the current VP, was mentoring him.

For Bryan and Lora, coming to the El Capitan State Campground north of Santa Barbara was a chance to enjoy both camping and the beach. During the day, they hung out by the ocean, catching waves on their boogie boards and taking in the sunshine. At nighttime, they sat by a crackling campfire, gazing at the stars together. It was their perfect getaway from the hubbub of life in Southern California—

certainly worth the long drive from their home in Carlsbad.

Bryan had suggested they both take a vacation day that Friday, leaving before sunrise to avoid the commuters clogging the freeways. Fortunately, they arrived early enough to snag a choice campsite near the beach with the surf pounding in the background.

When they planned this trip, he'd suggested it'd be a great opportunity to reflect on the past year as newlyweds and talk about their future. Bryan found it hard to believe they'd already been married a year. He'd met Lora at a co-ed softball game and then dated her for four years before popping the question. During the first two years of dating, he was busy working at KCI and taking college classes at night. Between work and his studies, their relationship had been slow to start. But since completing his degree, he'd spent as much time with her as he could, and the second two years were magical, leaving him firmly convinced he'd found his soulmate.

Even at the campground, it was hard for Bryan to separate his thoughts between work and home. There was a lot happening at KCI, and Bryan was right in the thick of it.

He and Lora had just eaten a pair of steaks cooked over mesquite and were relaxing with cups of steaming cocoa.

"I wanted to talk about us and our future this weekend," he said, gazing up at the stars he could never see in the city. "But there's a lot going on at work, and my mind keeps going back there."

"That's alright. Tell me about it," Lora replied.

Turning to face her, he continued, "Well, it looks like we have a real breakthrough approach to a procedure currently done through open-heart surgery. I learned about it at a project planning meeting yesterday, and last night we were so busy packing for this trip that I didn't get a chance to share it with you."

"Sounds pretty exciting. How will it impact you and your team?"

"For one, we're going to be sourcing a technology we haven't worked with before. It'll be new for me and my team. The challenge will be in finding out who's involved in this area and then selecting the best supplier with which to partner. It sounds like the future of the company is riding on this new product, which means we have to get our part of the project right. If all goes well, we'll likely be scaling up the business over the next couple of years."

"So far, it sounds good. But I'm detecting a bit of hesitancy," said Lora. "Do you see any downsides?"

"Yeah, our systems are really a bunch of homegrown, standalone spreadsheets that don't talk to each other. I'm surprised they've gotten us this far, to be frank. If we're to grow, we'll need much better foundational systems supporting us. That's one big concern.

"Also, we're still dysfunctional about how we get things done. The new president has spoken about it, and it might be too soon to say, but so far, other than a few new department heads on his staff, we haven't seen many changes. Nothing happens smoothly there, and if anything, the management style resembles my uncle Jack's description of a helicopter, which he called 'a bunch of loose parts flying in formation.'"

Bryan took a sip of his cocoa and then continued, "In the past, almost everyone in leadership worked autonomously, and the individual departments followed their lead, oblivious to the existence of the other functions. It seemed like each group would throw whatever they were working on over the wall to the next department in line, and then the finger-pointing would begin. The receiving department would complain that whatever work was completed was not done right, and the sending department would say it was right when they passed it on."

Lora smiled. "How did you guys ever get anything done?"

"Usually, the company president would come in yelling, and everyone would scramble. The main thing was you just didn't want to be the one left holding the bag."

"What do you mean by that?" Lora asked.

Bryan reflected on the crazy days when KCI was first starting up.

"We all spent a lot of time covering our butts, documenting who said what to who," he said. "Management spent more time trying to figure out who was to blame than trying to identify the root cause of the problems. So we each did whatever we had to do to make sure it didn't roll up into our lap, because we all knew it wouldn't end well."

"I think I get it now." Lora frowned. "That sounds like a blame culture. Are you sure this is the company you want to work for long term?"

Bryan pondered for a moment.

"I like what we do—making products that help people. And I like my colleagues, both on my team and, for the most part, around the company. We just need to work as a team. We need to care about each other's needs. And it needs to be modeled at the top first, or it's never going to get better in the rest of the organization. The walls between us won't come down until they knock them down in the executive conference room, if you know what I mean."

"I think I do," said Lora. In a bid to lighten the mood, she beamed. "Want to know what else I think, Mr. O'Conner? I think it's time for s'mores before this fire goes out."

"I couldn't agree more, Mrs. O'Conner!" Bryan laughed. "And thanks for listening and supporting me. I know I kind of hijacked the conversation tonight. Tomorrow, let's focus on us. And if we talk about anyone's work, let's talk about what's happening with you at the hospital."

"Sounds like a plan," Lora replied.

Jimmy Marino worked in the fast-paced distribution department at KCI. He'd been recommended for the job by his pal Gary Fox, who also worked in distribution. Jimmy's manager, Latecia Johnson, was a no-nonsense leader who was very specific in communicating her expectations: everyone arrived on time, which meant before your shift started; everyone hit their productivity numbers; and there were to be no mistakes made picking the products to be shipped.

Jimmy had heard Latecia reminding everyone that they were the last people at KCI to see the product before it reached the hands of the customer, so they must be sure they'd shipped the right product to the right hospital and that it got there the day it was expected.

Gary had told Jimmy about Latecia when Jimmy applied for the job. According to Gary, she'd grown up as the eldest of seven children in Chula Vista. Her parents had divorced when she was twelve, and she had to help her mom raise her siblings. Gary said that although she was a very *direct* person, Latecia seemed to have a soft spot for younger employees—whom she called her "kid projects"—who were trying to find their way.

That was encouraging to Jimmy. In fact, he'd already heard of many of Latecia's "kid projects" going on to bigger and better roles at KCI, something in which Latecia took a lot of pride.

Jimmy had no direction in his life so far. With a car payment, apartment rent (nothing was cheap in Southern California), and a new girlfriend, he needed a job to keep up with his increasing expenses. He'd taken a few classes at the local community college but had never really had a plan after graduating high school. He toyed with the idea of working in the trades, but after working at his father's shop the summer after graduation, Jimmy decided that it wasn't what he was looking for. He kept searching, hoping that he would find his niche eventually. He just didn't know how that would come about.

Before considering KCI, he'd worked at entry-level jobs, mostly in fast food, and didn't know anything about manufacturing—certainly nothing about medical devices. He had told his friends what a terrific opportunity he had at KCI and that he was hopeful to secure a good fit longer term.

Things were going well for him so far. According to Latecia, Jimmy had picked up the systems faster than anyone else had in the past. After two weeks on the job, Jimmy realized he was leading the productivity numbers Latecia posted each week. She'd already had a one-on-one discussion with him, to understand what he would like to do with his future. When they met, she revealed how pleased she was with his progress and added that his punctuality and positive attitude had not gone unnoticed. She offered her assistance in helping him find his path forward.

On the other hand, his friend Gary was not on the same upward trajectory. In the office, Jimmy had overheard Latecia comment sarcastically about how part of her job was anticipating what Gary was planning next.

Once, he overheard her sharing what she called her "classic Gary story." As the story went, it was about 4:15 p.m., with the shift ending at 4:30. Instead of picking orders in the warehouse, Gary was sitting at a desk, apparently keying in data. What Gary didn't know was that earlier in the day, there had been an electrical problem with the floor outlet servicing that desk—a problem Latecia had called maintenance to fix. She said she approached the desk, bent down, picked up the power cords to both the computer and the monitor, and then asked Gary if he believed the computer might work more effectively if it was plugged in.

She had quipped, "I always get a laugh when I tell this story."

Jimmy had heard the buzz around the company about a new product, which could create the opportunities he was hoping for. He had played a lot of sports throughout his younger years and was often named captain of his team. Whatever it was he ended up doing in life, he hoped it'd be something in a leadership position.

In the short time he'd been with KCI, he'd taken note of the company culture—or lack thereof—because it seemed to be different depending on which department you were in and the leader to whom you reported. As far as Jimmy was concerned, some departments were easygoing and employees had fun, while others had a tension about them, and no one dared to crack a smile. Distribution was somewhere in the middle of the pack.

Jimmy knew today would be interesting, not least because Gary had been caught in another shenanigan. He'd called in sick the day before but had told Jimmy that he really wasn't sick at all. Apparently, he'd seen the surf report—big waves expected at his go-to surfing spot, Tamarack State Beach—so he pretended he had a scratchy throat and skipped out on work.

The only problem was Gary had forgotten his sunscreen and came back this morning looking like a lobster. Jimmy thought that if he were in charge, he'd try to develop an atmosphere where when you woke up in the morning and thought about skipping work, you'd come in anyway because you didn't want to miss whatever was going on that day.

# 4

## LAYING THE FOUNDATION: PART ONE

The following Monday, Jason was again the first one in the conference room for this important meeting. He took the opportunity to enjoy the serenity of the view, as KCI's building sat high on a ridge in the hills of Carlsbad. From some vantage points, including the executive conference room, it was possible to catch a glimpse of the Pacific Ocean.

He gazed out at the blue sky and the ocean, which today was a rich shade of green and covered in wind-driven whitecaps. Such inspiring conditions could be useful with the task ahead of them: designing the future culture of the business. As his colleagues came into the conference room, they carried a tangible air of entering the unknown.

He'd invited Nelson Chow, KCI's production manager, to join the meeting in the perspective chair. Nelson was a mid-level manager with responsibility for about two hundred employees, the largest set of direct reports within the company, and Jason believed he could bring a valuable perspective to the meeting.

Once everyone had settled in, Jason opened, "We've got a lot to discuss today, so let's get going. I invited Nelson to join us in the perspective chair as he represents a lot of opinions across the organization. I'm confident he'll be a strong contributor to our discussion today. No pressure, right, Nelson?"

"Right, Jason. Thanks. I think."

Jason smiled and continued, "As I mentioned last week, the Thompson Holdings team will be excited to hear about the new product idea developed by Mike and his team. The next question on the executive leaders' minds, however, will be whether we can commercialize this technology successfully. If asked today, I think we'd be hard pressed to say we're ready, but the product development timeline is approximately two years, so we have time to do something about that.

"Our task today is to begin developing the framework for our company culture. When I was hired, my charter included restarting the product development engine and establishing and fine-tuning the rest of the internal workings, which were never developed fully. The work we are doing today falls right in line with those expectations.

"In preparation for this discussion, I asked you all to come ready to share your thoughts on culture and leadership. Specifically, what should the culture we develop look like? For my part, I've studied our own company's history and benchmarked some of the best companies out there, and I'll be sharing from those today as well as some learnings from my own experience."

Jason paused, noticing everyone leaning into the conversation. Based on his internal conversations throughout the company, he was sure this discussion was long overdue.

"We're going to explore a lot of information throughout the day," he added. "Rather than digging into tactics, let's keep today's discussions focused strategically on the overall framework. We'll circle back to the tactical in a subsequent meeting, but the goal today is to take the first step towards developing a set of elements that'll guide how we'll interact as a company. Does this make sense so far? Are there any questions?"

Jason again scanned the room and saw all approving nods.

"Let's start with your thoughts on culture and leadership models, and then I'll share what I've prepared. I'll be capturing the highlights on this flip chart. We'll start with Hannah and work our way around to her right. If there's a thought on your list that's a duplicate of one already mentioned, it's OK to acknowledge that. And if you have a related key point or additional example to share, please feel free to do so. Hannah, lead us off."

Considering Hannah's background and role with the company, it didn't surprise Jason that the first thing she mentioned was the importance of communications of all types: noting how critical it was to consider what information was shared, how it was shared, with whom it was shared, and the timeliness of sharing.

The second area Hannah brought up was trust. She gave an example of a previous employer where trust was one of the stated company values and noted that perhaps it was a benefit of being in a smaller company, but there, you could believe what people said and trust there were no hidden agendas. She explained that the company's CEO believed you could manage employees either by developing trust or by using fear tactics. He was of the opinion that it was both more productive and fulfilling for everyone when there was a culture of trust.

Jason captured Hannah's key points of "communications," with the sub-bullets of "what, how, who, and when," and "trust," with the sub-bullet of "vs. fear."

Cooper was up next, and he started off with the word "integrity."

He noted that integrity led right into Hannah's second point of trust and how both had been missing at KCI for years. He went on to explain that in his opinion, without integrity, no one trusted the management team—or, for that matter, even other departments. He cited the adage of "Say what you mean and mean what you say." He also tied it back to one of Hannah's comments, saying there had been a lot of personal agendas at KCI over the past years.

"Some, you were wise not to get in the way of," he said.

The second point Cooper brought up was the need to be a caring organization. He felt it had been missing.

"It's time to establish a culture where it's OK to openly show support for employees' work life and their personal life," he explained.

Jason captured the point of "integrity" and sub-bullets of "walk the talk" and "no hidden agendas," and then the second point of "caring" and sub-bullets of "work" and "home."

To Cooper's right was Victor, who focused his comments on the people-centric aspects of a company's culture. He said, "Successful companies establish a set of values to which everyone subscribes and employ more of a servant-leadership model."

He went on to share that he believed in a caring organization in which the leadership team listened to its employees.

Jason captured "values based," "servant leadership," and "listening."

Continuing around the table, Mike was next to share. His comments echoed Cooper's and Victor's in using the word "supportive," which Jason captured, but also linked it to "caring."

Mike explained that after the company's initial success, it seemed like management had milked what had been developed and described how in the interest of bolstering declining profitability, support for product development had dried up. The second point Mike brought up was the need to become an innovative company once again—not just in product development but in everything they did across all departments.

Jason wrote "supportive" and "innovative" on the flip chart.

Abby began by noting she also had "listening" and "caring" on her list, but her third item had not yet surfaced: "accountability." She observed that there were many different subcultures within the company; the company lacked a cohesive approach. It seemed like employees in each department looked out for themselves and no one was accountable for how their actions impacted other areas or KCI as a whole. There were a lot of nods around the room as she described this.

Jason noted "accountability" on the chart.

The last of the senior staff to contribute was Edward. He said he had a lot of the same points previously noted and had no additional comments for those but did add one final point to the list: having one set of standards for processes common to all departments—things like promotions, raises, disciplinary actions, etc. He explained that he had also worked in companies where employees memorized their core values and used them to guide their interactions.

Jason posted this last comment as he thanked Edward and then turned to Nelson. "You didn't really have a lot of advance notice on this, but do you have anything you'd like to add?"

Nelson replied enthusiastically, "First off, this is already an impressive list. What comes to my mind, though, is 'collaboration.' There are walls that have been erected between the departments, which I think was previously mentioned in different ways. Clearly, we need to work as one team throughout KCI."

"Thanks, Nelson," Jason responded. "That's an important add to the list. OK, let me summarize what I have up here from all of you."

- Communications
    - what, how, who, when
- Trust
    - vs. fear
- Integrity
    - walk the talk
    - no hidden agendas
- Caring
    - work and personal life
- Listening
- Values based
- Servant-leadership model
- Supportive
- Innovative
- Accountable
- One set of standards
- Collaborative

Jason stood back and looked at their list.

"This is a great start to our discussion today, and thank you for taking the time to think this through and share your thoughts." He smiled. "I also asked you to reflect on the state of our systems, and we'll cover that area in a follow-up meeting soon. I recognize those are in disarray, and as critical as they'll be to our success, I believe the topics we're covering today—culture and leadership—are at the very core of who we are and all we do. If those are off kilter, then, quite frankly, good systems won't be enough to save us.

"I've combined what I've picked up here at KCI as areas for improvement with both the outside benchmarking I've conducted as well as my own experiences, and I developed seven foundational tenets or elements that I'd like you to consider. On a positive note, after hearing your thoughts, I can already see that there's a lot of overlap between our collective thinking."

Jason gestured to the flip chart, adding, "We'll develop a first draft of the cultural elements coming out of today's discussion; then the next step in our process will be to solicit feedback from the rest of the leadership team and all the employees. Ultimately, we want to consider everyone's input before finalizing these elements, which goes back to Cooper's point of becoming a listening organization.

"Any questions or comments? Are we ready to move forward?"

"We're ready to go!" Hannah said, looking around the table.

Thumbs-up all around.

"Great," Jason continued. "Before we discuss the elements, I want to lay a bit of groundwork to help prepare our minds for the rest of the day. I'll be using both flip charts and the projector."

He moved to the flip chart and revealed the next sheet, showing a picture he'd taped to it of a lush tree above the ground with loads of hanging fruit and an elaborate root system intertwined below the ground [Figure 1].

Figure 1

He pointed to the fruit on the limbs, explaining: "You cannot get this . . . without this"—as he tapped the root system. In other words, you won't get 'fruitfulness' without 'rootfulness.' So, what we're talking about today is developing the right root system, or foundation, for KCI so we can position ourselves to support the growth of our business more effectively."

Victor piped in: "So we go deep before we go wide. Is that it, Jason?"

"Exactly, Victor. We start here this morning." He touched the root system on the diagram again. "Once we agree on the important foundational areas, we can begin discussing what we'll do to develop those with specific ideas or tactics."

He began writing on the picture.

"Taking this a little deeper, above the ground is 'what's seen' in a company: the people, its processes, its products of those processes, our interactions with it, maybe its profits, and certainly its achievements in the market—again, its fruitfulness as a company.

"Below the ground, though, is what's unseen: the company culture and its values, employee commitment to each other and the company, its failures, and perhaps its persistence and the sacrifices it makes to be successful—its 'rootfulness' that supports what's above the ground or what's seen and realized as a company [Figure 2].

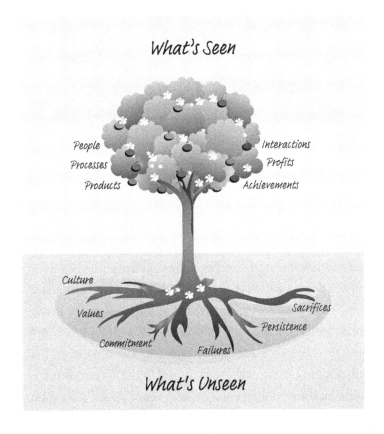

Figure 2

"I think you'd all agree, our current culture is disconnected. Right now it's the result of however each manager interacts with their respective areas. There's little or no collaboration between departments, nor any cohesive effort to develop a common bond among employees. Without an intentional plan, we're defaulting to hope or luck as a strategy. Although a little luck can be helpful, an intentional plan is the root system we'll need for our future."

Jason turned to the projector and advanced the slide.

"Take a look at this diagram I picked up a while back [Figure 3]. I'm sure you can guess which box we're in."

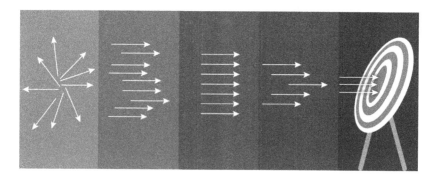

Figure 3

Jason paused to let the team consider the image before continuing, "One use of this diagram is to depict milestones of a business. However, in our case, it could represent the status of our culture, or it could also be used to show our past attempts at goal setting.

"The first box represents what could be many individual well-meaning plans, where they perhaps confuse activity levels with accomplishments. However, good intentions alone don't move the business forward. Our goal today is to take the important first step towards aligning the arrows, as depicted in the second box from the left—getting everyone focused on one set of goals. And then, over time, our objective would be to progress to the right, fine-tuning our methods with the objective of becoming a tighter, more focused and connected organization.

"Time-travel with me for a moment. After World War II, the

ongoing military influence led to a business leadership model of command and control. The culture within most companies was business-centric. Then, in the 1980s, we began evolving towards team-based concepts. After the turn of the century, the pendulum swung towards more 'people-centric' cultures in which everyone feels valued.

"What I am proposing today is an initial set of seven elements balancing both approaches: business- and people-centric. I'll be using the phrase 'both sides of the equation,' meaning the business and the employees or management and employees, to reflect efforts to encompass all perspectives. I believe either of these approaches—business-centric or people-centric—can be the foundation of a good, and perhaps even a great, company. However, I believe a culture balancing both creates the pathway towards becoming an exceptional or extraordinary company.

"I also want to get out in front of one thought that may be in the back of your minds. If not now, it'll likely pop up as we continue our discussion. We'll be talking about what some might call the relational side of business. The question is, will whatever we agree to also make good business sense? There's an excellent resource on this topic in a book entitled *Firms of Endearment*,[1] which studies companies who value and embrace a people-centric culture."

Jason advanced the slide deck. He continued, "This table [Figure 4] shows how both the US and international companies identified by the authors as 'firms of endearment,' or FoE, achieved a return on investment, or ROI, two to fourteen times better than both the 'good to great'[2] companies highlighted in Jim Collins's best-selling book and the overall S&P 500. The results were consistently better in the five-, ten-, and fifteen-year intervals they studied."

---

1 Wolf DB, Sisodia R, Sheth J, 2007

2 Collins J, 2001

## RETURN ON INVESTMENT

| Cumulative Performance | 15 Years | 10 Years | 5 Years |
|---|---|---|---|
| US FoE | 1681% | 410% | 151% |
| International FoE | 1180% | 512% | 154% |
| Good to Great Companies | 263% | 176% | 158% |
| S&P 500 | 118% | 107% | 61% |

Figure 4

After allowing the team some time to review the table, Jason continued, "Tackling the relational side of our business is good for our employees, supports our growth plans, and should strengthen our financial picture. I believe it's a win-win-win for any organization that embraces it. We purchased extra copies of the book, and they're on the back table. Help yourselves at the break or at the end of the meeting."

Jason continued, "That's the groundwork I wanted to lay. Are there any questions or comments?"

Mike responded, "All three examples were eye-opening for me." Many heads nodded around the table, and Mike continued, "I especially related to the arrows chart. That portrays accurately the way we've operated for many years. We had a great technology to start with, and as a start-up company, it got us sold. But we never aligned the arrows to sustain or build on our success."

"Thanks, Mike. I agree with your assessment," said Jason.

He took a look around the table for additional comments and, seeing none, he continued: "Let's dive into the first proposed element. We'll be examining seven elements in total. While I've put them in order, they're all interconnected and, I believe, vital to our success. We'll work through these and then make our conclusions together."

## ELEMENT #1: RESPECT FOR ALL EMPLOYEES

Jason began writing on a blank page of the flip chart. "The first element is respect."

He glanced around and asked, "How would you want to define respect at KCI? I'm not talking about the dictionary's definition or how other companies define it. Based on our collective experience, let's brainstorm a definition—right here, right now."

Victor was the first to offer his thoughts. "I think it can be as simple as treating everyone like you would want to be treated," he said.

"That sounds like something the HR guy would say, although I do agree with it," quipped Hannah.

Jason wrote Victor's response on a second flip chart.

"I'll keep a record of our discussion over here," Jason explained. "That'll make it easier for us to consolidate the input from both flip charts into a final consensus. Great comment, Victor. It's simple, as you rightly point out, but so true."

Cooper was next to share his thoughts.

"A bunch of us operations folks visited a company once that decided to make safety a priority as their way of showing respect to their employees," he said. "This facility had a horrible safety record, and leadership believed they could earn the trust of their employees if they showed them respect through a concerted effort to make it a safe place to work."

"How'd that work out?" Jason questioned.

"Excellent," Cooper replied. "It was the first step of a major cultural transformation for them. This facility was a union shop, and the relationship between management and employees was bad by all accounts. From the initial step of showing respect for employee safety, the company was able to build a foundation of trust, which led to a major overhaul of the business. Not only is the union–management relationship strong now, but through respect, they were able to work together as a team and turn around all the production statistics."

Jason smiled. "Great example, Cooper. Thanks for sharing."

"I'll throw something out there," Abby offered up. "Listening to people—actually, not only listening but then acting in the moment on what they're saying."

She continued, "It might be a response of 'I'll have to look into that,' or 'Great idea,' or even 'It isn't a good time to do that.' But *truly* listening to our employees and being accountable by responding to them. Let them know we respect them by showing we hear them and we value what they have to say. That doesn't show up as a separate line in our P&L statements each month, but it could become an underlying factor that positively influences it."

"Got it," said Jason as he wrote her comment on the flip chart.

Hannah jumped in next.

"Going back to Cooper's example, I'd submit we'll not be able to develop trust here without first showing respect to people. Those two are related, just like the company in Cooper's example found out. I think they go hand in hand."

"Absolutely, Hannah," replied Jason. "I agree. The relationship of respect leading to trust makes sense."

Jason thought this was a good time to share something he'd picked up along the way.

"All of what we've discussed is great so far," he said. "But I want to add one more dynamic to this discussion that I mentioned earlier: considering both sides of the equation. When the topic of respect comes up in a company, it's usually discussed from the perspective of management showing respect for employees. And, granted, that's important in any organization.

"However, looking at it from both directions, not only do we want to demonstrate respect for our employees in our leadership roles, but we also want to cultivate a culture of respect for management *from* our employees, and respect from each employee for every other employee, regardless of their role within the company. It's important we see and value our colleagues as equals.

"I believe our being in this room today is a function of the skill sets and experiences we've been fortunate to accumulate. And right now, many of our employees are also growing in their knowledge and experience. In the future, they could be in this very conference room, in one of these seats. In fact, if we could fast-forward ten years, it might surprise us to see who's joining us at the table."

Jason continued, "I could be one of those examples. In my first job out of college, I was working at a small medical device start-up right here in Southern California. On the Friday of the first week that I started there, I was asked to pick up lunch for the executives and deliver it to a conference room for a meeting much like this. I wasn't ready or skilled enough to be in the conference room that day as a participant. Heck, I was happy to be delivering lunch.

"As I placed the food on the back table, I scanned the room and wondered what it would be like to be one of those sitting at the table. I imagined they must be awfully smart people to be in there," he added with a wink.

"But now, twenty years later, here I am facilitating this discussion. I'll bet none of them ever pictured me in this role. We're all working our way through life, and my hope is we'll respect each individual where they are right now and support them in their journey."

Nelson chimed in, "I appreciate where this conversation is going. With a lot of employees reporting to me, and a few layers of management above me, I'm pretty much in the middle of the company. I like the idea of treating respect as something that's universal throughout our organization, regardless of position.

"One question I have picks up on Cooper's example. Is there any single area we should consider focusing on to begin building the element of respect here?"

Cooper zeroed in on Nelson's comment immediately.

"I think the answer is right in front of us," he said. "I've been around since the beginning, and each individual leader has been pretty much left to do whatever they wanted. I think that's why we have the mess we're in today. We're a mixed bag of cultures that change whenever you go into a different department. So, committing to a single set of standards for how we interact with each other as a company could be that big single area of change you're referring to. It's something we've never experienced here."

"Good point," Nelson responded.

Hannah shared a thought.

"I just finished a book called *Everybody Matters*,[3] by Bob Chapman, and it really hit the nail on the head for me. Chapman said something I think applies here. He said, 'We've paid people for their hands for years and they would've given us their heads and hearts for free—if we'd just known how to ask.'

"I think our employees do give us their hands, but if there was respect in all directions and it became a foundational element of our culture, they'd be more likely to give their heads and their hearts to help achieve the goals of the company."

"Wow, some great thoughts you've all shared. I think we have very similar thinking on this one," said Jason. "Let's summarize what's listed up here. The element is respect, and the key factors are as follows:

- Treat people the way you want to be treated.
- Listen and respond in the moment.
- Respect shown by all employees to all employees.
- Respect as the first step towards building a foundation of trust.
- Respect people and appreciate where they are today in their life's journey.
- Consistent use and application of respect throughout the company.

---

3   Chapman B, Sisodia R, 2015

"Make no mistake, we will revisit these thoughts many times in the future. However, I believe respect is the starting point in turning around our business. And years from now, when we look back, I think we'll find respect to be at the very heart and the real catalyst of all we accomplish."

Jason turned the page on the flip chart as he prepared to discuss the second element. "Excellent start, everyone. We got there quickly. Or perhaps Cooper snuck some Irish coffee into the pots. Let's build on this and move to the next element, which centers on relationships."

## ELEMENT #2: BUILDING AND MAXIMIZING RELATIONSHIPS THROUGHOUT THE COMPANY

Jason continued, "A thought hit me while considering how we—and by we, I mean business in general—have done leadership training typically. Tell me if this rings a bell.

"We determine an area we want to improve and hire an outside consultant to train our leaders on the topic. Once the training is completed, our leaders descend on their direct reports—doing whatever they've been newly trained to do. From the employees' perspective, it's another thing management tries that will likely fade over time. They just have to endure it for now.

"Reflecting on that revealed something I've overlooked for many years: we're missing half of the story! We're only effectively training one side of the equation, the leader. And leadership shouldn't be something leaders 'do' to their employees; it's a *relationship* between two people, two employees—one as leader, one as their direct report.

"Looking back at our discussion on respect, we agree we're equal as people, just working in different roles. So why treat one person as if they need special training to have a good relationship and leave the other person out? What if we took those same areas of targeted improvement and trained both sides of the equation?"

Jason could see them following along and felt they were ready to delve a bit deeper.

He continued, "OK, let's look at an example. Let's say we've decided to improve communications. In the past, we would've brought in a consultant to share the latest thinking and train our leaders how to communicate with their employees in the different situational circumstances they could encounter. They'd likely do some role-playing exercises, trying out the new approaches on each other. Then we'd ask them to try out what they've learned on their direct reports. So, while we took the time to educate the leader, nothing was done to help their direct reports understand how best to communicate in those same situations. Seems like a missed opportunity to me.

"If we really want to improve relationships within our company, we need to educate everyone. And as we consider how to go about this, I think it'd be optimal to begin with the leader–direct report relationship. In the short term, it could give us a great start towards becoming a cohesive team."

After allowing a moment for everything to sink in, Jason picked it back up. "I know I've been doing all the talking on this element, but let me lay out a few final thoughts, and then we can open it up for discussion. The reason I started with the leader–direct report relationship is because it's one of the most important relationships, if not *the* most important, we have in a company.

"Think about how your week typically goes, and your reaction to whatever your leader said to you. If they commended you, I'll bet it was the first thing you shared the moment you got home, or whenever you next talked to whomever was important in your life. Conversely, if it was a negative interaction, I'll bet it dominated your thoughts and attitude both at work and at home, and not in a positive way. Whether positive or negative, whatever happens between an employee and their leader is a big deal, and it impacts their life.

"I've heard it said that people don't typically leave a company—they leave their manager. In Gallup's published report titled *State of the American Manager*,[4] it says that more than half of the employees surveyed have left their job to get away from their manager at some point in their career. So, if we can find a way to build and strengthen all aspects of this critical relationship, I believe we're setting our employees, and our company, up for success.

"This also connects to our first element of respect by maximizing a vital relationship at work. As important as it is, I wouldn't stop there. I believe we can identify key aspects of the other relationships we have here and, again, train both sides of the equation.

"OK. That's a lot to take in. What questions or comments do you have?"

Edward cleared his throat and said, "Jason, this idea of training both sides of the equation—I never really thought of it that way, but it makes sense. My team in quality assurance oversees the documentation process, and when we, as a company, train employees on new work processes, we ensure that anyone who touches the process in any way, like your 'both sides of the equation,' is trained.

"We want to be sure everyone involved understands what they are doing and why they are doing it. I would agree that, historically, industry trains leaders but not individual contributors. Employees can be left in the dark to grapple with whatever new approach is being used on them. The approach you are proposing aligns with my training mindset. It is an easy fix, but there would be additional training expenses to consider. In saying that, I believe the benefits outweigh the costs. I know we are talking strategically right now, but perhaps you could share some of the tactics you saw during those company site visits. Did you see any examples of what others are doing in this regard, and did they share how it worked out for them?"

---

4   Gallup, 2015

"Good question, Edward," replied Jason. "Yes, I did, and I think sharing a few examples may shed light on this element. One company held a course on communications skills training—probably why I jumped right to that example earlier. This was a course that was perfect for leaders but was made more effective because it was opened to all employees. The business went one step further and took a unique approach by *not* making it mandatory. This was to ensure that, considering the time and the expense involved, each employee was genuinely interested in participating and not just stuck in a weeklong training course. In order to take the course, employees had to apply for it, and within the application, they were asked to state why they were signing up. Essentially, they had to want to be there and be ready to participate and learn."

He continued, "Each weeklong training had a mix of twelve employees from various departments and roles. The training began with the participants receiving the results of their Dominance, Influence, Steadiness, and Conscientiousness [DiSC] analysis—a personality and behavioral assessment tool rarely shared with non-leadership employees. I understand that was an eye-opening exercise in and of itself. They spent the rest of the week going through the key elements of communicating, did some role-playing, and even had a fun night out together."

Jason summarized, "The leadership team asked some of the employees who completed the training to share with our tour group how this experience impacted their lives. All of them said it was one of the more significant things they'd done in their lives—period. There were comments like 'I wish I had taken this class a long time ago; I'm now able to talk to my wife/kids/parents better than I ever have.' Or 'I'm able to work with another employee who I disliked immensely.' One woman made a new friend by applying her new listening skills.

"For all of them, the training changed how they related to other people both inside and outside work. It was a significant investment for this company and hugely impactful for everyone who participated.

Again, in the past, access to that experience was generally limited to those in leadership roles. The company would've missed the opportunity to improve and change the relationships—well, change the lives—of all who participated.

"Another example I'll share was a company that provided group personality testing, in this case the Myers-Briggs Type Indicator assessment. The organization wanted employees to better understand how other employees processed information and learn about their individual preferences for doing things. Essentially, participants learned about how each of us tick and that being different is OK.

"By the way, I'm not advocating any specific tool. There are lots out there, and if we decide to go in that direction, we should research them and select whatever best suits our needs and helps us accomplish our goals.

"There is one final example I would like to share. I visited a company in which all employees participated in a workshop titled the Five Languages of Appreciation in the Workplace[5]—based on the book of the same name—where employees discover how they best like to be shown appreciation.

"The leadership said celebration was a big part of their company culture but they realized their efforts were wasted if it was not done correctly. For example, think about calling someone up to the front in a meeting to celebrate something they did well. What if this person hates being in the limelight? What was supposed to be a positive experience to celebrate an achievement becomes a nightmare for the one being celebrated. The company wanted to be sure that when employees were shown appreciation, it was shown in a way that resulted in a positive experience for the person being celebrated.

"This course was especially helpful to leaders who, in the past, had simply used the same method of appreciation for all their direct reports. In fact, they may have thought it best to treat everyone the

---

5   Chapman G, White P, 2019

same or equal. Now that they knew each employee's preference for being shown appreciation, the company's efforts were much more impactful. And like the other trainings, it was a great relationship-building experience."

Edward had appeared pleased with the direction this element was taking when they discussed training both sides of the equation, but now Jason noticed a distinct change in his countenance.

"Edward, you have a concerned look on your face."

Edward squirmed in his seat. He seemed uncomfortable saying what was on his mind, but he finally let it out.

"You know I am big on training. That part makes sense to me," he said. "And areas like communications are a good topic for everyone to consider. But when you start getting into personality testing, well, that is where you lose me. I am not sure I want to do that. At least, not with a group of people I do not know. People tend to share some personal things in those settings."

Jason considered Edward's comment.

"Well, yes, that can be true," he replied. "But it's up to you, and everyone else who participates in this type of training. No one would be twisting your arm to make you share anything with which you're uncomfortable. What's your real concern?"

By now Edward was slumping. "Well, I guess . . . if I did decide to share something, my concern is what people might think of me," he explained.

"I understand, Edward, but they'd probably just think you're human, a real person, just like them," Jason said. "And how better to relate to people than as one human to another? No pretenses, no title or authority to hide behind—just one real person to another."

Edward listened intently. There would be more discussion in the future to help Jason prepare this team for what lay ahead, but it seemed like a good time to keep moving forward, so he asked if anyone had any further comments or questions on the element they were discussing.

Edward continued squirming. Noticing this, Jason went back to him. "Edward, more thoughts or comments?"

"Yes. OK, I do understand what you are saying about relationships," Edward proffered. "But personally, I have always thought it best to keep my distance from my subordinates, never getting too close or too personal."

"And why's that, Edward?"

"Well." Edward paused. "You never know when you might have to fire someone, and it would be much more difficult for me if I knew them personally."

Jason could see Edward was struggling to share this, but he was glad to get these topics out on the table with the whole group. He was silent for a moment while he thought about how to respond. Everyone else was quiet as well but appeared anxious to hear what he had to say.

"Before I address your comment, Edward, let me ask you a question: how would you describe the atmosphere in your department?"

Every time Jason did his walkarounds in the company, he picked up tension in Edward's department. That made Jason even more curious how he'd reply.

"I would describe it as a group who gets their work done," Edward answered in a matter-of-fact way. "It certainly is not party central like over in sales and marketing, or a bunch of back-slapping like in operations." He spoke without looking over at Hannah or Cooper. "We meet our commitments. Everyone can count on us to keep the company steady and straight."

Edward's comments raised a few eyebrows, especially, and not surprisingly, Hannah's and Cooper's. But this also presented an opportunity to share an alternative perspective—in this case, in an area about which Jason felt strongly.

Jason cleared his throat. "Edward, I hear you when you bring up the situation of termination. No one likes that part of leadership—

at least, no one I know. It's one of the hardest things we ever have to do in our roles. You call someone into your office, and their life is changed in an instant. And it's tough when you consider how it impacts them and their family. I get it."

Jason continued, "Here's the thing. If there's ever the situation when someone's employment is at risk, I want to be sure they've had the opportunity to be the best version of themselves in their job, and if that's not good enough, then termination may be a consideration.

"In saying that, my recommendation to you—well, actually to all of us—is to take time to develop authentic business relationships on an individual basis with each of your direct reports. I say 'individual' because each person is an individual, with different backgrounds and stories to share, as well as different needs. I also recommend we encourage each of them to likewise develop their individual relationships with their colleagues. We all don't have to become great personal friends, but we need to give everyone the opportunity to get to know us and each other.

"I believe when an employee is relaxed and feels cared for, they're free to be themselves. And from a work perspective, they're free to be the best version of themselves. If there's caution or tension in the air, it introduces fear into the mix, and it's hard to be at your best when you're fearful about whether you said or did the right thing moment to moment.

"To me, fear can result in drama, which is a distraction and could be considered another form of waste. All companies would like less of that in their culture. So, as their leader, I would feel even worse if I never provided the environment in which my direct reports could be their best. That's on me."

Edward nodded. Jason surmised that this was likely a fresh perspective for Edward to take in.

Jason took a look at the initial set of elements the staff had shared to open the meeting and added: "Looking at our first chart, I can see this discussion ties to what Cooper, Mike, and Victor brought up about caring for people and being supportive."

Then Jason asked them all, "How does everyone feel about this element in terms of the concerns Edward raised?"

Victor responded, "I'd like to applaud Edward for being open with his thoughts. We'll need that level of openness in order for us to grow together as a team. It's healthy for us to discuss these areas as other employees may have similar feelings. Jason, I think your recommendation to develop authentic business relationships is sound. Overall, I think this has been a good discussion."

Around the table, Jason heard comments supporting both Edward's openness and the recommendation to foster authentic business relationships.

Keeping up the pace, Jason continued, "Thanks, Victor. It looks like we are ready to move forward. Let's summarize this element." He began writing on the flip chart again. "For relationships, the key factors are as follows:

- Develop both sides of each relationship.
- Begin with the leader–direct report relationship.
- Expand to other key relationships within the company.
- It's important to get buy-in and ensure people are ready to participate.
- Create an environment where people can flourish and be their best.

"That wraps up element number two. Let's take a fifteen-minute break; then we'll head to element number three."

# 5

## LAYING THE FOUNDATION: PART TWO

A short time later, everyone reentered the conference room. Jason noticed that a few team members had stopped to talk with Edward, and that he appeared more confident afterwards. However, he noted that Hannah and Cooper walked right past Edward without saying anything.

During the break, some had gone off to answer emails or check phone messages, and as the team settled back in, Jason turned the page on the flip chart and wrote out the next element: "100 percent leadership buy-in."

### ELEMENT #3: 100 PERCENT LEADERSHIP BUY-IN

"Prior to the break, we covered the first two elements: respect and relationships," said Jason. "The next element, 100 percent leadership buy-in, comes from my own experience. I've seen it when it worked, when everyone bought into the agreed-upon cultural precepts. Conversely, I've seen when it didn't work, when it wasn't followed consistently throughout the organization and leaders acted independently.

"As you all know firsthand, the results can vary quite substantially. I think it ties right into Edward's earlier statement about having one set of standards throughout the company.

"As the president of KCI, I recognize I influence the way we do business, significantly. I can open the door to a more people-centric environment, or I can close the door and establish an autocratic approach. But that's really it. The president can set the tone for the company, but they cannot singularly ensure their intended approach is followed throughout the organization 100 percent of the time.

"And no matter which cultural elements we choose to subscribe to, once we do, we're likely to assume that everyone throughout the chain of command is likewise adopting and adhering to those same elements. However, that's not necessarily so, and it impacts the organization in a significant way. Because for each individual employee, the real culture of the company is reflected in whatever cultural elements their leader subscribes to and operates by on a daily basis. That applies whether their direct supervisor's title is lead, supervisor, manager, director, or even vice president.

"I can stand in front of the employees and promote these tenets we're developing, but the truth is, the employees will only believe what I say if their direct supervisor and the leaders within their department's chain of command also subscribe to and live by these tenets. If any link in their respective leadership chain doesn't follow them, then our efforts today and in the future—our efforts towards building a winning and consistent culture—are completely undermined. Imagine the breakroom chatter when that's happening."

Jason took a beat to let this sink in and continued, "So, we can talk about respect, building relationships, and the other elements we'll discuss today. But once we establish our standards, they'll only be as effective as the buy-in of the leadership team, one by one, including every single person who holds a leadership role."

He flipped the chart pages back to the picture of the tree.

"Our 'rootfulness'—our foundation—will depend on this, and subsequently our fruitfulness will be subject to the level of buy-in we achieve."

Victor spoke up. "Those are important points, and hard to argue against. But this leads me to the next question of what happens if someone *doesn't* buy in?"

Jason answered, "Fair question. If we end up agreeing on this as an element, we'll need to address that question in the tactical section, which is a future discussion. However, not to leave you dangling—whatever we decide here today and in the follow-up meetings, we'll be sure to share and discuss with the full leadership team, and with all employees. In fact, we'll be asking for everyone's input on the key cultural elements, and based on their feedback, we'll develop the final set. I also expect we'll be spending additional time and effort with some individuals to help them get on board.

"To be clear, our intention is to develop a culture centered on respect and care. If *any* leader doesn't want to be a part of that, then frankly, it's likely there's a better fit for them somewhere outside our organization."

Victor nodded, adding, "I agree with everything you've said, but we'll have to be thoughtful about how we communicate those expectations and determine how we'll ensure leadership buy-in across the board. On one hand, it could sound like an ultimatum, but I agree the success of any business culture depends on consistent application throughout the organization, no matter which door you open."

"Indeed," Jason replied. "And don't we currently assess the performance of our leaders? The difference is that we'll have a single set of standards to which every leader is held accountable, consistently throughout the organization. We owe that to our employees. It's one of the ways we can show them we genuinely care."

Victor nodded again and said, "Good here. I can't help getting ahead and thinking about specific tactics we can employ."

Jason responded, "Absolutely. I'm sure we're all thinking ahead to what implementing these elements might look like. However, I believe the employees would be encouraged to see this element, or something like it, making the list. Whatever direction we take, we have a lot of work ahead to achieve alignment and focus on that bullseye."

Nelson interjected, "I just wanted to add that this element fits well with our discussion on respect. We can show respect for our employees by providing a clear set of standards and holding everyone accountable to those standards—no exceptions; no separate agendas."

"Agreed, Nelson. Well put. Well, any questions on this element?" asked Jason.

Again, everyone seemed happy, their faces showing signs of optimism, Jason thought. He returned to the flip chart. "This element, 100 percent leadership buy-in, has the key factors of the following:

- 100 percent leadership buy-in to the agreed-upon elements
- Supported by sharing and the exchange of ideas (listening)
- Consistent and routine assessment of leadership performance

"We're making good progress. Three elements down, four more to discuss. We'll tackle this next element and then break for lunch."

## ELEMENT #4: TEAMWORK

As the marker squeaked across the flip chart, Jason explained, "The next element in our discussion is teamwork. A mentor of mine once told me, 'Without teamwork, two plus two equals three, because you lose what's possible when people don't work together, and the sum of their efforts is less than the whole.'

"The same mentor also told me, 'With teamwork, two plus two can actually equal five, because of the synergy it produces.' I know this may sound corny, but I've found it to be true time and time again. It's powerful what teamwork can do throughout, and for, an organization. It's like magic fairy dust being sprinkled over everything we do.

"Let me ask something here: is anyone willing to share their experience of being on a great team or perhaps what it was like to be on an underperforming team? This could have been in a work setting, or on a sports team or club, or any time where the element of teamwork applied."

Mike, who'd been quiet up to this point, spoke up.

"Jason, I've gotta say that I have a good team right now in product development. When you tasked us with reenergizing the new product pipeline, no one complained, and there were no defensive remarks. The call to action bonded us, and we were all rooting for each other to come up with a game-changing idea. And when this one idea came up, we rallied together to test out the concept. Amazingly, all our individual talents were drawn upon during that time. When we ran into an obstacle, someone used their knowledge or experience to figure out a solution. There were no individual agendas, just one common goal of turning the idea into a working concept.

"It's been a great experience so far; I find myself getting into my truck each morning a little anxious and excited to get to work. I can see that in the eyes of my teammates as well. The days go by fast, and yet we feel like we're moving mountains together."

Jason beamed. "Great example, Mike. Anyone else want to share?"

"I've got one to share," said Cooper. "Several years ago, I played on a basketball team in a city recreation league—obviously when I was much younger and in better shape."

"I am glad you qualified that, Cooper. I'm just saying!" Hannah interjected.

"Yeah, really. Today, I probably couldn't run from one end of the court to the other without stopping to catch my breath a couple of times. But I was surprisingly good in my time—and maybe just a tad slimmer.

"Anyway, we brought together some talented players from our high school days and thought we'd tear up this league. But when it was game time, everyone was out for themselves. Our offense consisted of one guy dribbling around the court, trying to create a shot for himself. The other four guys just stood around watching. On defense, we didn't help each other. We just pointed fingers when the other team scored.

"It was exactly what your mentor described. In this case, our five guys on the floor were probably equal to three, and the other teams let us know how much they enjoyed kicking our hotshot butts each week."

Jason laughed and thanked Cooper for sharing his experience, adding, "Those stories are good examples of both ends of the spectrum of teamwork. Now I want us to take a moment and do something together. It will be a short but powerful illustration. Let's stand up and make a circle around this conference room."

The team looked a bit bemused as they obliged, and Jason continued, "This circle depicts the way a lot of teams work, and it reflects accurately how our teams currently operate, which is problematic. You see, the real issue is we're all *facing* each other, watching what each other is doing, worried someone is going to let us down or maybe stab us in the back, or at least blame us for something we didn't do. We're so busy worrying about what's going on inside that we're not keeping up with what's happening outside."

He motioned to the windows and continued, "OK, now turn around, staying in our circle but facing outward. This is how our team *should* operate. We should be facing the outside, seeing the needs of our customers, aware of what is going on outside our four walls, ready to compete. More importantly, our backs should be turned to each other because we're confident they're covered. We should be able to trust we're all here with the same goal of supporting our teammates and delighting our customers.

"No backstabbing, no blame—instead, every member of the team pulling together."

With the exercise over, the team sat down, and Jason said, "If you look at where our company is today, we're missing an important piece of the culture puzzle: teamwork. Nelson described it this morning as a lack of collaboration. We have a lot of wonderful people here, but we're all stymied by the internal politics and individual agendas, and the sum of our efforts is well below what's possible.

"We're like the diagram with the arrows going in many directions, good intentions that haven't added up to much—at least in recent years. In fact, we're a good replication of the basketball team Cooper talked about, and instead of bringing out the best in each other, we're working in the opposite direction. I don't think we need more talent; rather, we need to find a way to work together to maximize the talent we have."

It had been a packed morning, and they'd covered a lot. Jason wanted to cover one more aspect of this topic before breaking for lunch. As he scanned the room, he saw the wheels were turning.

"What are your thoughts on teamwork? Any questions or comments?" he asked.

Hannah spoke up. "We're going through a lot of concepts today, and it's easy to see how teamwork applies to us. I agree we have a lot of great people, but we certainly aren't a great company. I feel good about my department, but that's where it ends. I want to feel good about the whole company, and everyone we work with and depend on. I mean, what you're describing as teamwork sure sounds like a better way to spend the day—like what Mike described for his department, but companywide."

More nods around the room.

"OK, one last thought I'd like everyone to consider regarding teamwork," said Jason. "This is an aspect, or dynamic, that doesn't get much attention. Let me start by asking you a question. As you came into the conference room today, which team did you consider yourself to be a part of?"

Jason looked around the conference table, his eyes stopping with Edward, who seemed ready to share.

Edward answered factually, "I represent the concerns of the RA/

QA department and that body of knowledge within the company."

Everyone appeared supportive of Edward's reply.

"Alright," Jason answered. "Then, in this meeting—right here, right now—where would you say your primary allegiance is when it comes to a specific team?"

Edward came back quickly.

"Overall, my allegiance is to the company, but my primary and first allegiance is to my department, the RA/QA team," he said.

Again, there were nods of agreement, although Jason thought they appeared more cautious this time.

Jason added: "Let me share another way of looking at this and see if it resonates with you. In this room is the senior leadership team for KCI. Are we a *team*, or are we a collection of representatives?"

He paused to let the question sink in before continuing.

"If we're a collection of representatives, then what team is directing KCI? Or perhaps you consider yourselves a group of representatives, and that would make me a team of one directing KCI. Can you see where I'm going with this? Because it applies not only here in this room but also to each of your departmental teams.

"As an example, when Edward holds his weekly RA/QA staff meeting, do his managers come together as a team responsible for directing the activities of the RA/QA department, or are they a collection of representatives for the various areas they manage?"

Looking around the room, Jason saw quizzical looks on some faces.

"Here's the difference," he elaborated. "First off, yes, we are all part of KCI, the greater team. That's where our ultimate allegiance lies. However, when participating in a team meeting, I believe your primary allegiance should be to your highest level of responsibility in that situation. So, in our case, everyone here, save Nelson, should have primary allegiance to the senior leadership team.

"Imagine how difficult it would be to operate as a highly efficient team, much less guide KCI at a high level, if your only participation here is as representatives of your respective departments. In that case, you might choose to disconnect and tune out any part of the executive staff meeting that doesn't relate to your area. Yet everything that's discussed at this level has the potential to impact every department here, including yours. While I do take responsibility for all that happens at KCI ultimately, I see this as the 'team' making those decisions based on our collective knowledge and experience.

"It's important that when you come into this conference room, you enter as a member of the senior leadership team, fully connected to each other, with responsibility and accountability for the activities and results of this organization.

"The same applies throughout the company. Your respective staff meetings should be comprised of the team responsible for directing your functional area—but responsible and accountable not only for the direction but also for the results. It shouldn't be a collection of representatives with you as the leader.

"Can you see the difference in those models? As a representative, you don't have the same accountability for team decisions or outcomes. Worst-case scenario, a representative could attend this meeting, caring little for the items unrelated to their department and intending to merely protect their departmental interests.

"At the same time, as a full team member, you participate in and own each of these decisions as much as I or anybody else in this room. So, when we talk about teamwork, to me, it's not just the ability to work together for the common good of the organization. It's about groups of people functioning in teams to guide, direct, and perform the activities here with full responsibility and accountability."

Victor still looked confused. With scrunched eyebrows, he said, "I've never heard this concept before, and it's intriguing. So, I want to be clear that I understand what you're saying. Let me repeat it back to you in my own words. When I enter this conference room, you want me to take off my VP of HR hat and essentially put on a hat that says 'Senior Leadership Team' on the front? And I should concern myself with everything going on here as if I'm an owner of the company?"

Jason smiled. "Yes, I think that's a good start, Victor."

Victor continued, "So, when I have my departmental staff meeting, the managers should drop their individual hats, whether it be employee relations, benefits, or recruiting, and all of us put on our HR hats. Is that basically it?"

"Yes," said Jason. "Once they enter the room, they're part of the team planning and executing the HR function. They bring their expertise and share their experiences, but their goal in participating should not be to maximize what they can get for their respective sub-area—employee relations, benefits, or recruiting. Instead, they should be focusing on maximizing the impact of the HR function throughout KCI. Their respective areas are individual tools in the collective HR-team toolkit, just as the HR function is one of the tools in our senior leadership team's tool bag when you enter.

"Is that making sense to you? And to everyone now?"

Everyone nodded in agreement. However, Jason made a mental note to do a deeper dive later when they put this into practice.

"This is an aspect of teamwork that can both separate and elevate our organization," he said. "Many people think teamwork is everyone getting along. While that's an important part, it's equally important for everyone to understand how a team functions and their role in making it work. It's critical then for everyone to clearly understand what team or teams they're on and their specific role in each of those. If we can accomplish that, we'll have a shot at maximizing my mentor's teamwork equation of two plus two equaling five.

"Well, it's beginning to smell like a taco shop in here, so let's summarize this element and break for lunch. The element is teamwork," Jason said while making the notations on the flip chart. "And the key factors are as follows:

- Without teamwork, 2 + 2 = 3, but with teamwork, 2 + 2 can = 5.

- Teamwork allows us to face the outside, trusting that we have each other's backs.
- Team allegiance is to the highest level of responsibility for the team on which you're participating.

"All right, time to eat. Let's plan to start back up in forty-five minutes. Thanks for a great morning and a lot of excellent discussion."

Excitement was building in the room as they made their way to the food line.

It was summertime, so over lunch, Jason enjoyed listening to his colleagues sharing their vacation plans with each other.

Victor, a father of five children, told everyone about a family vacation he'd planned at an Airbnb near Lake Tahoe. He was looking forward to hiking and river rafting in the Sierra Nevada mountains.

Mike shared with everyone that his wife's home-craft business was taking off and that she might be looking into a storefront soon. He also said that they were planning to combine business with pleasure by showing some of her work at a huge craft fair in the Napa Sonoma Valley in Northern California. In addition to the fair, they planned to take in the scenic valleys and "taste" as much wine as they could at the world-famous vineyards there.

Hannah and her husband were planning what she called a "romantic getaway" to Maui where they'd laze around the beach and do a little snorkeling.

It seemed to Jason like the conversation was flowing much more freely than it had been earlier in the day. He was also glad he'd invited Nelson to sit in the perspective chair. Nelson was an important connector between management and many employees.

Jason had been filled in on Nelson's background by Cooper. The production manager had effectively grown up in this organization and progressed to his current role. He was very mechanically skilled and had been a valuable member of the production team initially. In Nelson's younger years, he and his dad restored old 1960s and

1970s muscle cars, and he'd learned a lot about mechanical assembly without ever having any formal training. The real bonus was he was great with people—a natural-born leader. In all the conversations Jason had had with the employees in production, everyone spoke highly of Nelson.

From all Jason had learned about Nelson, he was confident today's topics would resonate with both the production manager's way of thinking and his leadership style. Jason expected him to be one of the leaders of the cultural transformation at KCI.

Jason thought Cooper was fortunate to have strong players on his operations team, including Nelson leading production and Bryan O'Conner in the supply chain manager role. Both were significant contributors; however, Nelson had indicated he wasn't interested in being considered for Cooper's vice president of operations role in the future, while Bryan clearly was.

Jason was aware that Cooper was spending extra time with Bryan, teaching and grooming him for that future opportunity. As for Nelson, apparently he just didn't have a taste for the responsibilities that came along with the VP role.

As they neared the end of lunch, Jason prepared the flip chart to signal the session was recommencing and kicked off the afternoon by moving to element number five on his list.

## ELEMENT #5: EMPLOYEE ENGAGEMENT

"The next element we're going to discuss is employee engagement," he said. "You've probably heard a lot of buzz about this over the past several years. How important do you think employee engagement is to our success?"

Victor jumped in. "Without it, I don't think we stand a chance at achieving real success, and certainly not to the level that Thompson

Holdings is expecting," he said.

Jason responded, "Agreed, Victor. So how engaged do you think our employees are?"

Victor answered without hesitation, "My opinion varies. There are times or areas where I'd say engagement is high, but then, I do see a fair amount of apathy around the company. Or to use a term you've been using today, employees are disconnected from the organization. Considering the elements we've covered so far, well, none are being fulfilled like you've described. Employees are probably just going through the motions. Based on that, overall, I'd say we're not a highly engaged company."

"Nelson, you manage the largest number of employees here. How would you respond to the question?"

It didn't take Nelson long.

"I agree with Victor's comments," he said. "We've tried to establish and maintain some level of employee engagement in production, but with inconsistencies everywhere, that's been difficult. It's interesting, because when you asked the question, the first term that came to mind was exactly the one Victor used: apathy. And as stated earlier, it really depends on which department you're in and how it's managed."

Nelson continued, "If you have kids at home, you can probably relate to what's happening here. In your neighborhood, there are always those kids who don't have any boundaries, and your kids wonder why they have to live under such different rules. There are so many subcultures here, it's left many employees in a state of mind where they don't care anymore. They come in, do their jobs, get their paychecks, and go home. You can call it apathy or being compliant—but it certainly isn't engagement."

Jason took in what Nelson was getting at.

"So, it's good-news-bad-news time," he replied. "The bad news is we're leaning more towards an unengaged workforce. The good news is we're not much different from other companies. With focus and effort, we can change that. Gallup, the company known for conducting public opinion polls, has done a lot of work in this area. It updates its employee engagement statistics every year based on the survey information it receives."

Jason turned back to the projector and queued up the next slide [Figure 5].

Figure 5

After allowing the team some time to take in the information in front of them, Jason explained: "First off, you can see Gallup has developed three categories of employee engagement: engaged, not engaged, and actively disengaged. I've paraphrased the three descriptions for this chart.

"It's disconcerting to see that two-thirds of the classifications are negative, isn't it? Well, as concerning as those definitions are, the percentages of employees in each category are even more alarming. As of early 2022, in US-based companies like ours, only 32 percent of the employees surveyed were engaged; 51 percent fell into the not-engaged category; and 17 percent are actively disengaged.[6] So,

---

6  Harter J, 2022

not only are two-thirds of the classifications negative, two-thirds of the employees fall into those negative classifications.

"Let me paint a picture for you of what that might look like. If you entered a race with a ten-person rowing team, there would be roughly three people in the boat rowing to win the race. There would be five people checking their social media accounts or reclining in the boat, taking a nap—oblivious to the fact they're even in a race. Incredibly, there would be two people in the boat throwing anchors into the water or coming up with ways to capsize the boat and lose the race.

"How do you think your team would fare against the other competitors?"

Cooper quipped, "Well, if the other teams are as bad as us, hmm. But probably best not to count on that!"

As those numbers sank in, Jason spotted looks of shock and concern. He surmised everyone was thinking about their own teams—about which category individual employees might be in, and perhaps which category they *themselves* were in.

He picked up the conversation.

"There's a consolation," he said. "Those numbers are the averages of all the companies surveyed in the US, which means companies across the country are dealing with this same issue. And lest you think it's different elsewhere, the numbers do vary by global region, but right now, the US and Canada have the highest percentages of engaged employees. So, this is an issue for companies everywhere on the planet, and this information should generate a call to action to anyone who's listening.

"But if, and this is a big *if*—if we can develop an intentional plan to improve employee engagement, how might that impact our ability to compete?"

Hannah spoke up. "I'm speechless, which you all know is a rare occurrence. Those statistics are exactly what you described: alarming. But on the other hand, what an opportunity if we can pull together and actually do something about it. How does Gallup go about measuring employee engagement?"

Jason answered, "After years of research, Gallup identified twelve foundational elements of employee engagement that predict high team performance. From those elements, it developed a twelve-question survey, aptly named the Q12. With only twelve questions, it's not difficult to take the survey and monitor progress on an ongoing basis. There's also another measurement of employee engagement called net promoter score, or NPS."

"Oh, sure," Hannah replied. "We use that to measure customer loyalty."

"Right," said Jason. "You can also use NPS metrics to measure engagement by asking employees if they would recommend working at KCI to their friends or family.

"At some of my past companies, I've used a less sophisticated way to monitor employee engagement. It's simply called 'committed versus compliant.' For comparison, I believe those employees who fit into Gallup's not-engaged and actively disengaged categories are most likely compliant in their duties for the company. In other words, they just do what they are told, no more, and in some cases, maybe less.

"Those in Gallup's engaged grouping are the equivalent of someone in the committed category. As you can imagine, the committed employee is the one who goes the extra mile without being asked. Those are the employees who have their colleagues' backs and are probably the people who show respect to other employees.

"Like I said, in the past we simply asked leaders to classify their employees into one of those two categories. They know their people best; it was quick and easy and completed on a quarterly basis. If they had an employee in the compliant category, we requested the supervisor develop an individual plan to help their employee progress into the committed category. We kept it simple, but you'd be surprised at its accuracy, and how useful it was in cultivating an environment where teamwork could flourish within the company."

Victor posed a question: "Jason, during the time you've been a

CEO, have you ever classified one of your senior leaders as compliant? Generally, I'd expect to see them in the committed category."

Jason thought for a moment before replying, "You know, Victor, I have. Like you said, it's rare. Senior leadership is typically highly committed. But where they weren't committed, you could say there wasn't strong alignment to many of the elements we've been discussing. Ultimately, our senior leadership team must be a model of everything we agree to here; we absolutely have to walk the talk."

Jason finished writing "committed vs. compliant" on the flip chart and turned back to the group.

"I got a little bit into the weeds," he laughed. "But I hope the example was useful. Sticking with employee engagement, I believe there's a second, less obvious side we should explore."

Those around the table did not seem surprised that he had an alternative perspective, but this time they appeared anxious to hear it. He'd known up to this point that some folks weren't sure about his leadership style: was he a hands-off leader, soaking it all in, or just quiet? However, the energy buzzing around the room was a good indicator that they were on board with these discussions and probably enjoying seeing this side of him.

Jason pressed, "So, having seen Gallup's survey results, what area of improvement do you think executives focus on when they see these employee engagement results?"

Cooper was first to answer.

"Generally, I'd say their goal is to increase productivity. They're hoping to get more out of their employees through engagement," he said.

"Exactly!" said Jason. "Engagement and/or commitment generally results in more output, better quality—hopefully more or better everything. Then, what does the employee get out of being engaged or committed?" Jason polled the room.

No one had an answer.

After what seemed like a long silence, Abby finally said: "Maybe a raise, or a future promotion?"

"Possibly," Jason remarked.

He could see they were a bit stumped with this question.

"I think what employees are looking for, and what the company owes an engaged or committed employee, is fulfillment," he explained. "I believe that's a fair exchange. The company receives higher productivity throughout the day, and the employee gains the opportunity to go home fulfilled each day. It should be a two-way street requiring effort by both parties. It takes effort and commitment for employees to be engaged. Likewise, it takes effort and commitment by the company to help employees achieve a sense of fulfillment. It's also our chance to show we genuinely care about them.

"When companies see those alarming Gallup statistics, many leaders focus on possible causes for the productivity losses they represent. And while they see the opportunity to improve productivity through engagement, they don't consider the responsibilities the company might have in exchange for engagement.

"As I mentioned, I believe there's great value when we look at both sides of the equation and strive to maximize the benefit to both the company and its employees. In this case, engagement and fulfillment go hand in hand. When we agree to couple them, we have a chance at improving on those dismal Gallup numbers and then sustaining it."

Hannah blurted out, "What if this element had a goal statement? Something like 'Engaged throughout the day and fulfilled when we end it'?"

"Brilliant, Hannah. I love it!" said Jason. "You've captured the essence of this."

Everyone nodded their approval, and Jason chalked up one more nudge in the right direction for this team.

He continued, "When we move to tactics, we can develop specific plans to cultivate and improve employee engagement. Does anyone have anything else to add to our discussion? Does everyone agree with this element's goals so far?"

Hannah led the way. "This just keeps getting better. I'm all in." She beamed as everyone else again nodded their approval.

Jason moved back to the chart. He summarized, "The element is employee engagement, and the key factors are as follows:

- On average, only three out of ten employees are engaged.
- On average, seven out of ten employees are either not engaged or actively disengaged.
- Our desire is for employees to be committed vs. compliant.
- Goal statement of 'Engaged throughout the day and fulfilled when we end it.'

"Excellent work, everyone—five elements down, two more to go. We're going to take a quick ten-minute break to get some refreshments."

Jason knew it had been a long day for everyone, but a sense of purpose had taken hold in the room. They had a long road ahead of them and a lot at stake. He needed the foundation of their plan developed when he went to the quarterly meeting at corporate.

At the back of the room was a table filled with drinks and snacks. Jason grabbed a soda for a little caffeine boost before the final discussion. Three team members were gathered around Mike, sharing a laugh over something Jason could not quite make out. He thought about how good it was to see laughter in the group even after an exhausting day. Jason joined in for a moment and then herded them all back to the conference table.

# 6

## LAYING THE FOUNDATION: PART THREE

With everyone reseated in the conference room, Jason began, "OK, we've discussed five elements so far: respect, relationships, 100 percent leadership buy-in, teamwork, and employee engagement. The sixth element is continuous improvement.

### ELEMENT #6: CONTINUOUS IMPROVEMENT

"Looking back, in KCI's early days the company touched success, but it was fleeting. An effective way to sustain and build on success is by becoming a continuous learning organization, improving daily. The world around us is changing at a faster rate than ever before. Our ability to learn and adapt can become either a strategic weapon in the competitive landscape or a noose around our neck if we are unable to keep up.

"We've probably all heard of the Toyota Production System, or the Westernized version called 'lean manufacturing.' It originated within Toyota after WWII. Long story short, Toyota was strapped for cash and couldn't afford to purchase inventory. It developed a continuous flow production methodology revolving around a pull versus a push system, which enabled the company to consume materials and resources based on actual customer demand—pull, or sales—which in turn minimized its required inventory pipeline and the cash required to support it.

"Toyota also empowered its employees to improve work operations, giving them the authority to stop production anytime a quality issue was detected. TPS blossomed into a full-blown companywide approach, the Toyota Way, which has sustained Toyota over the years through this mindset of continuous improvement.

"At the heart of this thinking is *respect* for the individual and *trust* in everyone's desire and ability to improve their work processes each day."

Jason wrote down those two key words before continuing, "You can see the connection to our discussion this morning. Like employee engagement, both the company and the employees benefit from this continuous improvement mindset. The company gains productivity and quality improvement, and the employees gain the opportunity to make their work life better each day. Coupled with engagement, it enhances their ability to achieve a sense of fulfillment through their work."

Hannah had a question.

"I've been told about companies using this lean approach to improve their manufacturing operations, but I've heard it's more of an inventory reduction strategy that results in backorders. Then the sales team gets to spend hours trying to keep their customers from leaving," she said. "Is that what this element boils down to: reducing inventory so our numbers look better to Thompson Holdings?"

"I've got this one," Cooper replied, looking over to Jason. "Hannah, there are many aspects of lean that make it a viable strategy. Conversely, there are many myths. You've hit on two of the myths. The first myth is that it's no more than an inventory reduction strategy—which it's not; rather, inventory reduction is a benefit realized through continuous improvement.

"Here's a simple example that might help you see this clearer. Let's say we have a process with ten steps in its cycle. And for ease of calculation, it takes one week for the product to go through each of those ten steps. Based on that scenario, how much inventory would you have in the product pipeline I just described?"

Hannah answered, "Ten steps, and each step processes for one week—I'd say ten weeks of inventory?"

"Correct," said Cooper. "Now, imagine through continuous improvement efforts that you're able to reduce both the total number of process steps and the length of time each step takes. Let's say we've successfully brought the total steps down from ten to five and reduced each individual step's processing time from one week to one day. How much inventory would you now have in the same product pipeline?"

Hannah answered, "Well, five steps at one day each would be five days of inventory?"

"Right again," said Cooper. "We started with a complex process resulting in ten weeks of inventory filling the pipeline. Through our continuous improvement efforts, we streamlined the process and its associated pipeline from ten weeks to five days. A benefit of the process improvement was a 90 percent reduction in inventory.

"The goal was not to arbitrarily reduce inventory and then hope for the best outcome, which in the early days was what some thought lean was. The real goal is to simplify and accelerate the process—and inventory reduction is one of the benefits of doing so. A better and faster process also provides a higher level of service and quicker response time to our customers. If done with the right goals in mind, I suggest there'll be less backorders instead of more. Make sense?"

Hannah was nodding.

"Yeah, the way you explain it does make sense," she said. "Even to a nonmanufacturing person like me."

Cooper continued, "You can imagine the overall impact if we are able to simplify our processes across production. Again, our strategy would be continuous improvement resulting in a production cycle with less touches, higher quality, and a quicker throughput time—with one of the benefits being inventory reduction."

Abby jumped into the mix.

"Right now, we have more than one year's total inventory on hand, which is high for any company," she said. "That's a sizable amount of cash tied up in something that's parked on a shelf in the warehouse or sitting on a rack in production. If we could do what Cooper described, it could free up significant cash, which could be invested in growing this new product, whether it be for equipment, people, systems—or all of those."

"There's a lot more to this," Cooper went on. "And once we get into the tactics, we can go deeper. Before we move on, I want to address the second myth I alluded to, which says lean or continuous improvement is something we do only in operations. The truth is that the most successful companies are adopting this strategy on a companywide basis. Everything we do in business is a process, so this can be applied to the processes in every department.

"We can improve accounting, customer service, or new product development. We'd be crazy not to target every facet of our business, right? I guess you can tell I'm passionate about this. I've brought this topic up a couple of times over the years, but it was always met with resistance. I was told we didn't have the time or money, and we'd consider it down the road, which never happened until today."

Cooper turned to Hannah, adding, "By the way, Hannah, I did hear of a company that analyzed its selling processes and estimated the total 'value added' time in a typical salesperson's day to be 30 percent—'value adding' meaning when the sales rep was actively selling product. The other 70 percent was spent in 'non-value adding' activities like driving, filling out paperwork, making calls, and so on. That's a startling statistic on its own, although probably seen across all selling processes in general.

"So, let's say again through continuous improvement efforts you were able to enhance the selling process and raised the daily time spent in value adding activities from 30 percent to 50 percent. What could that mean for our sales numbers? Simply put, it'd be like adding an hour of customer facing selling time to every salesperson's day."

Thinking out loud, Hannah said, "That could be huge, Cooper. Hmm."

Cooper continued, "Imagine the edge we'd have if our competitors are dabbling in continuous improvement but limiting it to operations, while we apply it companywide. What could that do?"

"It would be a significant advantage for us, and I'm liking where this conversation is going," Hannah said. "I also have to say something, Jason, going back to our conversation about whether we're representatives in this room or participating team members with full accountability. When you said the element was continuous improvement, my first inclination was to tune out and do a quick check of email. I figured this topic was for Cooper and Nelson. This is a great example of the rationale behind staying tuned in as a participant. And, Cooper, excellent job of pulling us all in. Thank you for that."

Jason was energized as the discussion touched all the right areas. He'd wanted to impress the notion that continuous improvement was an enterprise-wide strategy, not just for operations. Cooper certainly hit that nail squarely on the head.

"Hannah, thanks for the question. And, Cooper, great examples with which we all can identify," Jason said. "As Cooper stated, continuous improvement is used optimally as an enterprise-wide strategy. I think it can be an impactful element in our future. I want to share a couple of additional examples, and then we'll move on to the final element.

"I had the opportunity to see some interesting approaches to continuous improvement through many of the company tours I attended. I also heard of instances where continuous improvement or lean created confusion. That's something we want to avoid, hopefully through thoughtful planning and good communication.

"One takeaway for me was the different approaches companies used to launch their continuous improvement journeys. This *is* a journey, and if done properly, it never ends. We'll strive for perfection; however, we can always improve.

"In lean's early days, companies typically began by setting up a process work cell in production. They also might have begun with the 5S toolkit; either way, they were trying to establish a success story they could build upon. Sometimes it worked, but many times it was localized to those who participated firsthand. Often, the efforts to build upon their work were met with resistance, and the whole idea would become a battleground within the company.

"People can be resistant to change, and at times, they can feel like these concepts are being forced upon them. Once they go on the defense, it's tough to break down the barriers.

"I was intrigued, though, by how some companies are going about it more recently. The first step in their approach has been to develop the culture of the company, building a foundation on—you might have guessed it—respect and trust. With those in place, they then launch the tools of continuous improvement. In fact, one company I visited spent two years establishing its culture. Just prior to our tour date, it began launching the tools.

"Remember earlier when Cooper was telling us about the company that first respected its employees by focusing on safety improvements, then began implementing continuous improvement tools. Both ways considered, it makes sense that if you can first establish a culture of respect and trust, then resistance to change is minimized and the tools of continuous improvement are more easily accepted. I'd also bet those improvements will be more sustainable over the long term. If, or when, we initiate our continuous improvement efforts, I'd recommend we consider the sequence of activities surrounding its launch and let the cultural changes lead the charge."

Abby interjected, "Jason, I know you tried to head this off with your 'Firms of Endearment' slide earlier, but doing this on an enterprise-wide basis concerns me. We are just able to squeak out a decent profit today, but nowhere near what the other Thompson Holdings medical companies are generating. In the short term, I can't see any way this element will improve those numbers. More likely, it will increase overall expenses. I hope I'm not being too negative, but all I can picture is our building lifted into the air with money leaking out everywhere. How are we going to finance this?"

"Great question, Abby—also perfect timing," said Jason. "My second example comes from a company I visited that decided to start every work shift with a half-hour period of what they called 'lean and clean.' Its employees were given the choice to spend the thirty-minute period either working on a 'two-second lean' improvement, inspired by the book[7] of the same name, or being on one of the teams cleaning the common areas, including hallways, the lunchroom, and, yes, the bathrooms.

"The CFO of the company told me that he panicked once he estimated the productivity losses associated with this decision. But productivity quickly gained momentum, and the company ended up netting a solid return on its investment through the incredible number of improvements implemented daily.

"By the way, this also ties into respect. I'll give you an example. On the facility tour, I asked a few of the employees how they felt about the thirty-minute lean-and-clean time and which option they typically took: lean or clean. The response I got was they'd do a mix of both options. One employee said, 'Hey, where else can you be side by side with the company president, cleaning a toilet?' So, the janitorial cost savings, combined with the productivity improvements they implemented each day, more than offset the lean-and-clean productivity losses. At the same time, mutual respect increased, and trust developed within the company.

"Abby, I'll connect you with the CFO there so you can pick the brain of someone who's been through this. They had a high degree of confidence they were on the right side of the ledger in this activity."

"That'd be great, Jason," Abby replied. "In my mind, the math just doesn't add up for us—at least, not right now. I'll talk to this guy,

---

7   Akers, P, 2016

and hopefully he can show me how it makes good financial sense."

Jason made a note to send Abby the contact details and then moved on.

He explained, "Another company I visited used the phrase 'earning the right to go on to the next continuous improvement tool.' That meant the employees had to agree they had the current tool or countermeasure well established and were ready to take on the next one. It also gave staff the opportunity to ensure their improvements were generating enough savings to help fund the next tool's implementation—in other words, not putting the cart before the horse. Is this making sense to everyone?"

Nelson and Cooper nodded in agreement, but it was Nelson who spoke up.

"Earlier you mentioned employees thinking management was bringing in programs they could just wait out and those programs would fade over time," he said. "The way we're talking about this today, especially in terms of continuous improvement, well, for the first time, I see a path forward that isn't filled with potholes. By the way, I visited a company that forced these concepts on their employees, and it didn't go well. This sounds like the right approach."

Cooper nodded in support again, so Jason kept going.

"You know, this may be getting too tactical, but there's one more observation from my site visits I want to share," he said. "I liked the way the company in this example laid it out, setting up its continuous improvement activities under three pillars. In fact, these three pillars align well with the elements we're discussing today, but in essence, they're the tenets this company chose to guide everything related to continuous improvement. The three pillars are 'equipped,' 'empowered,' and 'engaged.'

"For equipped, the company wanted to be sure, before setting any improvement goals, that employees were equipped with the tools of continuous improvement. All employees were provided training, but with each tool, the employee had to be certified as both competent and confident—competent meaning they'd successfully completed the training course, and confident meaning they were able to demonstrate to their immediate supervisor that they could successfully use the tool in a real situation.

"I thought this was insightful. Often, we expect people to make things better without giving them the tools to do so, or we run them through a quick training exercise, and although they've heard the concepts, they may not be confident enough to use the tool in their daily work life. Without confidence, the tool will likely sit on the shelf and never be used—or at least not to the level everyone hoped for. This is the first pillar: equipped, with the caveats of competent and confident.

"The second pillar is empowered; employees were given the time and environment to continuously improve. Like the company that did lean and clean, this company started each shift with fifteen minutes of continuous improvement time, which applied to everyone in the company. The fifteen-minute period accounted for the time aspect, while the environment aspect was the support they received from their leader and/or fellow employees to complete their improvements. This created an environment in which continuous improvement was a good thing to do throughout the company. So, the second pillar is empowered, and the caveats are time and environment.

"Continuing on, the company also recognized the importance of placing these tools in the hands of engaged employees and providing them with the opportunity to do something positive. That's the third pillar: engaged. When this team drilled down on engagement, they found that they were doing a lot of company-sponsored activities for their employees: celebrations, recognition, and fun events; however, most were episodic in nature. Those were fine as individual activities, but the real goal was daily engagement with every employee.

"The first step in achieving this was a daily, twenty-minute, all-employee update meeting where participants shared company results and celebrated improvements. Employees hosted the meeting on a voluntary basis, and time was provided for anyone to share something they were grateful for. It was a short meeting, but purposeful and engaging. So, the third and final pillar is engaged, and the caveat is daily connection."

Jason paused to let the information percolate with the team. He added, "I got tactical once again, but I wanted to get you thinking about this element. I believe each of the elements we're discussing are important aspects of our cultural transformation, but if we agree on continuous improvement as one of those, it will ultimately be the biggest undertaking. All right, does anyone have any comments or questions?"

Cooper went first this time.

"To be honest, Jason, I'm impressed by your knowledge and understanding of continuous improvement," he said. "Most company presidents don't take the time to fully understand either the impact or what it takes to get it right. They completely miss that it's an enterprise-wide strategy, and, if anything, it's relegated to operations only. The fact we're talking about this as a senior leadership team already puts us ahead of the competition. I'm pumped."

Nelson joined in: "I'm with Cooper. It's going to be a lot of work, but knowing there's support at this level will make the long hours worthwhile."

Abby was next to add a comment.

"I know I probably came across as a naysayer," she said, "but I'm only making sure we do this in a way where we still hit our numbers. Thompson Holdings will be excited about what we're doing, but they'll expect it to contribute positively to our bottom line."

Hannah chimed in, "I'm all in on this. Cooper got my attention with his selling analogy."

Mike continued the parade of comments: "Me too! If we can apply this approach to how we develop new products, it could have a huge impact on the organization."

Edward nodded his approval, although Jason got the feeling he was hesitant.

Jason moved to the flip chart to bring closure to this element.

He summarized, "The element is continuous improvement, and the key factors are as follows:

- Companywide implementation
- Respect for people is central.
- Culture first, tools second
- Pace is important.
- Positive overall ROI
- Equipped, empowered, and engaged

"We've covered a lot of ground today, and by now you're probably seeing the connection between these elements. So, let's look at the final one."

## ELEMENT #7: TRANSPARENCY

Jason flipped over the chart and explained, "The Wikipedia description of the word 'transparency' accurately sums it up for our application. It says, 'Transparency is operating in such a way that it's easy for others to see what actions are performed. Transparency implies openness, communication, and accountability.'

"Let's go back to our discussions from earlier today. We agreed we want our employees to be committed, not just compliant. Our goal is for them to be in Gallup's 'engaged' category. We want them to connect to this company and feel like it's theirs—to operate as if they're an owner. I believe the only way this happens is if we share all pertinent information related to our company.

"Some may argue there's proprietary information which cannot be discussed publicly, and that's a real possibility. When that occurs, we simply call it what it is and share why we're not able to discuss it—just be up front and *transparent.*

"Many companies treat information as if it's a closely held secret; yet mid-to-senior-level executives often have access to this information, and it's common for them to change jobs *within* industry. The fact that they've had access to high-level information generally doesn't impact or damage the company they just left. And if you're curious, it's not hard to find out how a company is doing; just look at their market share data trends, or look at their filings if they're public—heck, look at their parking lot, and you can see which direction they're headed. I think the value of keeping our employees informed far outweighs the downside of any information leakage."

"What information are you thinking of sharing and how often?" Abby questioned.

"Since we have quarterly reviews with Thompsons Holdings, it'd make sense to share our information quarterly with our employees," Jason responded. "That would include a high-level P&L, our strategic plan, and the corresponding key result areas, or KRAs, along with updates of our performance against those KRAs. I'd also share any other key business metrics we identify and, of course, significant projects or activities within the company as well as any future obstacles or hurdles we're anticipating."

Abby quizzed him again. "Do you really think everyone in the company will be able to understand a P&L statement?" she said.

Jason was ready for this discussion based on similar approaches he'd taken in the past.

"Yes, I do, Abby, if we keep it basic and teach them how to read and interpret the information we present to them. Taking the first tenet from the company example I shared on continuous improvement, we 'equip' everyone with the knowledge and then teach them how to use it. I don't think you can operate as an owner if you don't know what's happening inside your own company. It also serves to hold us—and every other employee—accountable for our actions. In the end, this element is an important step towards showing respect to our employees and building trust throughout the company."

"OK," said Abby. "It's probably doable, but I'd like to be involved in this activity once we get going. And frankly, if we could get our three hundred-plus employees acting as business owners, that'd be one change I'd support."

Jason nodded. "Thanks, Abby; no doubt your participation will be key in this element. Without getting deeper into tactics, the Wiki definition really sums up transparency: openness, communication, and accountability. If we do those three effectively, this will go a long way towards engaging our employees and providing them the opportunity to be fulfilled each day.

"However, in terms of transparency, what we've talked about so far only scratches the surface at the very top level. It should extend to developing and maintaining scorecards for each department and their sub-areas and holding routine performance updates and discussions. These would be held based on whatever cadence is appropriate—monthly, weekly, daily, or even hourly. We'd want to ensure employees receive timely feedback on their individual and departmental performance metrics and help them realize the impact they have on the achievement of the overall company goals. We should be able to walk into any area and visually know if everything is on track."

"I agree completely," Cooper remarked. "That fits in with continuous improvement practices as well."

"Thanks, Cooper," said Jason. "Well, that's what I have on transparency. Are there any comments or concerns before we summarize the discussions for today?"

Most shook their heads. To Jason, they looked tired from the day, yet optimistic. He wrote one more time on the flip chart.

"The element is transparency, and the key factors are as follows:

- Openness
- Communication
- Accountability

- Equipping employees with the tools to be competent and confident with the information shared with them
- Ability to visually see in real time if areas are tracking to their goals

"Let's take a moment and summarize the seven elements or tenets we've discussed in depth today:

- Respect
- Relationships
- 100 percent leadership buy-in
- Teamwork
- Engagement
- Continuous improvement
- Transparency

"In most of these elements, we expanded on the traditional company view and included what we described as both sides of the equation.

"For respect, we expanded it to respect for all employees, going in all directions—to direct reports, to leaders, to each other.

"For relationships, it's educating all employees on how to maximize our working relationships—beginning with the leader–direct report relationship and expanding to all relationships within the company.

"For 100 percent leadership buy-in, we require 100 percent buy-in and commitment from all those who are in leadership roles. We must achieve consistency throughout the organization to establish a winning culture.

"For teamwork, we discussed having each other's back so we can face the outside world and then participating as an engaged and accountable teammate and not merely as a representative.

"For engagement, we considered both productivity at all levels for the company and fulfillment for our employees.

"In continuous improvement, we want to go companywide, centered on respect, and establish our cultural principles before launching the tools.

"And finally, transparency means we share all the information we can with our employees while being accountable to each other visually."

A collective sigh of relief seemed to fill the room. Perhaps the magnitude of the potential impact and the excitement of working in this kind of environment was sinking in. Jason was pleased that it appeared to resonate with everyone in the room.

"Now, to tie this all back together, let's go back to your list from this morning and see where the crossovers are. As we review each one, I'd like the person who shared it to determine if we covered their comment within the seven elements, or if it's a sub-bullet to one, or perhaps you feel strongly it should be considered as an additional element. I am going to place the two flip charts next to each other so we can see both lists side by side [Figure 6].

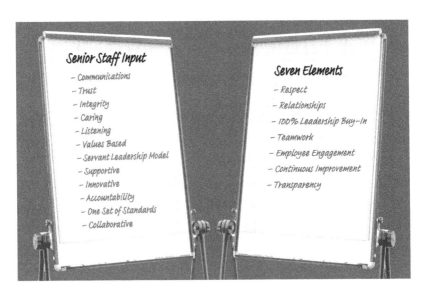

Figure 6

"First up is Hannah's initial point of communications. Hannah, what are your thoughts? And go ahead and keep the floor for discussion on your second point, trust."

Hannah paused for a moment before explaining, "I think communications is a part of transparency. Jason, you copied down my sub-bullets of what, how, who, and when, and I think those will be covered in the next round of discussion when we develop tactics. You can check that one off.

"I think the same for trust. I'd be happy if we included it in the tactical discussion for respect, and if we were to make earning and developing the trust of our employees the goal of our work in respect, then I think it's well covered."

"You got it," said Jason. "Cooper, you're next up with your comments of integrity and caring."

Cooper cleared his throat. "I think integrity could be a separate element, but it might be redundant. I think it's an integral part of respect, relationships, 100 percent leadership buy-in, employee engagement, teamwork, and transparency, so I'm not sure it merits additional element status. The same goes for caring. We show we care through all seven elements. That's my two cents' worth. I would say check them off."

"Thanks, Cooper. Victor, how about listening, values based, and servant-leadership model?"

"Yeah, Jason, listening is included in respect, relationships, engagement, and for sure in continuous improvement, so it's well covered within the seven elements. Let's see. Values based is what the seven elements are all about, so check there. And you answered the goal of targeting the middle of the leadership models by using a blend of both business- and people-centric approaches. Check, check, check for me."

"Excellent!" said Jason. "Mike, how about supportive and innovative?"

"Well, supportive is an easy one. It's another way of being a caring organization, and as Cooper noted, it's inherently part of all seven elements you presented. As far as innovative, I think what we discussed today is very innovative. But I was thinking more along the lines of the systems we develop. So, I am on the fence with this one. Innovation could be its own separate element, it could be combined under the continuous improvement element, or it could be a major component of the upcoming systems upgrades meeting. If it is covered under one of those, I'm good."

Jason agreed and thought about how best to include Mike's point.

"Let's go ahead and place it as a sub-bullet under continuous improvement and make it an important consideration when we consider upgrading our systems," he said. "I also want to see how the rest of the leadership team and the employees respond when we ask for their input on culture. If this gets a lot of hits, maybe we should carve it out as its own element. Is that acceptable to you, Mike?"

"Yep, works for me."

"OK, Abby: accountability."

Abby was ready. "I think this is well covered in both 100 percent leadership buy-in and in transparency. That's a check, Jason." She smiled.

"That was quick. Thanks, Abby. Edward, how about one set of standards?" asked Jason.

"I'm good too," he replied. "It's well covered in 100 percent leadership buy-in and just overall by having these seven or however many elements we finalize on."

"Alrighty," said Jason. "And last but not least, Nelson. You brought up collaborative. What say you?"

"Glad to be able to wrap this up as I'm standing between continuing this discussion and everyone going home tonight! It's covered under respect, relationships, teamwork, and continuous improvement. Good here."

Jason went on, "As Nelson stated, it's getting late, and I want to thank you for your attentiveness today. These first steps we're taking are critical to our future. We've been in survival mode for years now, and we must continue to not only survive but also to thrive. Thanks to Mike and his team, we have a significant opportunity to do just that. Unfortunately, we have a lack of credibility with our corporate group and not a lot of time to repair it. We need to move quickly and efficiently. Our next step will be to involve the rest of the leadership team and all the employees. You've all received an invitation for our next meeting with the full leadership team, which is scheduled for the end of the week. The draft agenda looks like this:

- Review our company status.
- Discuss the role of a leader at KCI.
- Solicit comments on key cultural elements from all leaders in attendance.
- Go out into the company and ask employees what's important to them in a company culture.

"Once we've gathered and analyzed the feedback from the leadership team and our employees, we'll be able to finalize the foundational elements and begin working on tactics for each. I'll be prepared then to share our initial revitalization and commercialization plans at the upcoming quarterly meeting at Thompson Holdings. Sound like a plan?"

Jason noticed during his summary that Hannah was busy doodling in the red leather-bound journal she carried everywhere. She finished whatever it was and looked Jason square in the eyes with a smirky look of satisfaction.

"Hannah, care to share with the whole class?" he asked.

Hannah seemed proud of herself and went up to one of the flip charts. "I *would* care to share."

She began writing the two words Jason had just mentioned: "survival" and "thriving."

She motioned to the flip chart and said, "You are right in saying we've been in survival mode the past several years, and we want so badly to be a thriving company. I think I have a name for what we've started here today."

"And what's that?" Jason asked patiently, though he was drained from the day's discussions.

"Surthrival!" she answered proudly as she wrote it across the top.

Jason realized what she'd come up with was perfect, and a perfect way to end the day—a word that could bind them together in this journey.

"I love it, Hannah! It's a bit hard to pronounce, but it accurately reflects where we've been and where we're going. What does everyone think about using 'Surthrival' as the name for our journey?"

Thumbs-up all around the table.

Jason glanced around and said, "It's a go. That's what we'll call it. With that being said, let's call it a day. Thanks everyone for staying so engaged today and for all the great discussions."

There were a few questions about timing and logistics for the next meeting, and then everyone headed out the door and back to their offices.

Jason could see the change in how the senior leadership left versus how they'd arrived. The transformation from representative to team member was already taking place, evident as well in the small bits of chatter he picked up as they left.

Nelson stayed behind and approached him.

"Jason, I want to thank you again for including me in today's discussion," Nelson said. "We would've heard a lot of this from Cooper, but being here today, getting to contribute, and hearing firsthand—it was invaluable. We've all been waiting and hoping for a discussion like this. I can't tell you how excited I am that it's happening."

"You were a big contributor today, Nelson, and I'm glad you joined us. Let me ask you a quick question: do you see any downsides to what we talked about today?"

He thought for a moment.

"Well, like we discussed earlier in the day," he said, "there are a lot of subcultures throughout the company and there are some—I won't mention any names, but some—who won't want to give up running things their way. They've been autonomous for a long time. So, I imagine there'll be resistance, but I'd also guess you've been through this before and perhaps anticipated it."

"Yes," Jason replied. "That can occur to some extent. Everyone hopes it'll be minimal, but we won't find out until we get into it. People can dig some deep trenches. We'll plan for the worst and hope for the best. Thanks for sharing with me, and again, I appreciate your comments and participation today."

"You got it," Nelson said with a look of support.

Nelson headed out to production while Jason retired to his office and contemplated the next steps in this process. He thought about the line of questioning he'd receive at Thompson Holdings. Adam had already prepped him for those discussions.

Over the next couple of days, Jason followed up individually with each of his team members. He felt like all were on board, apart from perhaps Edward, who had couched his replies with cautious optimism.

Anticipating Edward's hesitancy, Jason had begun developing plans for how he would work closely with the VP throughout the rebuilding process. For the rest of the team, Jason was gaining confidence that these were the changes for which they had been hopeful when Adam Drake announced his decision to recruit a new president to revitalize KCI.

He looked forward to hearing from the rest of the leadership team and all the employees on what type of a culture they'd find engaging and motivating.

# 7

## LET'S HEAR FROM EVERYONE

The end of the same week heralded the planned follow-up meeting. Jason had invited everyone in a leadership role at KCI, from area leads to the senior leadership team—a total of fifty-five people.

His first objective was to provide these leaders the opportunity to share what they valued in a company culture; his second was to send them out on a mission to interview the rest of the employees and listen to their thoughts on the desired cultural attributes.

Everyone squeezed into a training room that normally seated forty-five. Around the room, Jason noticed expressions ranging from eager expectation to impatience.

He began with a summary of the struggles the organization had faced in recent years and shared his charter from Thompson Holdings to revitalize KCI. He continued with the challenge he issued to the product development team and the resulting new product opportunity. He then shared details about the upcoming meeting at Thompson Holdings for which they were preparing. With all the leaders present in one room for the first time since he had joined the company, Jason also took the opportunity to outline his own thoughts on leadership.

He stated, "I believe the role we have as leaders can be summed up in a modified quote from an excellent book by Rick Warren titled *The Purpose Driven Life*,[8] in which he states, 'Life is a test, life is a

---

8   Warren, R, 2002

trust, life is a temporary assignment.' If you replace the word 'life' with 'leadership,' it would be, 'Leadership is a test, leadership is a trust, leadership is a temporary assignment.'

"You're in this room today because you're in a leadership role. Leadership is a test because whether you realize it or not, as a leader you're under constant evaluation by our employees, especially your direct reports. You're on stage for everything you say and do. Today represents a step towards developing the foundation of our desired culture, but just know that whatever we determine it to be, you'll be under scrutiny as to whether you walk the talk or just give it lip service. Leadership is a test of what you believe in and how well you live it each day—measured not only by what you say but, more importantly, by what you do.

"Second, leadership is a trust. As a leader, you've been entrusted with the lives of the employees who report to you. I'm not using the word 'entrusted' as a point of control but rather as a responsibility. This leader–employee relationship is not only an important relationship from a business perspective; it's an important relationship in each of our employees' lives. Everything you say and do is impactful to them, just as it is between you and your leader. I don't know of anyone who wants a tyrannical boss, so be the leader you would want to work for. And be careful not to take these relationships for granted. It's important you respect and cultivate each one.

"It's also important to remember that leadership is a temporary assignment. We don't know how long each of these lives will be entrusted to our care, so make the most of what time we have together. In summary, be a role model in all you do, respect the role and the lives in your care, and make a positive impact while you can."

For the next hour and a half, Jason solicited input from the leaders in the room on what they thought comprised the key elements of a winning culture. Capturing everything on a flip chart, he explained they'd be combining their input with the feedback and information they gathered from the other employees in the next activity and described how it would all be used to develop the final set of cultural elements.

Victor then took the floor and explained the process of going out and interviewing the employees. These interviews were intended to create a dialogue by asking the employees what was important to them in a company culture—a culture they'd find both engaging and motivating. He explained that the employees had been asked in advance by HR to consider this question and to be prepared to share their thoughts.

One of the leaders raised his hand. "Victor, why are we spending the large part of a day interviewing all the employees? It seems a bit manual. Couldn't we just use a survey to capture this information?"

"That's a great question," Victor responded. "We did discuss that and felt the company has been too impersonal over the years. As leaders, we need to take the first step towards creating authentic relationships with our team. We want employees to know that they're valued, and that we care about what they think. We're planning to conduct surveys in the future, but we wanted to be sure this first time that we got out of our offices and connected with every employee. Make sense?"

"Yes, thanks for explaining it to me."

Victor then divided the leaders into teams of two and handed each team a packet containing a list of around ten employees to interview. He advised everyone that they would be interviewing employees from departments outside of their own. He instructed them to capture the raw feedback and ask questions for clarification, further depth, or to help narrow down the response. He gave each team three hours to accomplish the task and then return to share what they'd heard. He also let them know that he'd already requested the remote working employees to make themselves available for a video call to complete their interviews. He explained that each leader's packet included instructions for those video calls. Victor intended to capture the remote working employees' data within their operating departments but also as an individual group to identify any unique needs or requirements they might have.

Three hours later, the teams were back, and the room was buzzing with stories of their experiences. Victor questioned the leaders and for the most part found that everyone had a positive experience.

From several teams, the comments were consistent in reporting that the employees were pleased to be asked their input. Interviewers had received such comments as "Finally, someone cares about what we think."

One interviewing team shared that an employee in the machine shop had taken this opportunity seriously and developed a two-page document listing elements, examples, and supporting rationale. However, the teams also gave reports of people not caring enough to put any thoughts together and winging it on the spot.

Many of the interviewers commented that the exercise had been a good opportunity to make connections with employees they'd never met before, which they all agreed was a positive start towards transforming the culture.

Jason thanked the leaders for their candidness and for making the effort to reach out to their colleagues. He advised how HR would be analyzing their interview notes and looking for common themes.

At 6 p.m. on Tuesday of the following week, an email from Victor popped into Jason's inbox. The note explained how the HR team had spent the previous two days reviewing both Jason's notes from the leadership team discussion and the notes taken in the employee interviews.

From there the team used sticky notes to develop affinity diagrams from the data sets, and they were able to identify five themes emerging from the input. The email included a meeting invitation to review those findings the following morning at 9 a.m. in Victor's office.

Jason checked his calendar and accepted the invitation, anxious to hear the outcome.

The next morning, he was excited to meet with Victor.

"Hey, Victor. After seeing your note last night, this morning couldn't get here fast enough. Thanks again for taking on this big data-analysis task on such short notice. I know everyone appreciates it," Jason said.

"Actually, it was a great exercise for the HR team," Victor replied. "And since our primary function is to support and promote the people aspect of our business, it gave us an opportunity to see and feel the emotions of the employees in one quick snapshot. We rarely get a chance to do that, so my team was grateful for the assignment."

Jason nodded. "How broad was the range of input? Was it difficult to see what the employees are looking for?" he asked.

"Not really," said Victor. "Initially, we set up two affinity diagrams: one for the leadership data you captured and one for the employee interview data. The themes were clear, and it was encouraging to see how closely the employee themes reflected those of the leaders. We also set up a third affinity diagram and took a separate look at the remote working employees as an individual group. There were clear messages from them as well."

Jason was delighted.

"The next step is to bring the senior leadership team back together to develop the final set of elements based on our original discussion and the summary you've just developed," Jason said. "You know, upon reflection, I hope I didn't overstep with the senior leadership team by laying out the seven elements. I wanted to jump-start our transformation process, but I've been wondering if I should've taken it slower. And if I'm honest, I'm surprised you were all so agreeable to what I proposed."

Victor was quick to reply: "Listen, Jason, we've desperately needed leadership, and you're providing it. I don't think anyone disagrees with your initial set of elements. They're happy we're finally moving in a positive direction."

He continued, "And I don't want to diminish anyone, but there isn't a lot of experience in the room in terms of developing these types of foundational thoughts. They may have read about them or discussed them with friends and colleagues, but for many, this is their first time participating at the ground-floor level. Heck, Mike and Hannah have worked their entire careers at KCI, which as you know hasn't shown them many examples of a strong culture or inspiring leadership. I'll tell you what: if you get off base, we'll be sure to let you know. Just keep leading."

"OK, well, thanks, Victor. I appreciate your feedback," said Jason. "Hmm. You know, rather than sharing your summary with me now, I'd like you to facilitate the first part of the meeting and take the team through the information you've assembled, and then through the discussion finalizing the cultural elements. I'll listen to the conclusions and be a participant just like everyone else. I want them to realize their input is just as important as everyone else's on this team—including mine—and that we're equal partners in this work. I have my opinions, so you'll need to manage me just like the others. Are you up for this too?"

"Yes, and I'm encouraged you'd trust me with this responsibility."

"I know you'll do your best, Victor. After your review, we'll assign a leader to each element and discuss the logistics of developing their plans. I'll facilitate that part of the meeting."

"Sounds good, Jason. I look forward to it."

The next day, the senior team and Nelson Chow (again in the perspective chair) gathered in the conference room. Jason noticed a few looks of surprise when he announced Victor would be facilitating the initial discussion.

Victor opened by outlining the process they'd be using to develop the final set of elements. First, they'd refresh their minds by reviewing the flip charts from their first meeting, which listed the senior staff's input and Jason's proposed seven elements. Next, they'd be reviewing the summaries HR had developed from the leadership team's, employees', and remote workers' data sets, including the themes that emerged and highlights of any supporting comments. Then, together, they would compare the summaries and develop the final set of elements.

The team moved through the review portion quickly and then on to the summary of the second meeting. Talking from slides, Victor began, "A quick FYI: we set up affinity diagrams for the leaders' input, the employees' input, and one also for the remote workers' input."

Cooper quickly raised his hand. "Victor, sorry, but what's an *in*finity diagram? I'm not familiar with that term."

"Infinity diagram. I love that, Cooper!" Hannah quipped.

"Oh, sure, Cooper," Victor intervened with a mock-stern look Hannah's way. "It's an *aff*inity diagram, by the way, and it helps organize a large number of ideas into their natural relationships. It's applied to create outputs following a brainstorming session like we had.

"In this case, we wrote a sticky note for each idea that was captured and stuck them on the wall. Then we began grouping them according to their affinity, or similarity. Once they were grouped, we were able to see an emerging theme and labeled that group accordingly. It all came together quite nicely. That's pretty much it."

"OK, I get it. Thanks for explaining." Cooper smiled, shooting a glare Hannah's way that cracked into a smile.

"Absolutely," said Victor. "So, the themes that emerged were similar across those three groups. How about I share the themes and some of the supporting comments, and then open it up for discussion and/or questions?"

Heads nodded and Victor continued.

"In all, five cultural themes emerged from the data that was captured: care, communication, consistency, teamwork, and organizational pride—or being the best.

"Under care, the comments centered around wanting to know the company cared about the employees, both professionally and personally. This was a strong theme within all groups. In fact, it was the strongest overall theme in the complete data set.

"There were comments about the agendas of some of the past leaders. Employees were made to feel used and taken for granted. They felt their personal lives didn't matter. The focus was on the company success, at any cost. Remote working employees feel detached from the company and not considered or cared about generally. This theme also contained some of the harshest comments we received, so there was a lot of passion surrounding care.

"In the second theme, communication, our people want to know what's happening at the company. Not surprising, is it? Many said they have no idea where the company stands and if we're even going to be around next year. They want to know when challenges or opportunities arise so they can be part of the solution, which was encouraging to hear. They want to know what's happening in other departments. They want to know if we have goals and objectives as a company and how their roles connect to them. And importantly, they want to know how we're performing against those goals and objectives.

"Perhaps what we considered to be apathy during our first meeting has emanated from the issues brought up in these first two themes. Our employees don't know what's going on; they're disconnected and feel like nobody cares about them, so why should they care about the company? And remote employees have no idea what's going on and commented that they also don't hear any of the gossip anymore. The latter probably isn't a bad thing, but overall, they're in the dark too.

"Feedback on the third theme, consistency, mirrored many of our comments. Employees are very aware there are different ways of doing things in each department and each individual leader pretty much does what they want. There were several comments about inequity across departments in terms of pay rises, promotions, and even disciplinary actions. They're looking for consistent policies and consistent application throughout the company.

"The fourth theme is teamwork, and like us, they cited the lack of cooperation between departments. They feel like they can't 'trespass' into other domains, so they keep to themselves. One person gave an example of being reprimanded by their leader for helping another department. According to the employee, the leader said that he should 'let them figure that out on their own.'

"That statement helped me better understand Jason's mentor's comment on teamwork, where in some cases, two plus two only equals three. Remote working employees don't have a sense of being on any team, just 'hanging out on their own, flapping in the breeze,' as one person described it.

"And we gave the last theme two names, organizational pride and being the best, because it surfaced in two different ways, but we thought the message was the same. Our employees want to work for a winner, and they want to be proud to work here. They feel the organization was once considered an innovative leader in this field, albeit many years ago, but now it's pretty much 'roadkill,' as some called it.

"Our employees want to feel good when they say they work here. They want us to be a relevant company once again.

"That's a quick summary, but before I open it up for questions, let me share some additional input that was voiced by our remote workers. Overall, they fell into the same response categories as the employees and leadership team, talking about care, communication, and teamwork, but there were specific comments we need to keep in mind, especially when we begin developing tactics.

- They shared feelings of not being respected. They sense employees in the office don't think they work all the time

and imagine that they struggle with focusing on their work. Their response to that is that they work long hours—in fact, maybe longer—because their workstation is accessible day and night. And they feel they can focus even better without all the distractions at the office.
- They're also out there on their own and can feel isolated. They miss being included in those 'in the moment' type discussions. And when they need an answer to a question, they cannot just get up and drop into someone's office to get it. So, they wait . . . and wait, until we get back to them.
- Conversations they participate in are all pretty much work related; but they would like to have personal discussions with their leader and peers, just like when they worked on-site.
- They want their leader to be the remote workers' champion and their lifeline to the company. They want to be kept up to date on what's happening here.
- Remote workers still want to progress in the company, and they would like to see clear steps mapped out for their career progression.

"We need to be sure to consider these comments when developing tactics. Are there any comments or questions on the information I presented?"

Hannah spoke first. "First off, on the remote workers, that's a lot to take in. But they represent some incredibly good insights into what it's like for our folks—or for anyone working remotely."

"Yes, they do," Victor replied. "And we need to keep this group in mind as we develop our overall culture plan. Any other questions or comments on either remote workers or the thematic summary I presented?"

Jason asked, "Based on the input, do you think our employees care enough to help turn this around?"

"Overall, yes. I think they like what we do, just not how we do it," said Victor. "The general feeling is that—in the past, at least—all efforts went towards making a few individuals a lot of money and there was no consideration for the long-term health of the company or the future of the employees. If we show our employees that we care, if we're transparent and accountable and we demonstrate we're in this for the long term, then yes, I believe the majority will be excited to help with the transformation. However, with so many observations of fiefdoms within the company, I anticipate there will be some battleground areas."

Cooper asked, "Were there any other comments worth mentioning?"

"A couple," Victor said. "Even though the focus was on culture, there were a lot of comments about the state of our operating systems. It seems that many employees put in extra hours just to make our work-around systems productive enough to get by. The upcoming systems review will be a lively discussion. There were also concerns about how Thompson Holdings views us and whether they are in it for the long term. Will they support us through the changes we need to make? And ultimately, they want to know if the senior team will stick around now that they've seen how disconnected we are as an organization."

"Wow, those are some heavy thoughts!" Jason said.

"We've exposed a lot of our warts," Hannah noted. "It's agonizing to see so much pain in the organization but good to get it out on the table so we can begin addressing it. What's next, Victor?"

"If there are no other questions on the information I presented, then let's begin working on the final list of elements. I've prepared a comparison chart [Figure 7] for this part of the discussion.

## CULTURAL ELEMENTS COMPARISON

| Seven Elements | Senior Staff Input | Employee Feedback Summary |
|---|---|---|
| Respect | Trust | |
| Relationships | Listening | |
| 100% Leadership Buy-In | One Set of Standards, Values Based, Integrity | Consistency |
| Teamwork | Collaborative | Teamwork |
| Employee Engagement | Caring, Supportive | Care |
| Transparency | Communication, Integrity, Accountability | Communication |
| | Servant Leadership Model | |

Figure 7

"I did my best to align the input using Jason's seven elements as the starting point. You can see there are a lot of similarities in what everyone is looking for in our culture. The quickest path may be to knock out the elements that are clearly similar and then tackle those that require more discussion.

"Let's take 100 percent leadership buy-in first. I would submit that if we achieved that, it assumes and/or satisfies the comments from the staff and the employees regarding one set of standards, values based, integrity, and consistency. We are establishing one set of standards to buy into, they are values based, including integrity, and with 100 percent buy-in, they would be consistently applied throughout the company. Would you all agree?"

Everyone agreed.

"OK, that was too easy! Next, let's look at teamwork, which has the two associated comments, 'collaborative' and 'teamwork'—essentially the same. That's an easy keeper, right?"

Again, agreement across the board.

Victor continued, "Like I said, there's a lot of similarity. Moving next to continuous improvement. We agreed in our staff meeting that 'innovative' could fit in there, and Mike also asked us to consider innovation in our systems review meeting, which we all agreed to. Looking at the employee comments, being the best and pride in the company seem more like goals to which we can aspire rather than elements, and I think continuous improvement will drive us towards both of those. What do you all think?"

Abby spoke up. "I agree, Victor. Through continuous improvement we can set a goal of being the best, which, as Cooper described, will be an ongoing journey. As we get better and better, we'll begin developing more pride in our work and in our company naturally."

"Well said, Abby!" Cooper added.

Victor saw everyone else nodding in agreement and checked 'yes' there. He moved on.

"The next one that's straightforward is transparency," he continued. "The comments from the other groups that fit are 'communication,' 'integrity,' and 'accountability.' I propose we expand this element to incorporate the term 'communications.' And if we *do* provide transparent communications, we'd be in a better position to demonstrate both integrity and accountability. Like keeping innovative as a subset of continuous improvement, we'll incorporate the caveats of integrity and accountability in the tactical discussion. Sound reasonable?"

Jason jumped in. "It looks like you've done your homework on this. I agree transparent communications is a good blend of the input for that element. But let's not overlook that transparency can include areas like visual management to make the status of a process obvious and transparent; developing a culture of vulnerability and challenge, which we are working through now; and having the managerial courage to address tough topics. There are many facets to transparency, but again, I agree with adding the word 'communications' as I believe it incorporates the input we've received."

"Thanks, Jason. That makes sense, and we'll need to consider those thoughts when we move into the tactical discussions."

While Jason noted the addition, Victor looked around the room for other comments and received the thumbs-up from everyone.

He moved to conclude. "All right, the remaining element to discuss from the employee summary is caring. Conversely, we have three of the seven elements we have not yet touched: respect, relationships, and employee engagement. I would suggest these remaining three are broad elements yet specific ways to show employees we care. In fact, I believe all seven elements reflect a deeply caring organization, which addresses the employees' last element.

"All in all, I believe the seven elements, with the one expansion to transparent communications, reflect a culture all employees want to see here—one which would be well supported. I probably could have started there, but I wanted you to discover this the same way my team did, while reaching this point. I propose this as our final set of cultural elements."

He advanced to the next slide [Figure 8].

## CULTURAL ELEMENTS COMPARISON

| Seven Elements | Senior Staff Input | Employee Feedback Summary | FINAL SET OF ELEMENTS |
|---|---|---|---|
| Respect | Trust | | **Repect** |
| Relationships | Listening | | **Relationships** |
| 100% Leadership Buy-In | One Set of Standards, Values Based, Integrity | Consistency | **100% Leadership Buy-In** |
| Teamwork | Collaborative | Teamwork | **Teamwork** |
| Employee Engagement | Caring, Supportive | Care | **Employee Engagement** |
| Transparency | Communication, Integrity, Accountability | Communication | **Transparent Communications** |
| | Servant Leadership Model | | |

Figure 8

Hannah was the first to speak.

"That was a lot more straightforward than I thought it would be," she said. "But on the other hand, it's good to see we value many of the same things in our work lives. And it feels good that we, the senior staff, didn't just decide this in a vacuum. We asked and listened to all employees who wanted to share their thoughts. That's a step in the right direction!"

"Great, thanks, Hannah," Victor said. "OK, before I hand it over to you, Jason, I have one last slide. But before I advance to it, let me give you a little background. One of my staff members had an idea, and the whole HR team stayed late to work on it together. The idea was to turn the elements into an acronym that could be easily remembered by everyone in the company. So, with a little adjustment to the element titles and by changing their order slightly, we were able to come up with this [Figure 9]:

## FINAL SET OF ELEMENTS

| Element | Leader |
|---|---|
| **R**espect | |
| **E**very Leader Buys In | |
| **S**trong Relationships | |
| **P**urposeful Teams | |
| **E**mployee Engagement | |
| **C**ontinuous Improvement | |
| **T**ransparent Communications | |

Figure 9

"As you can see, we were able to produce the acronym RESPECT, which, if I remember correctly from our first meeting, Jason, you stated that you believed 'respect will be at the very heart of, and the real catalyst of, all we accomplish.' So, we thought this was an appropriate acronym to land on. What do you all think?"

"Wow," Hannah said. "How did you guys think to get there? That is so perfect. Great job."

Mike added, "You and your team nailed it. I support your recommendation all the way."

Jason, looking dumbstruck, said, "I wasn't expecting that, but I'm so impressed with what you and your team came up with. How does everyone else feel about it?"

Once again there were thumbs-up all around.

"Looks like we have a green light all the way on this one, Victor," Jason said.

"OK, Jason, then I'm handing the meeting over to you now," Victor said.

Jason took over. "Victor, you did an excellent job of getting us here. Well done. I see you already had this slide prepared in the deck. You had a hunch we'd land here, eh!"

Victor laughed. "It seemed clear cut to my staff and me, so yes, I took a chance and made up the final slide."

Jason began applauding Victor, and when the rest of the staff joined in, he noticed a glaze in Victor's eyes.

Jason continued, "I believe we've hit on a set of core values our employees desire in their work lives: respect, fulfillment, consistency, and an opportunity to be a part of something special, something larger than themselves. Coming back down to earth: our next step is to assign a leader from the senior team for each element. Your role as leader will be to form a team and develop an implementation plan for your assigned element. Once we determine who has which one, we can go into more details on the path forward. However, rather than me assigning those, I want to open it up to you. If you are passionate about an element, make your case to lead it."

Immediately, Cooper jumped in. "Jason, I have been waiting a long time for us to invest in continuous improvement. I'd be thrilled to take that one."

Looking around the table and seeing nodding heads, Jason said, "By all means, Cooper. It's yours!"

Victor raised his hand, adding, "Jason, I think 100 percent leadership buy-in, or now 'every leader buys in,' could get into some sensitive HR areas. It might make sense for me to take that one."

"Good point, Victor. We'll put you down for that element."

Abby spoke next. "In our staff discussion, I said I'd want to be involved in transparency, so I'd like to take on transparent communications, if that's OK with everyone."

Once again, all heads were nodding. "Makes perfect sense, Abby. It's yours."

"Since I came up with the goal statement for employee engagement, I feel close to that element," Hannah said. "I'd like to take that one if everyone is OK with that."

"Everyone in agreement?" Jason saw everyone was. "I'm putting your name down, Hannah."

Mike stepped up next. "I already shared about my team working together and how I see the possibility of two plus two equaling five, so I'd like to take teamwork—or purposeful teams, as it will be called."

"That makes sense, Mike; you got it. Can you handle it along with this major product development project?"

"I think so—mainly because of the team I have. I'll let you know if I feel like I'm sinking at any time."

"Fair enough, Mike."

Jason realized that left Edward and himself to choose between the remaining elements: respect and strong relationships. He recalled how Edward had struggled in the discussion on relationships, and rather than force him into that leadership role, he thought he would give him the choice.

"Edward, this leaves you and me, and the two elements remaining are respect and strong relationships. You take your pick, and I'll take the last one."

Jason knew it probably wasn't lost on everyone that Edward was in a bit of a pickle. He could see them watching with curiosity.

Edward wiggled in his chair and cleared his throat. "Jason, put me down for respect."

"OK, Edward, you are on respect. I'll take the last one: strong relationships. We're all set with our assignments."

Filling out the final chart that Victor had shown [Figure 10], Jason said: "This is what it looks like.

## FINAL SET OF ELEMENTS

| Element | Leader |
|---|---|
| **R**espect | Edward Eggleton |
| **E**very Leader Buys In | Victor Delacruz |
| **S**trong Relationships | Jason Bailey |
| **P**urposeful Teams | Mike Montgomery |
| **E**mployee Engagement | Hannah Parker |
| **C**ontinuous Improvement | Cooper Collins |
| **T**ransparent Communications | Abby Mills |

Figure 10

"Let's talk about next steps. First, I'd like each leader to form a team of four to six people. Use Victor as a clearinghouse for names so we don't double-book anyone. He can also help you with recruiting members for your teams.

"Just like our data, we want to get broad representation on these teams. Make sure members come from different departments and various roles within the company. Also, include one or more remote working employee on each of your teams. Plan to form these within three days. Also, within three days, be sure to schedule a one-on-one meeting with me so we can review possible directions to take.

"Then call your first team meeting and come up with a strategy or goal statement for your element. After that, you can begin brainstorming ideas. Victor's raw data can be used as a starting point. Next, begin to research options and benchmark best practices where possible. Lastly, start developing specific ideas or tactics to action. Be sure your tactics support the strategy or goal you've developed.

"Your target is to generate five tactics for your element in one month, of which three will be prioritized for initial launch. We'll plan to have a second round of one-on-one's somewhere in the middle—let's say in approximately two weeks. Then we'll review your progress and answer any questions you have. Let's get this group back together in one month to review the plans for each element. By then, I'll be back from the Thompson Holdings quarterly review and can provide additional feedback.

"Tomorrow will be the all-employee meeting to share the final set of elements, along with our plans and time frame to develop these. I think that's it for today. Any questions, comments, or concerns?"

Hannah spoke quickly. "Is Nelson automatically assigned to Cooper's continuous improvement team, or is he a free agent? Just asking!"

"Nelson is locked up, tightly!" Cooper responded.

"Outstanding work, everyone!" said Jason, and he closed the meeting.

After the meeting, Victor walked with Edward back to his office.

"Edward, have you got a couple of minutes for a quick chat?"

"Sure, have a seat, Victor. What is on your mind?"

"I just wanted to do a quick check-in with you and see how you're doing," Victor said.

"I am fine. Is there something specific you want to discuss?"

"Well, you've got a big element on your hands there in respect. How do you feel about that?"

"I have not had much time to consider it. I know it is significant, and, well, we all are leading one, and this is the one I got."

"Well, it's not only significant, but I'd say it's probably the most important element of the seven. You have both a challenge with this and an opportunity to make an impact on our culture and the overall future of KCI. I want you to know that if you need to bounce ideas or questions off someone, I'm available. Any thoughts on where you might start?"

"Not immediately. I guess I will get my team together and begin brainstorming ideas about respect."

"Yep, you have to put a team together first. I also might suggest that, once together, your team starts by defining respect. We began work there in that first senior leadership meeting. Building on those comments could point you in some interesting directions. Just a thought."

"Absolutely. Thanks. I appreciate your stopping by. I will consider your suggestion and likely take you up on your offer to listen to our ideas for tactics."

"No worries, Edward. Anything to help. I'll see you later."

# 8

## SPREADING THE WORD

When the leadership team discussed how to roll out the seven elements, they were intent on creating an event that marked a clear change in direction for the company. One aspect they agreed on immediately was to try to bring as many employees on-site as they could. Their goal was to send one consistent message about the future plans of the company and begin this journey as one team.

Logistically, it was not easy bringing three hundred-plus people together into one place, but it being early summer in Southern California was a big help. They decided to set up a large tent on a grassy area adjacent to the KCI building, complete with a small stage and two large screens flanking the speaker.

The plan was to bring all the employees together at 11 a.m., share an hour-long company update, and follow the more formal proceedings with an informal, picnic-style BBQ lunch. The departmental teams were encouraged to meet together after lunch to discuss the seven elements and work towards establishing positive momentum on day one.

Around 10:50 a.m., employees began filing out of the building and filling up the chairs under the tent. As Jason had seen from experience, the seats filled up from the back moving forward, leaving the front rows empty. He wondered why no one ever wanted to sit closer to see and hear better. Sometimes a few brave souls would come forward, but the best seats were usually left empty.

After double-checking his mic was on mute, Jason moved

around, greeting employees as they found seats and being sure to look everyone in the eyes and warmly shake their hands. He was beginning to remember employee names and even a few personal tidbits he could ask about. A couple of employees thanked him for providing the opportunity to weigh in on the cultural elements.

With the smoke of the BBQ wafting in, Jason took the stage. After welcoming everyone and acknowledging the folks connected via video, he opened with a quick review of the rich KCI history and how the company had "stubbed its toe" and fallen into the current rut.

He shared his overall plan to propel the organization back into a market leadership position—a plan centered on people, culture, products, and systems.

- *People*: the first step was to fill in the holes left behind on the senior leadership team—now completed.
- *Culture*: build a winning culture based on foundational elements consistently deployed throughout the organization—in progress now and a more detailed update to be provided later in the meeting.
- *Products*: assess the product portfolio and restart the engines in product development—work initiated that has resulted in a significant development project in the wings.
- *Systems*: update the operating systems to a sustainable and scalable level—the next significant task on the horizon.

Jason continued, "I want to ask you all a question. When you came to work this morning, did you think of anyone here at work as an enemy? Think about it for a moment. If an enemy in your mind is another department or another employee or even a supplier, I want you to reconsider.

"The real enemies of KCI are the diseases and illnesses the doctors and patients in our field of work are battling each day. Our reason for being is to help improve their outcomes. The challenge we have is how to focus our talent, our strengths—our three hundred-plus minds—on working together each day to make that happen. I shared the four key areas of people, products, culture, and systems. However, when it comes down to it, we can have great products and great systems, but without great people in a winning culture, we'll never realize our full potential. And I believe we have great people right here under this tent and online."

As Jason spoke, he noticed one of the machine shop operators sitting about halfway back with his arms tightly folded. He was glaring intently at the back of the chair in front of him.

Jason mentally tucked this observation away and continued, "The next step, then, is to build a winning culture that enables us all to flourish. We asked for everyone's help in determining the key elements of our desired culture, and I want to thank you for your input and insights. This is our culture; we own it. We want to be sure that whatever we develop meets the needs of this organization, right here, right now. Using everyone's input, we arrived at seven elements to focus on as a company.

"They are respect, every leader buys in, strong relationships, purposeful teams, employee engagement, continuous improvement, and transparent communications."

Jason proceeded to go through each element with emphasis on the first one, respect, saying: "Respect is where we start this journey today, and from the input we received, it's the center of what we are looking for in our culture. As such, we believe that years from now, when we look back, we'll see that respect is the heart of who we've become as a team and all that we've accomplished."

After he shared a summary of each element and the support each one had received through the employees' input, he said, "Teams will be forming over the next couple of days to begin work on specific tactics to develop and sustain each element. By the way, thanks to Victor and the HR team, we were able to slightly tweak the element names and their order so the first letters spell out the acronym

RESPECT as a way for all of us to remember them more easily. Here's a slide showing what that looks like along with the team leader who will be managing the development of each element [Figure 11]."

## FINAL SET OF ELEMENTS

| Element | Leader |
|---|---|
| **R**espect | Edward Eggleton |
| **E**very Leader Buys In | Victor Delacruz |
| **S**trong Relationships | Jason Bailey |
| **P**urposeful Teams | Mike Montgomery |
| **E**mployee Engagement | Hannah Parker |
| **C**ontinuous Improvement | Cooper Collins |
| **T**ransparent Communications | Abby Mills |

Figure 11

He continued, "If you have an interest in serving as a member on one of these teams, I encourage you to contact the team leader listed to the right of the element or to get in touch with Victor Delacruz in HR, who will be helping manage the assignments."

Jason had decided that since the new product development project was pending Thompson Holdings' approval, he would not share the details at this meeting. He simply alluded to a significant new product, and hopefully project approval at the upcoming meeting would create an opportunity for another celebration. Regardless of which way Thompson Holdings' decision went, the organization needed to get moving on building its culture.

Jason took time to recognize employees for specific accomplishments and celebrate significant work anniversaries. There was a brief open Q&A, and then he brought the meeting to a close.

Concluding, he said, "Thanks for listening today. We have both a fantastic opportunity and a big challenge in front of us. Let's not kid ourselves; this will be hard work. It won't be smooth, and it won't be perfect. In fact, this drawing [Figure 12] depicts what our plan will look like in the first pane, and in the second pane what reality will likely deal us."

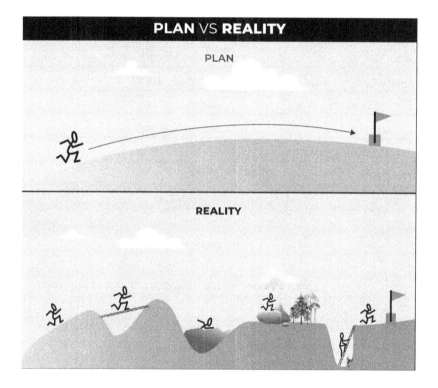

Figure 12

He paused to allow everyone to take in the illustration, before adding, "As a company, we've been in survival mode for the past several years. We must get out of the rut we are in. I believe that if we work together, we *can* become a thriving company again. In that regard, the work in the seven elements will be under the banner of 'Surthrival.'

"This is not a project with an end in sight. We expect it to be an ongoing effort for as long as the company is here. This banner will remind us of our commitment to each other and to our customers."

Jason advanced the slide to reveal the banner designed by

Hannah's marketing team [Figure 13].

Figure 13

"We'll need all the talent we have under this tent and online to be successful. I believe we can do it. I believe we *will* do it," asserted Jason. The employees stood in unison and applauded the new direction for the company.

Jason sent everyone off to lunch. He encouraged his senior staff to spread out and sit at tables where no managers were present. He decided to grab a seat with the machine shop operators and perhaps follow up with the one he had noticed in the audience. In fact, he was able to sit right next to him, which initially didn't appear to go down well with the operator. Jason introduced himself to everyone at the table, asked their names, and then asked them what they thought of the meeting.

Surprisingly, the guy with the folded arms spoke up immediately.

His name was Anthony, but he said Jason could call him Tony. He shared how he didn't have much respect or trust for anyone in management. Jason asked him why.

He responded, "We heard the original group—who, by the way, put us in this situation—all walked away with big fat checks. They were obviously in it for themselves, and I imagine you aren't much different."

Jason glanced around the table and replied, "I understand all that happened before, and I am committed to changing our culture to one that embodies what you said you don't have much of: respect and trust. If we can't trust each other, this is never going to work."

Jason paused for a beat and added, "Listen, Tony, I'd like to connect with you and this team personally to see how we are progressing as a company. Maybe we could meet weekly?"

He could see that he had their attention now.

"But if we do, I'll need you to be open and honest with me. Are you all up for something like that?"

Tony replied, "Yeah, but you may not like what you hear."

Jason responded immediately, "I'm willing to take that chance. I'll set it up."

Everyone at the table relaxed a bit and began digging into the BBQ lunch. They ended up in a deep discussion about college basketball—something about which Jason was passionate. One operator's younger brother was a member of the San Diego State basketball team, which was expected to be nationally ranked in the AP Top 25 this coming season; and UCLA was on their pre-conference schedule. That made for some fun banter. Jason looked forward to his future discussions with Tony and this team.

From what Jason perceived, the meeting had been a success. It felt like the company had a pulse once again. Hopefully, many of the departments would be able to hold review discussions soon after the meeting while the information was still fresh in everyone's minds.

Jimmy thought it had been an excellent meeting and couldn't help but think about the potential opportunities that might come up if this company started growing.

Latecia called the distribution team together for a debrief. Fortunately, they'd completed the large and important shipping orders earlier that day. He helped bring chairs into an open area to form a circle while Latecia passed out a summary of the seven elements that Jason had shared. Once they settled in, she asked them for their thoughts on what was presented or if anyone had any comments about how the elements were developed.

Gary Fox, still showing remnants of a peeling face from his sunburn, commented how "one of the bigwigs" had asked him what was important in a company culture when the leadership team was out interviewing everyone, and he said he'd answered, "Everybody doing it the same way in every department when it comes to raises and promotions."

Gary said he was pleasantly surprised to hear that having a consistent approach throughout the company made the final list in Jason's presentation today under the element of every leader buys in.

Jimmy thought about what he had heard earlier and wanted to get involved in some way.

He spoke up. "Latecia, I don't know if this is possible, but I have a request. The employee engagement goal statement of 'Engaged throughout the day and fulfilled when we end it' really spoke to me. Jason practically invited anyone and everyone to join one of the teams that are forming. Is there any chance I could be on that team?"

Latecia responded, "Anything's possible. If you're serious, I'll give Hannah Parker a call after this meeting and see if there's an opening."

"I'm definitely serious, and thanks for doing that for me."

There were a few more comments about the meeting and about the upcoming systems review; then they wrapped it up. Jimmy, filled up after the big lunch, was relieved the orders were light for the rest of the day.

Bryan O'Connor likewise gathered his supply chain team together for a similar discussion. He was pleased to hear that his staff believed that he personally modeled a lot of what was now being advocated. There were comments about the seven elements being right on target. Many times, this department had been caught in the middle of the turf wars. The thought of KCI working as a team was refreshing to all of them.

That evening, Bryan was anxious to get home and share the new direction with his wife. Something smelled good as he came in through the garage. Lora greeted him with a quick hug, telling him his timing was perfect as she proudly pointed to the grilled chicken on the table.

"I see you got home early from work," Bryan said. "Thanks for getting dinner going."

As they sat down, Lora said, "Yep. It was light this afternoon, and I got to take off a little early. So, how was the big meeting today? I want to hear all about it."

Bryan, too excited to eat, put his fork down. "It was great! Remember when we were camping and I said not much had happened since the new president joined us? Well, a lot happened today, and it's evident Jason's been doing his homework."

"Jason is the new president, right?"

"Yes." Bryan then outlined some of Jason's opening summary, the four key areas for revitalizing the company, and the seven elements of the cultural transformation.

"Wow, you seem pretty pumped about all this."

"I am. My department is in the middle of a lot of what goes on there, and like I said at the beach, we're a dysfunctional company at best. So, not only do we have a new product that could take off, but now we also have a plan to fix our broken parts so we're positioned to manufacture and sell the new system successfully. By the way, it gets better!"

"Oh yeah?"

"Well, this afternoon I received a call from Mike Montgomery. He's heading up the purposeful teams element and asked if I'd be a member of his team."

"Now, that's right up your alley."

"I know, and if I could have my pick of teams to serve on, that'd be my first choice—although any team would've been great. Our first meeting is in a couple of days, and the task is to figure out what we can do to cultivate teamwork throughout the organization. And we still have the upcoming meeting to review the state of our systems. It's going to get crazy busy for me."

"Careful what you wish for!" Lora quipped.

"Amen to that!"

# 9

## THE MEETING AT CORPORATE

Four weeks after the initial meeting with his senior staff to announce the product development breakthrough, Jason was on a late-morning flight from San Diego to San Jose for the quarterly update meeting at Thompson Holdings. Upon arrival, he caught an Uber to his hotel in Palo Alto. He had plenty of time to spare before the evening dinner, which Adam Drake was hosting for the medical company presidents.

Adam had begun this pre-quarterly-meeting dinner ritual to create an opportunity for the medical company presidents to get together in an informal setting where they could share openly and get to know each other. Jason also figured it gave Adam a chance to prepare the presidents for any questions from the Thompson Holdings executives who would be attending the meeting the next morning.

It was Adam's quarterly review, but he'd told Jason that key executives from Thompson Holdings were always welcome to sit in and ask questions as the medical device world had many complexities their other businesses didn't operate under. Jason noticed that Adam made a point of sitting next to him this evening.

"Ready for tomorrow?" Adam asked Jason.

"As ready as I'll ever be."

"Great. Well, I was able to schedule the meeting you requested with the CEO and CFO for tomorrow afternoon to go over the new product timeline and budget proposal. No need to get into those details in our review meeting tomorrow morning. As a matter of fact, when it's your turn to share, I know you'll have to be a bit cryptic in your description of the new product opportunity. Everyone understands the need to keep it that way, so no worries there."

"Got it," Jason replied.

"But I do have one request," Adam added. "I appreciate how you went about developing the cultural elements—specifically how you involved all the employees. I also subscribe to the approach of developing a culture that's both business- and people-centric. Would you share some of the related details tomorrow? I'd like to see all our medical companies heading in that direction. Your talking points will provide openings for me to discuss this topic with the other presidents."

"Absolutely," Jason replied. "I planned to touch on it briefly, but when I get back to my hotel room tonight, I'll add more details. You know, the next area we're tackling is our operating systems. If we have time tomorrow, I'd be interested to hear what operating system everyone else is using, especially if the systems are tailored to medical device companies, and if they're happy with the platform they're on.

"It could save us time if we can identify systems that work well and perhaps be able to benchmark their best practices. I don't know if any of the companies are using the same operating system, but if so, do you know if they have user groups within Thompson Holdings?"

Adam replied, "Not that I know of, but it'll be a good discussion to bring up under new topics tomorrow."

"OK," said Jason. "So, what can I expect in the meeting with you and the Thompson Holdings folks tomorrow afternoon? How did they respond to the advance information I sent on the development project? Anything I need to be concerned about?"

Adam smiled. "Are you kidding, Jason? They're doing cartwheels over this opportunity. I was able to go through it briefly with them, and they'll run you through the typical line of questioning, but nothing you can't handle."

"Well, I know this is a significant opportunity, and I wondered if they thought we were up to the challenge."

"Listen, Jason, we brought you in for a reason—to get KCI moving forward again," said Adam. "It took two sets of recruiting candidates to find you, but everything I've seen so far reinforces that we made a good choice, and I believe the rest of Thompson Holdings feels the same. We're behind you and your team 100 percent.

"You've been at KCI long enough to see the whole picture, and it isn't pretty. On our last phone call, you told me that every time you turn over a new rock, a bunch of cockroaches run out. I can only imagine what you're finding. You can count on our support, but you and your team will have to do a bit of a balancing act as you work your way through this. We have capital to invest, but there needs to be a solid and timely return on investment.

"Also, there are questionable financial areas at KCI needing to be addressed, such as overhead costs, having lower margins than the other medical companies, and I am sure we both agree inventory is well above what it should be. We'll want to see progress on those as you work on the culture and develop this new product. No pressure, right? Just a small hill for a mountain climber like you!"

"Great," said Jason. "It's encouraging to know we have support. And yes, we have a lot of issues, but I believe we can and *will* overcome those. You've been through this before. It's two steps forward and one step backward—never a straight line to the winner's circle!"

Adam nodded. "Very true. About the afternoon meeting: I'm pretty sure there's one question on the product development project they'll ask. In your P&L projection, the sales of the new product line look a bit conservative. Do you think you'll do better than your projection?"

"Well, as you know, Adam, a projection is just that: a projection—a little science and a lot of hope. But once you put a number out there, it's no longer a projection. It becomes a commitment, etched in stone. I'd rather under-promise and over-deliver. Even at the conservative level we've submitted, it'll be a huge boost to our sales and earnings."

Adam nodded again. "I expected that'd be your answer, and I support it. Thompson Holdings knows that too, but they'd rather show the shareholders a bigger projection and then try to squeeze it out of you later. I think you're wise to take this approach, but expect to be questioned about it. Before I forget to ask, how's your leadership team coming together? And how is it going with Edward? You shared some concerns on the phone a month ago. Any progress?"

"About the same. Overall, the team is good and coming together. Edward is still a bit of a mystery, but I'm working with him."

Dinner tasted a lot better to Jason now that his stomach wasn't turning somersaults. Adam's support and his heads-up for the afternoon discussion were both helpful and reassuring. The medical device companies had a good group of presidents. Jason could tell from the conversation that this group of company leaders shared the same ethics and commitment to both their businesses and their employees.

Meanwhile, that same afternoon back in Carlsbad, Latecia had asked Jimmy and Gary to go on a late run from the KCI office to the airport with international shipments their freight forwarder hadn't been able to pick up. Gary grabbed the van keys and jumped in the driver's seat. As they neared the airport area, Gary took an early off-ramp and pulled the van into the parking lot of a craft brewery house.

A bit startled, Jimmy asked, "What's up, Gary? What are we doing here?"

Gary replied, "Oh, I always stop in here on these runs. They don't know how long it really takes us, and if there's any questions, I just tell them I got caught in traffic."

Jimmy was concerned.

"I'm not comfortable, Gary," he said. "Can we just make the delivery and get back to the warehouse?"

"Just relax. It'll be cool."

Once seated inside, a server came over with the drinks menu.

"Welcome, guys. I'm the manager here, and it looks like you're stuck with me because we're a bit short on staff today," he said jokingly. "What can I get for you?"

"You can get me out of here," Jimmy responded.

Gary interjected, "He's just nervous because technically we're out making a delivery for our company, but our boss doesn't really know how long it takes."

"Wow. Where are you two guys so lucky to work?"

"We work up at Keyhole Cardiovascular in Carlsbad," Gary said.

"Seriously? My brother works there too, although he's only been there a few months."

"Oh yeah? What's his name? Maybe we know him," Gary said.

"Jason. Jason Bailey."

Gary tried to pretend like he didn't know Jason, while Jimmy's head sank into his hands.

The next morning, Jimmy was called into Latecia's office.

She said, "I've already talked with Gary, and he let me know that yesterday's late-afternoon excursion was all his idea."

"I hope this isn't going to be too big of a black mark against me," Jimmy replied.

"Nah, this has Gary written all over it. If I send you out with him again, I'll be sure to give you the keys. You must have died in your seat when Jason's brother revealed who he was."

"You can't imagine."

The next morning, the quarterly review meeting flew by for Jason.

As it turned out, a couple of the medical device companies were using the same operating system as each other, and it was tailored to medical device requirements. They were willing to share their knowledge with Jason's team and welcomed the idea of starting up a user group among the companies.

Jason thought the afternoon meeting with Adam and the Thompson Holdings execs went as well as he could've expected. The execs seemed elated with KCI's new product opportunity, and just as Adam had speculated the night before, they had questions about the project financials—specifically the sales forecast.

When Jason shared the same response he had with Adam, that a projection was a little science and a lot of hope, the new corporate CFO pressed him a bit harder. He questioned the "hope" part of the sales projection, citing the years of experience KCI had in this market. Jason countered that with KCI not being competitive for the past several years, he wasn't sure how responsive the market would be to a new product, hence the conservative initial forecast.

As a concession, he agreed to revisit the plan six months after product release and reforecast based on the early sales trends. He knew the Thompson Holdings executives hoped for more, but he didn't offer it up. Tucked away in his mind was a comment Adam had once made that it wasn't their style to force a commitment on any of their companies, something Jason appreciated.

Later in the meeting, Jason was pleased when both Adam and the Thompson Holdings execs applauded KCI's plan to develop a new culture. The consensus was that it was long overdue.

They were also curious about any insights into the operating systems analysis he could provide, saying they wanted advance warning if a significant request for funding would be coming out of their internal review. Jason acknowledged the antiquated systems and need for significant upgrades to sustain the company over the long term. He explained that a systems review meeting was scheduled for early the following week and that he would advise Adam of their initial direction.

As expected, the new corporate CFO brought up the financial performance issues that Jason and Adam had discussed at dinner the previous night. Jason responded by saying he would present a plan to address those at the next quarterly review.

That evening, he flew back to San Diego with signed documents approving the product development project. Now he could turn Mike and the cross-functional development team loose. He felt good about his relationship with Adam, and after this second interaction with some of the Thompson Holdings execs since accepting the opportunity, he had a better feel for their expectations. He'd become comfortable with the job opportunity during the interview process; still, it was a relief to get through this meeting.

There were a lot of obstacles ahead, but now he was confident that he had the backing he'd need. It would've been a lot tougher taking on those obstacles while fending off corporate.

It was full steam ahead. For now, Jason eased his seat back, adjusted his headphones, and turned up his music.

# 10

## THE WORK BEGINS

Two weeks later, Jason began reviewing the teams' progress in his staff one-on-ones. He had advised each team to brainstorm ideas, research the latest thoughts, benchmark where possible, and consider any overlap between their ideas and what another team could be considering; while there were seven distinct elements, they were all interconnected. He'd also requested they consider remote employees in each of their tactics.

His first check-in was with Mike to review the progress on the purposeful teams element.

Mike let Jason know that there had been no shortage of reference materials online and that his team had generated several ideas for tactics that they were developing further. He also mentioned that Bryan O'Conner had impressed him, both with his insights and how he handled himself within the team as a member and as a leader. Mike had assigned Bryan the lead role in online research, and Bryan himself had generated multiple ideas for tactics.

Mike added that the new product development project was taxing him personally, so he was thankful that Bryan had stepped up. Mike pointed out that Bryan also had a significant role on the product development team, so, from his perspective, Bryan's efforts on purposeful teams were well beyond his expectations. Overall, Mike was confident his team would be ready for the report out.

Jason's second check-in was with Hannah to review employee engagement. It was no surprise to hear her team was on track.

She shared an interesting story about being contacted by Latecia Johnson regarding a distribution associate, Jimmy Marino, who wanted to participate on her team. Latecia said he was a recent addition who was inspired by the goal statement that Hannah came up with.

Hannah commented how in her first team meeting, she'd asked everyone to share why they were on the team. She said Jimmy's response was "I've thought about what I'd do if I was in charge, and I'd create an environment where no one ever wanted to miss a day because they didn't want to miss out on whatever was going on." She continued, "He said, 'Your goal statement of "Engaged throughout the day and fulfilled when we end it" seemed to be kind of the same thing, at least to me.'"

Hannah had been taken aback by Jimmy's comments and asked him how, if he were in charge, he would go about establishing such an environment. Jimmy had responded that he would make it possible for every employee to know how their work impacted either the customer or the company's ability to meet its goals.

She told Jason, "He said, 'It's important for all of us to understand the significance of what we do, and even better if we could somehow see, by some type of measurement, how our work contributes every day towards meeting our company goals.'"

Hannah added, "My jaw dropped when he made those comments. There are people in leadership roles who don't get that."

Impressed as well, Jason commented, "Jimmy sounds promising. Keep an eye on him while he's on your team. We should talk more later."

"Well, as an FYI, he did stay after one meeting and asked for advice on how he could progress in his career," said Hannah. "I told him first, he should share his goals with Latecia, his supervisor, so she can help guide him along the way. As far as things he could do, I advised him to be the best at whatever he is currently doing, because she will notice that.

"Second, I encouraged him to start working on his college degree at night and take advantage of our tuition reimbursement program. And third, I suggested he meet with Victor to see if he could work shadow in some different areas and figure out where his interests lie."

Jason smiled. "Good advice, Hannah. Let's see how he responds."

For Abby (transparent communications), Cooper (continuous improvement), and Victor (every leader buys in), their teams were also on track. They shared with Jason how much they enjoyed hearing the feedback and ideas coming from their cross-functional teams and getting to see the reactions to all the concepts they discussed. One of them commented how excited employees were for the new direction the company was heading. They noted that overall, teamwork across all departments—and notably within their respective element teams—was beginning to take hold.

The last person to schedule his one-on-one was Edward, who was leading the element of respect.

During the review, Edward was forthcoming in explaining that he'd been slow in filling out his team initially but was at full strength now. The next comment he made was how he felt it would be a challenge to enforce respect throughout the company.

The hairs went up on the back of Jason's neck when Edward used the word "enforce." Jason cautioned him that *enforcing* respect was not the best way to address this element. He explained that respect was a central theme of the feedback they'd received from everyone: staff, leaders, and employees. Rather than enforcing respect, modeling and peer pressure would be strong motivators.

Edward acknowledged his point and vowed to be more careful with his choice of words.

Other than those two comments, Edward communicated that he was pleased with the overall progress of his team. He said he'd been skeptical about their ability to pull something comprehensive together at the outset, but he felt they'd since come up with creative ideas that would surprise everyone.

Just to be sure they were on the same page, and remembering the old saying of "Trust but verify," Jason asked for a couple of examples of what the team was considering. After hearing those ideas, he was pleasantly surprised and encouraged Edward to keep going.

Jason had asked each team to generate five tactics for their element and to prioritize three of those to launch initially. He recommended they prioritize the tactics based on sequencing them in the right order and not necessarily by impact.

He explained that this was because their initial goal would be to establish positive momentum; impact would come over time. He also shared that in the follow-on meeting, they'd develop the overall sequence of these first twenty-one tactics, primarily so they didn't overwhelm the organization and create confusion or ambiguity.

He looked forward to hearing what each team came up with.

# 11

## A FRAMEWORK TAKES SHAPE: PART ONE

Jason thought about all the meetings this senior leadership team had been in recently. He knew they must be tired, but they all showed resiliency and a growing commitment to each other. It was gratifying to see this across the group, and he wanted to be sure to support them as best he could.

The seven teams had been working together for a month on their respective elements, and today they would be sharing the tactics they had developed to help launch the cultural transformation. Word had leaked out on some of those tactics under consideration, which he felt had created a spark within the company. Before all this started, the activity level had seemed sluggish at best. Now it felt like the whole company eagerly anticipated what was coming next.

Jason opened the meeting. "First, thanks for the work you and your teams have put into this. I'm sure you would've liked more time to develop these tactics, but none of this is set in concrete. We can adjust our plan along the way. The good news is our product development project is on schedule—so far. We need to keep Surthrival moving right alongside it.

"We don't have anyone sitting in the perspective chair today. However, I propose we consider our employees' points of view as we move through the teams' recommendations. I requested each team generate five tactics and then prioritize the first three of those to implement. We'll go through your three priority tactics today. As noted in the meeting invite, extra chairs have been brought in so that when you're presenting the recommendations, your team can join the discussion. We also have the laptop hooked up for the remote employees. They'll be able to see the screen and presentations, and anyone who's speaking.

"I know the logistics for this aren't ideal, but hopefully we'll be able to keep to the published schedule. As you probably noticed on the meeting invite, the order of presentation will follow the spelling of the acronym RESPECT. Lastly, I'll use the flip chart to track any overlaps we identify between elements. At the end, we can review and decide how best to manage those.

"Let's get started. First up is Edward and his team with R-E-S-P-E-C-T," he said, spelling it out Aretha Franklin style.

"Jason, can I bring up one thing before we get started?" Hannah asked.

"Sure, what is it, Hannah?"

"One of the tasks you charged us with was coming up with a goal or strategy statement for our respective elements. I thought it would also be good to have an overall goal statement for Surthrival that encompasses all our efforts. I wanted to run this by you and the team and see what everyone thinks."

"Absolutely. Let's hear it."

"OK, the goal statement I came up with is 'To develop a connected culture based on *respect* that is engaging and fulfilling, creates alignment and accountability, and maximizes the potential of every employee and the company.'"

Jason pondered. "I like the words you used: 'connected,' 'based on,' 'creates,' 'maximizes.' I like this a lot," he said.

Victor added, "I think you covered it well, Hannah. I don't have anything to add."

"Agree completely. That says it all," said Abby.

Jason scanned the room and asked, "Do you all agree?"

He saw agreement across the board. He looked to Hannah and said, "Go ahead and add it to the Surthrival graphic your team designed. This statement will complete it. Thanks, Hannah. That's an excellent way to start this meeting. Edward, let's bring in your team and begin with the element of respect."

## ELEMENT #1: RESPECT

Edward opened the door and welcomed his team into the room. He introduced each member and began sharing.

"We did not know what we were getting into when we came together as a team. I certainly did not realize what I had signed up for—and I mean this in the most respectful and positive way, no pun intended.

"As we examined the element of respect, we recognized quickly why it was the first element on your list. We see respect as the hub of the wheel. It is at the core of each of the elements. From our perspective, it would be almost impossible to achieve sustainable success without respect throughout the company. Using your word, Hannah, respect *connects* and *aligns* the elements and all of us. Therefore, our goal is to cultivate a culture of respect in all directions throughout our organization.

"With that in mind, we agreed our first task as a team would be to develop a definition for respect at KCI."

Edward glanced towards Victor, who nodded back.

He continued, "Upon researching the word 'respect,' we found it originates from the Greek word '*timēsate*,' which means 'to honor or value.' So, if we are going to show respect for each other here at work, we believe it means we honor and value the rights and equality of every employee.

"As part of our research, we found that Toyota takes an active and personal approach to respect by defining it as listening to people and acting upon their ideas. In fact, Abby expressed those very same sentiments when we initially shared what respect looked like to us. In the end, our team realized that respect, or honoring and valuing each other, could be shown in many ways, which resulted in some interesting ideas for tactics within our team.

"The first tactic we would like to share is publishing guidelines for respect. We recommend adopting a publication by the University of Texas Medical Branch as our initial guideline. We can add or subtract to it as we see fit over time, but we thought this would be an excellent starting point. Here is a copy of its ten guidelines for you to read along with me [Figure 14]."

1. **Say something.** If you see disrespectful or unsafe behavior that undermines the work environment, speak up. Everyone deserves to be treated respectfully.
2. **Smile.** Empathize and be considerate of others. Make it a routine to smile and greet everyone as you arrive at work—it's a sign of courtesy and kindness.
3. **Say "thank you."** It may seem like common sense, but many people forget to say thank you or don't say it with sincerity. Show gratitude often by making sure people know you appreciate them and their actions. Give encouragement to show you value your team's contributions.
4. **Be considerate and discreet.** Be mindful of your surroundings. If you work in an open workspace and need to make a phone call, make sure to control your own volume and respect your neighbors.
5. **Apologize.** If you make a mistake, take responsibility and have a corrective action plan. Saying "I'm sorry" (without excuses) is courageous and proves your commitment to your colleagues and to your job.

6. **Participate constructively.** Make sure your contributions in meetings are on topic and respectful. Avoid interrupting others, and give others your full attention.
7. **Respond in a timely manner.** Answer emails and phone calls promptly—this shows people you value their time. Ensure that information is communicated and shared openly as appropriate. Sharing information signals trust and confidence.
8. **Go the extra mile.** Sometimes your team needs additional help to get the job done. Offer to pitch in and share the load. If a co-worker has helped you in the past, then returning the favor is a good way to show both your respect and gratitude.
9. **Be reliable.** Follow through on your commitments and responsibilities. Keep your word. Make task lists or reminders if needed and avoid distractions that make it easy to lose sight of deadlines. You'll earn your co-workers' respect when they know they can count on you.
10. **Feedback is a gift.** Praise much more often than you criticize. Share your expertise respectfully and be open to growth and learning. A collaborative workplace where everyone shares their ideas and offers creative solutions is one that thrives.

Figure 14

Edward allowed a few moments for the team to look at the guidelines, then asked, "I know this is your first glance at it, but what is everyone's initial reaction?"

Victor responded, "It looks like a great starting point. It promotes respect in many ways. Great job."

Jason smiled to himself. The meeting was off to a good start. He was also happy for Edward, who early on had seemed cautious with this element but today was beaming with confidence.

The rest of the staff gave the thumbs-up, and Jason encouraged the team to continue.

Edward picked up where he'd left off.

"Excellent," he said. "The second tactic we are proposing is to set up a recognition and celebration program. We believe recognizing and celebrating success is a way to show we value our employees and their contributions. Through a contact the team made, we benchmarked a local company that developed an interesting approach.

"The first thing this organization did was to put together a company store and stock it with many different consumer items of modest value, from T-shirts and hats to mugs and umbrellas. All the items are marked with the company logo.

"At the beginning of the quarter, each leader is given an allotment of what they call company bucks. The goods in the store are all priced in these bucks, so you can see where this is going. If a leader observes a good behavior or a significant accomplishment, they can celebrate within their department by awarding bucks to their employees.

"Prior to launch, the HR department developed guidelines for the leaders with examples of actions that could be considered for an award and the suggested amounts for those different activities. For each award, the leader fills out a form describing the situation, fills in the amount, and turns it into HR. HR then tracks how the awards are handed out—how much is given and for what reason. This ensures that all the leaders are participating while also monitoring them for equality.

"Employees are recognized and celebrated for doing something good, and they can use the award to purchase something of use. Those items happen to have the company logo on them as a reminder of the great place they work. We would like to develop and implement a similar program. Comments or questions?"

Abby asked, "Can employees purchase from the company store if they see something they want there?"

"Yes. Even though everything is priced in company bucks, one buck equals one dollar, so they can also come to the store and buy merchandise for the cash equivalent. From what we heard, the cash purchases account for about 30 percent of the store's activity."

Cooper also asked a question: "Do their leaders have to use up all of their allotment each quarter?"

"No, they do not. But HR tracks the activity, monitoring how much is distributed. If they do not use up their allotment, they carry over extra bucks into the next quarter. Also, if they don't hand out any in a quarter, HR has a discussion with that leader to better understand the situation."

Cooper added, "I don't know about this. Anytime money is involved, things can get a bit dicey."

Edward replied, "I hear what you are saying, Cooper. We did discuss that aspect and agreed that we would emphasize the recognition and celebration aspects. We would also keep the dollar value—the amount awarded and the store-item cost—at a minimal level to mitigate those concerns."

"OK. I appreciate that the team considered this aspect. If we go forward, we can always amend the program if it gets out of hand."

"Fair enough," Edward said.

Jason brought up a point. "Hannah, I can see where this could overlap with employee engagement. Did your team have a recommendation along this line?"

"You're right, this program would be a great employee engagement tool," said Hannah. "However, it's not something we thought of, so if it gets implemented, it'll serve double duty."

Jason made a note and nodded to Edward. "Carry on, Edward. You're on a roll."

"Thanks, Jason. OK, well, our third tactic was inspired by the example Cooper shared in our first meeting where the company showed respect for their employees by going after safety in the workplace. We asked ourselves if there was something significant we could do here for all employees. The area we identified was wellness. Again, showing employees we care about their physical and mental wellbeing shows how much we value them.

"When we researched this, we found companies that started their own on-site clinics. In some companies, it was accessible for the employees, and others also included the families of their employees. That seemed like a big bite for us, so we decided to focus on a component of wellness by implementing an exercise facility. We can start with a small footprint and gauge the interest level, expanding our offering as driven by usage. We have identified potential locations within our building that could house this and facilitate future growth as well.

"Also, through benchmarking a local company doing the same thing, we have the names of coaches who can help out a couple of days a week by developing workout plans. We do recognize that on the face of this, it is all cost. But we believe in the longer term, healthier employees could translate into lower medical insurance costs to the company and better attendance. Questions?"

Abby commented, "Our healthcare costs seem to go up every year, so, yes, this tactic could help us there. I also like the approach of starting out small. We can see what the take-up rate is and, as you say, scale up if—or hopefully when—merited."

"Thanks, Abby. Any other questions or comments on this one?"

Everyone appeared genuinely excited.

Edward continued, "OK, well, thank you for your support on what we have presented this morning. Before I summarize, if I can, I would like to address one more point that was brought up in our prior discussions: how respect relates to trust.

"As a team, we believe respect will lead to trust. Although you do not see any specific tactics related to trust, we believe everything we are doing in the seven elements will contribute towards building trust in our organization. It will be a natural byproduct. Does that make sense to everyone?"

Victor replied, "I'm glad your team considered it, and your take on it makes perfect sense. Well done!"

"Excellent, then to summarize, our three priority tactics are as follows:

1. Guidelines for respect at KCI
2. Recognition and celebration program
3. On-site exercise facility

"That is what we have to share today. Are there any other questions?"

Hannah spoke up. "This was amazing, Edward! Who are you, and what have you done with our Edward?"

Edward laughed with everyone else. They gave him and his team a round of applause.

Jason kept the meeting moving. "Thanks again, Team Respect. Great job! The next element is every leader buys in."

As Edward's team exited, Victor's team entered and settled in.

## ELEMENT #2: EVERY LEADER BUYS IN

After introducing his group, Victor began, "The definition of success and our goal for this element is embodied in its title: every leader buys in. That's 100 percent of the leaders buying into 100 percent of the elements. While we would like to see immediate buy-in across the board, we recognize that leaders will need a better understanding of what we're trying to accomplish through the seven elements, and then they can better determine what that could look like in their area.

"We see our role as taking them through a deeper dive into the seven elements with both information and examples, positioning them to then craft an implementation plan for their area. To get the ball rolling, we've identified three initial tactics:

1. Review the elements and tactics with the leadership team, including the rationale for implementing them, and elevate any concerns.
2. Leaders develop area plans and communicate to their team.
3. Track progress through ongoing Q12 surveys every six months.

"Once we complete today's work, we'll develop the material for this deep dive training on the seven elements, including the twenty-one tactics from today, along with the role each leader has in transforming the culture. The important step here, though, will be helping our leaders not only to see the real-world impact of the seven elements and their associated tactics but also to understand the impact that our three hundred-plus employees going in the same direction can have on our organization.

"We have to help them see how this cultural transformation will help solve some of the biggest pain points they encounter. If we can do that successfully, it'll go a long way towards establishing buy-in. We are targeting to have the prep work completed within two weeks."

"Are you confident you can complete this that quickly?" Jason asked.

"Yes, we believe we can," said Victor. "We've already started on the overall benefits to the company and the impact of the seven elements. Now we can layer in the twenty-one tactics and tie it all together."

"OK, you all have your work cut out for you," Jason commented.

"We recognize that and are committed to making it happen," Victor replied. He continued, "At the end of the training session, and once we've addressed any concerns that are raised, we'll ask each leader to develop an implementation plan for their area. It'll be due two weeks after that and should be inclusive of both on-site and remote workers. Their managers will review, and once they're both in agreement, they'll both sign it as approval.

"I'll be copied on each of the plans so we can share best practices across the leadership team. I also suggest that each functional leader reviews and monitors the plans within your respective areas. Once each area's plan is approved, the leader will share it with their team and post it both in their primary work area and on their team portal.

"After that, we'll ask each department to review their progress to their plan at least monthly in team meetings and develop corrective measures where needed. That's the second tactic.

"The third tactic is the measurement or follow-up part of this. We'll track the progress through Q12 surveys every six months. The option exists to code them to receive feedback by leader, and, of course, we can roll it up to both the overall functional and company level. It's important to complete an initial survey as soon as we can so we have an established baseline before beginning any activities. That's the third tactic.

"What questions can I answer for you?"

Cooper was first to respond.

"How will you identify leaders who are not engaged?" he asked.

"I believe the first opportunity will be through the implementation plan they develop, and in the ensuing review discussion they have with their manager," said Victor. "Their plan will provide an excellent tool for ongoing follow-up discussions with their manager. The Q12 surveys will also provide feedback. I think once this is launched, there will be strong peer pressure throughout the organization as well."

Jason said, "OK, we all need to be involved in the review process and be mindful of any early indicators."

"Actually, there has been some fallout already," said Victor. "Nelson came to see me about a production supervisor and their assistant who told him that they were fine doing it their own way without the seven elements."

"Where did that end up?" Jason asked.

"Nelson set up a meeting between the four of us and Cooper for tomorrow morning. I'll let you know how it turns out. Cooper, you were out at a site visit yesterday, but I know Nelson included you on the meeting invite and was planning to catch up with you after we get out of this meeting today."

"OK, I'll be there. Thanks for the heads-up."

"Anything else?" Victor asked.

There were no more questions, so Jason took the lead. He was impressed with how Victor and his team had approached this potentially sensitive area.

"Wow, that was an excellent start for this element. I know I always expect areas like this to change overnight, and it just doesn't happen that way. I appreciate your team helping our leaders make the transition. Well done."

Victor moved to the flip chart and summarized:

1. Review the elements and tactics with the leadership team; elevate any concerns.
2. Leaders develop and communicate their departmental implementation plan, then post.
3. Track progress through Gallup Q12 survey twice yearly, initial survey to be taken ASAP.

Victor said, "Thanks, team; you can go back to work. Jason, it looks like we're right on schedule so far."

Jason replied, "Speaking of which, we're scheduled for a fifteen-minute break now. Then we'll pick it up with my team and the third element, strong relationships. I'll let my team know we're right on time and we can all meet back here in fifteen minutes sharp."

# 12

## A FRAMEWORK TAKES SHAPE: PART TWO

Once everyone was back in their seats after the break, Jason restarted the meeting. "OK, so far this morning, we've covered the elements of respect and every leader buys in. The third element, which we'll cover now, is strong relationships."

### ELEMENT #3: STRONG RELATIONSHIPS

He then introduced his team and began, "For strong relationships, our team recognized that the ways in which employees work, perform, and behave depends significantly on the relationships they have with their coworkers. Further, we anticipate that relationships will be the vehicle for how we'll accomplish our goals as an organization. As such, our goal statement is simple: to develop all relationships within the company while focusing initially on the leader–direct report relationship.

"As a team, we wanted to pursue all five tactics immediately, so getting down to three was a challenge. I guess it means we have some great ideas waiting in the wings. Like Edward's group, our presentation begins with a simpler tactic and will grow in complexity as we move through the others.

"The first of our three priority tactics is conducting the Five Languages of Appreciation in the Workplace workshop, which was an example I shared in our first meeting. It's a great way to kick off the area of improving both the leader–direct report relationship and relationships in general. We liked the concept of showing appreciation to our employees in the best way that works for them. We also get the opportunity to learn a little more about each other in a nonthreatening environment.

"The company will have to identify an internal trainer to facilitate the workshops, but again, the up-front training process is reasonably short and concise. We propose this workshop for all employees. It's not time consuming nor too costly. We'll put together a budget for review and approval before planning the launch.

"Are there any questions on our first tactic?"

Everyone appeared good to go. Jason moved along.

"For the second tactic, we benchmarked a company that, for several years, has been at the top of the Best Companies to Work For ranking. One of the factors differentiating it was the range of company-sponsored outside activities available to employees. This business believes the time spent together in a different and relaxed setting outside of work is beneficial to developing both departmental and cross-functional relationships. The benchmarked company offered several different activities, from sports teams to book clubs, quilting groups to camping outings. These outings are optional to the employees, and yet they have a high participation rate.

"We'd phase this in over time, launching fresh activities as and when they are driven by employee interest, allowing the activity level to build on its own. Questions on this idea?"

Victor asked: "Who managed the activity groups in the organization your team benchmarked?"

"At that company, HR helped launch each new group, then kept the information updated and available for anyone interested. Each group named a volunteer employee leader and were self-managing for the most part."

Abby asked, "What about employee liability for the physical activities?"

"Good question, Abby. Employees are required to sign release forms before participating. We have a copy of their form and can run it through our own legal review."

"Thanks," said Abby. "And are there costs related to team activities?"

One of Jason's team members answered this question: "This company paid the entrance fees associated with leagues, but employees purchased any equipment or uniforms they required, minimizing the overall cost to the company."

"Other questions?" Seeing none, Jason continued, "We see a potential overlap on this idea with employee engagement, so I'll note that. Our third tactic is more complicated, and it's another one we discussed previously: the communications workshop. Our team had further discussions with the company I visited. We heard how impactful and meaningful it's been for every participant. It literally changed lives. We recognize it's a significant financial and time commitment on behalf of the company and employees. It's a big ask but one that we believe will be worth it."

Abby was the first to ask a question. "Any estimate of the total cost and over what period? That's got to be a big-ticket item."

Jason nodded. "I thought you might ask that, Abby. The timeline would be about two years to take all employees through this. We're still working on the costs, but like our first tactic, if we employ the 'train the trainer' approach, we can minimize the total outlay. We also must factor in the productivity loss of every employee participating for a full week. Once we have the full cost estimate, we'll develop a budget and present it to the staff."

Victor commented, "I remember your excitement when you shared this example in our first meeting. It sounded compelling then, and I hope we can find a way to do this for our employees. I know it'll test the budget and the payback is in the future, but I too believe it'll be worth it. Let me know if I can help in any way when you work up the budget."

"I'd like to help out on that budget as well," Abby interjected.

Victor continued, "One quick question, though. Would you approach it like the company you benchmarked and make it voluntary for all employees, or would the training be mandatory?"

"First, thanks for the offer to help on the budget—both of you. That's much appreciated," replied Jason. "As to your question, our recommendation is to follow their example and offer the training on a voluntary basis. We would use a similar approach by providing an opportunity for employees to apply for the weeklong class. We believe that best fits with the first element of respect. Using Edward's terms from earlier, we'll honor and value each employee's personal journey of engaging with the cultural changes we're advocating."

"I like that. Thanks, Jason."

"You got it. One last quick FYI: we did consider our remote working employees for each tactic. For communications training, we'd ask the remote working employees to come on-site that week. For the Five Languages of Appreciation in the Workplace training, our plan is for the remote workers to participate via video link. OK, any other questions about this one or the prior tactics?"

Everyone was quietly nodding. Jason summarized, "Our three tactics are as follows:

1. Companywide workshop on the Five Languages of Appreciation in the Workplace
2. Company-organized outside activities
3. Companywide communications training

"We're making great progress today," said Jason. "Let's complete one more element before breaking for lunch. Next up is Mike and the purposeful teams team—sorry for the redundancy."

## ELEMENT #4: PURPOSEFUL TEAMS

Mike's team filled the extra seating along the sides of the room. For most, it was their first time in the executive conference room, and Jason saw the newness of the experience reflected in their eyes.

Mike completed their introductions and began, "We had a fun time working on this element, and I can say with confidence that every member of our team is passionate about establishing purposeful teams. There was a lot of information available online that we enjoyed sharing with each other. We thought we'd share two pieces with you today before we move into our tactics.

"The first is from an article by Indeed, a job-recruiting website, which was titled: '12 Reasons Why Teamwork Is Important in the Workplace.'"[9]

The list of twelve flashed up on the screen:

Teamwork results in . . .

1. More fun
2. Less stress
3. More communications
4. Less confusion
5. More creativity
6. Less fear
7. More personal growth
8. Less burnout
9. More motivation
10. More diversity
11. More relationship building
12. More resilience

---

9   Herrity J, 2021

"Those are great," Abby said.

"We thought so too," Mike replied. "They all embody what we are attempting to accomplish with the seven elements and through purposeful teams in particular."

He continued, "The second piece is a quote from Patrick Lencioni and his book *The Five Dysfunctions of a Team: A Leadership Fable*,[10] in which he says, 'Not finance. Not strategy. It is *teamwork* that remains the ultimate competitive advantage, both because it is so *powerful* and so *rare.*' This statement got our attention and truly incentivized us throughout our work."

"That is powerful," Hannah and Jason echoed each other.

Mike responded, "Fantastic. We're glad it impacted you as much as it did us. And thanks for letting us take extra time to share those two. Moving on, then, the goal statement for our element is taken from the insights Jason shared from his mentor: achieve a scenario in which teamwork within KCI results in two plus two equaling five. With that brief introduction, let's go to our first tactic. It was a suggestion Bryan O'Conner made, so I am going to ask him to share it with you. Bryan."

Bryan addressed the group. "I was camping at the beach with my wife when this hit me. We are all part of a lot of teams—some formal, some not. I thought it'd be helpful if we took a moment to list the teams of which we are a part and spell out our role on each team. Every employee could do this with guidance from their leader. To help accomplish this, we've developed a form with a few key questions."

Bryan passed out the forms, which read:

- What is the team's name or the makeup of the team?
- What is the charter or primary goal of this team?

---

10   Lencioni P, 2002

- Is this a formal or informal team?
- What is your role on this team?
- What is your deliverable?

Allowing everyone a few moments to read the form, Bryan added: "This questionnaire should generate healthy discussion between leaders and their direct reports, which could improve those relationships. It should also help existing teams evaluate whether their charter or primary goal is clear to everyone, both on and off the team. Team leaders can then have discussions with team members relative to their individual roles and expected contributions. It's a great opportunity to reset the table on existing teams and ensure alignment across the board.

"Overall, it's a simple task, and we think it'll open some eyes by helping them see their contributions to the bigger team here. That's it. Any questions?"

Hannah had a comment. "I think this idea is insightful and perhaps leads to setting up guidelines for our teams, like Edward's guidelines for respect."

Mike jumped back in. "Exactly, Hannah. You just named our next tactic. Before we move on to that, are there any other questions or comments for Bryan?"

With nothing but positive comments for Bryan, the team agreed to move to the next tactic.

Mike continued, "Thanks, Bryan. The second tactic we're proposing—and thank you, Hannah—is to develop guidelines for setting up teams and framing up the behaviors within them. We also found examples we thought could work well. If we agree to use them as a starting point, they can be tweaked later as needed."

He gave everyone a handout from MIT [Figure 15], which was a guideline for setting up a team:

---

### CHECKLIST FOR TEAM START-UP

**How to use this tool:**

The following checklist contains questions that should be answered early in the start-up phase of a project team. Ideally, the project sponsors will discuss these matters with the team leader or team members <u>prior</u> to the actual team formation. That information, along with any relevant unanswered questions, should be part of the team's kick-off activities and discussions.

### A. Driving Issues

13. Why is this team being formed?
14. What are the critical issues the team should address?
15. What is the team's scope? (Has the scope been set by or approved by the team's sponsors?)

### B. Goals

1. What are the specific project (or process improvement) goals?
2. What constitutes success?
3. How can we make these goals measurable? If they are not quantifiable, how can we look for qualitative data about improvement?
4. How do these goals support the overall mission of our department, the project, the company?

### C. Roles and Responsibilities
1. Why has each member of this team been selected? What skills/expertise does each team member bring?
2. What is the role of the team leader?
3. What is the role of the facilitator?
4. What is the role of our sponsor?

### D. Deliverables/Timeline
1. What is the output/product for this team?
2. What is our timeline overall?
3. Are there mid-point milestones or approval processes?
4. What is the deadline for deliverables?

### E. Commitment
1. How much time are we expected to spend on this effort?
2. Do all team members need to be available for each meeting?

Figure 15

Mike also shared an example of operating guidelines for teams [Figure 16].

## OUR ATTITUDE & CULTURE

- We treat each other with respect.
- We intend to develop personal relationships to enhance trust and open communication.
- We value constructive feedback. We will avoid being defensive and give feedback in a constructive manner.
- We strive to recognize and celebrate individual and team accomplishments.
- As team members, we will pitch in to help where necessary to help solve problems and catch up on behind schedule work.

## TEAM MEETINGS

- We will hold a regular weekly meeting on _____.
- Additional meetings can be scheduled to discuss critical issues or tabled items upon discussion and agreement with the team leader.
- All team members are expected to attend team meetings in person or via video connection unless they are out of town, on vacation or sick. If a team member is unavailable, he or she should have a designated, empowered representative (another team member, a representative from their functional organization, etc.) attend in their place.
- The team leader can cancel or reschedule a team meeting if sufficient team members are unavailable or there is insufficient subject matter to meet about.

- The team leader will publish and distribute an agenda by email by 12 p.m. each Monday. Team members are responsible for contacting the team leader or leaving a voice message or email with any agenda items they want to include by _____. Agenda items can be added at the meeting with the concurrence of the team.
- Meetings will start promptly. All members are expected to be on-time. If, for extenuating circumstances a member is late, he/she will need to catch up on their own.
- An action-item list with responsibilities will be maintained, reviewed in meetings, and distributed with the meeting minutes.
- No responsibilities will be assigned unless the person to be assigned the responsibility accepts it. If a person to be given a responsibility is not able to attend the meeting, the team leader must review that assignment or action item with the person before the responsibility is designated.
- The responsibility for taking and distributing meeting minutes will rotate monthly among core team members.
- Meeting minutes will be distributed within __ hours after the meeting.
- We will emphasize full discussion and resolution of issues versus sticking to a timetable

Figure 16

After reading through the two handouts with the meeting attendees, Mike added, "This is a starting point. We can develop KCI versions of both frameworks within a month for review, prior to distribution to all employees. Any questions on our second tactic?"

Victor commented, "Mike, this is good foundational work, and it's been missing here. Participating on a team has been high-adventure theater in the past. We can use the checklist and ground rules when we form a new team, and perhaps we can get our established teams to adopt these as well. Heck, these are good for staff and department meetings too. I applaud what you're doing to develop the structure first. Well done."

"Thanks, Victor. Any other comments or questions before we go to our third tactic?"

There were a few head shakes. Everyone was in agreement.

Mike continued, "The third tactic is a big step towards tearing down the walls or silos we've erected between departments. We're proposing that over the coming twelve months, each department selects a minimum of two other departments to meet with individually. Preferably, the two selections would include a major internal supplier to the department doing the selecting, which could mean supplier of parts or forms or information, and a major internal customer to whom the selecting department delivers parts or forms or information as the next step in the overall process.

"In this meeting, each group would share what their primary role in the organization is, how they do it, why they do it, and what their goals are. The departments would then discuss constructively what works and doesn't work between them. Ideally, the department leaders would meet prior to this discussion, anticipating some of the more contentious points, and develop plans to guide the discussions towards positive solutions.

"It's been commented we have an over-the-wall mentality here, so this is a great way to begin breaking down those walls and start working together as one team with a common mission. Again, we're open to comments and questions."

Jason spoke up this time. "This is interesting. The part of understanding what each other is trying to do is important. If we can begin tearing down the walls we've erected here, that'd be a huge plus for the organization. It's a solid idea, but I don't think two meetings per department will be enough."

Victor jumped in. "I think two meetings is a good starting point, Jason. They can always ramp up from there."

Jason responded, "I'm just saying that we have a lot of years to overcome, and two meetings might be light."

"I don't think we want to put too much pressure on the departments. They'll have a lot going on," Victor replied. "I'll bet they'll see the value once they get going."

Jason thought for a moment before adding: "OK, I'm good with this for now, Mike. Victor has a point; you can always add more if they are as impactful as I believe they will be. Again, great idea."

Everyone was on board with this as well. Mike continued, "All right then, to finish our part up, the three tactics for teamwork are as follows:

1. Each employee clarifies their teams/roles.
2. Develop a team checklist and establish guidelines for team operations.
3. Each department to conduct two interdepartmental meetings—one with a key supplier and one with a key internal customer of the department.

"That should wrap things up."

"Thanks, Mike," Jason said. "Great start this morning. We're right on time and have three elements left to cover, plus the discussion about any overlaps we see. Let's break for lunch, and then we'll be back at it."

Jason and Victor stayed behind as everyone hit the lunch buffet.

Victor leaned in to speak to Jason. "I agreed with what you said just now, but I wanted to show everyone it's OK to challenge you. It's important that they know you won't shut them down for thinking and voicing their opinion."

Jason smiled. "You had me going there for a second. You're right. I do want everyone to feel comfortable enough to share their thoughts and know they're safe to do so. Thanks."

Victor stood and patted Jason's shoulder. "You got it, Jason."

Jason added, "Hey, before you go, Victor, I want to thank you for how you do what you do."

"What do you mean by that?"

"Well, I believe HR should play a key role in helping maximize the people aspect of the business, whether that is in our culture or through leadership. I see how you're working behind the scenes to move us forward and, in many cases, out front pulling us along. I appreciate that."

"Thanks, Jason. That means a lot that you've noticed."

Jason smiled. "My turn to say you got it."

After lunch, Jason welcomed everyone back into the room, "Hannah, you and the employee engagement team are up. You have the awesome task of being right after lunch!"

## ELEMENT # 5: EMPLOYEE ENGAGEMENT

Hannah completed her team introductions and began, "In the first meeting, we established a goal statement for this element, which was 'Engaged throughout the day and fulfilled when we end it.'

"This statement resonated with every member of our team. We agreed it was critical to establish a baseline measurement of employee engagement before we began any work. To accomplish that, our first tactic was to complete the Gallup Q12 survey. Since Victor's group already has this on the table, we're going to pivot and present our second, third, and fourth tactics. Thank you, Victor. It looks like we get a bonus one in."

Victor gave her a thumbs-up.

"Before I get to our tactics, I want to share some meaningful information we found on the Gallup website relative to the impact employee engagement has on overall company performance.

"In comparing the differences between the top-quartile and bottom-quartile business units or teams in terms of employee engagement, the top-quartile group had the following statistics:

- 81% less absenteeism
- 28% less shrinkage or theft
- 18% higher productivity
- 64% less safety incidents
- 41% less quality defects
- 10% higher in customer loyalty or engagement
- 18 to 43% less employee turnover depending on the type of organization
- And 23% higher profitability

"As you can see, employee engagement plays an important role in our future success. Once we realized the extent of its reach, we all committed to staying on this team through the implementation of an indefinite list of tactics. Again, it points to the relationships between these seven elements. It's astonishing."

"And so are those results," said Cooper. "Can you send that list out to all of us? I'd like to have a copy of that."

Hannah smiled. "Absolutely."

Jason noticed Hannah's entire team beaming with pride.

Hannah continued, "Let's get started with the first tactic. It was suggested by Jimmy Marino, and I'd like him to share it with you."

Jimmy wobbled a bit as he stood to address the staff.

He cleared his throat. "We felt it was important for every

employee to understand each day how their work contributes to the achievement of both their departmental and our overall company goals. We thought if they were in sync with those, they wouldn't want to miss work unless something drastic happened in their life."

Looking to Hannah for support, he added, "We're proposing that leaders sit down with each employee and develop an individual plan and scorecard. We *tell* employees their work is important to the organization's success, but we need to *show* them how their work contributes to the achievement of our company goals. This plan and scorecard, then, should tie into their departmental goals and, where possible, be linked to our company goals as well.

"The scorecard should have daily targets, so if they hit those, every day every employee can achieve a sense of fulfillment. And this fits with our goal of engaging employees daily. That's pretty much it. We recognize there's a lot of work ahead in creating those plans and scorecards. Are there any questions we can answer on this?"

Jason smiled towards Hannah and responded, "First off, great idea. Thank you, Jimmy. We may have to coach some of the leaders through the plan development stage. Have you thought about that?"

Victor jumped in: "I think my team can help there and provide mentoring to the leadership team."

"Perfect! Thanks, Victor."

"This idea dovetails into one of our ideas for continuous improvement," said Cooper. "I will explain the connection when we're up."

Hannah stepped back in to take over. "Great job, Jimmy. Our first tactic creates daily engagement while our second one creates episodic engagement. This tactic complements the relationships team's organized outside activities with organized inside activities.

"We propose establishing an activities committee, providing a budget, and requesting they develop an annual calendar of events. This could include activities like potlucks around the holidays, BBQs, health fairs, and family events like a summer picnic or a holiday party. We want to see this organized and planned strategically to nurture employee engagement. Any questions on this one?"

Jason commented, "I agree this is a good complement to the outside activities. It's a lot of activities overall, but if they are strategically planned and coordinated, they could create powerful links to the company, and to engagement. It'll also build on the positive feedback we heard when the leadership team met with all the employees to conduct the culture interviews. When you work through this, be sure to consider our remote working employees. It may take some creativity, but I am sure you'll come up with the right approaches."

"Yes, absolutely, Jason. We discussed the remote employees and have ideas for including them. Any other comments or questions?" Hannah asked.

Seeing none, she moved on.

"Our third tactic is for leaders to connect with each of their direct reports daily. It doesn't have to be a long discussion, but it should be a daily activity. If we can achieve this simple step, we believe employees will feel cared for and valued.

"In fact, research shows that 94 percent of employees who feel cared for say they are personally engaged in their work.[11] This also fits in with showing respect and developing relationships. Again, this will be easier for employees in the office. For our remote workers, we suggest a daily morning team check-in via video and an individual call at least twice weekly. Any questions on this?"

There were thumbs-up all around.

"You're too easy on us," laughed Hannah. "Then to summarize, our three tactics are as follows:

1. Develop an individual daily plan and scorecard for every employee.
2. Organized internal activities.

---

11   Hamilton K, Sandhu R, Hamill L, 2019

3. Leaders connect with employees daily.

"Thanks for listening, everyone."

Jason beamed. "Thanks, Hannah. Next up is Cooper and the continuous improvement team. However, looking at the schedule, Victor had asked me to add in a quick ten-minute break to go to the lunchroom for a birthday celebration for Bryan O'Conner. Right, Victor?"

"Yes, and it's great that we're right on schedule today. We can sing 'Happy Birthday,' grab a piece of cake, and come right back."

# 13

## A FRAMEWORK TAKES SHAPE: PART THREE

The team reconvened after the birthday celebration.

Jason said, "OK, back to it. We've really done a good job of staying on task today. We covered the first five elements so far and have two to go. Next up is Cooper and the continuous improvement team."

## ELEMENT #6: CONTINUOUS IMPROVEMENT

Cooper began, "It's been a good day so far and fun to see what everyone has come up with. Our team enjoyed working through this element. We agree with something Jason said in our first meeting: this element will be the most complex to implement and one we should phase in over time. We also agree on allowing the cultural transformation to take hold first before launching into the tools of continuous improvement. And we support the focus on respect for people wholeheartedly and believe it will provide a solid foundation to build upon.

"One other point to share: we embraced the idea of coming up with a way for employees to control the pace of each phase of continuous improvement by developing a mechanism whereby a panel of associates could monitor the status of the current tool or countermeasure being implemented and advise when the company is positioned to successfully launch the next one. This mechanism is something our team will continue working on."

Cooper continued, "This element is not a project; like Surthrival, it's a journey. Our plan is to implement continuous improvement on a companywide basis.

"And one final comment before I share our three tactics. Hannah has a goal statement for her element, and we would like to have a guiding statement for continuous improvement. I was listening to a podcast about three weeks ago, and the person being interviewed was asked what his favorite continuous improvement quote was. He replied that although the quote was not originally meant for continuous improvement, he thought it applied well. He quoted legendary UCLA basketball coach John Wooden when he said, 'Be quick, but don't hurry.'

"We think this statement captures the essence of what we want to accomplish through our continuous improvement efforts, so we'd like to adopt it as our banner."

"You know I love it," Jason quipped.

Everyone around the table agreed, so Cooper continued.

"Here are our three tactics. The first one is the development and implementation of a cascading strategy deployment process, which is an important umbrella to our continuous improvement plans and relates back to the slide Jason showed with the arrows coming into alignment. It is a way to *align* the company to one set of goals so our work adds up to significant forward progress as an organization. This process would start at the top of our organization with a long-term strategic plan.

"We're recommending the plan be a five-year lookout. The five-year strategic plan would then cascade back through the organization to a set of one-year company key result areas, or KRAs, to achieve the five-year plan. Those KRAs would be supported by one-year functional plans—functional meaning operations, sales and marketing, etc.—and one-year goals and objectives by their departments and subgroups, all in alignment to the company-level plan. In some companies they call this their 'line of sight' plan.

"As detailed as that plan sounds, there are more sophisticated approaches; but we decided that this would be a good first step for our organization—essentially walking before we run. Some of you like to see something like this drawn out, so here's a depiction we developed to make it easier to see the entire process [Figure 17]."

Figure 17

Cooper allowed the team to look at the diagram and asked, "Does this help everyone see how this tactic aligns the organization? We recommend quarterly report-outs to ensure both alignment and accountability. There are more details to this. It's a big undertaking but an important one if we are to maximize the resources we have. You can also see where the recommendation from the employee engagement team to develop individual plans and scorecards and link them to our company goals fits in perfectly."

Jason had a question. "This really helps us begin driving the organization to the right on the arrows diagram, right towards the bullseye of total connection and alignment to our goals as an organization. Has your team selected a tool to accomplish this?"

"We're still exploring those options," he added. "But when we get the go-ahead, we'll tackle that first. There are more details, but you get the gist of the recommendation. Are there any other questions or comments on our first tactic?"

There were a few comments about the complexity of this approach, but the other leaders also said that they were encouraged by the direction it would take the company.

"Hope you didn't start with the easy one," Hannah commented.

Cooper assured her, "It's not the easiest one but is one we believe we should start on right away.

"Our second tactic is to adopt a companywide problem-solving tool. The benefit here is developing a common language within the company as we go about solving problems and improving our work processes. We've selected the A3 problem-solving tool, which is a structured approach first developed by Toyota. It typically uses a single sheet of ISO A3-size paper, hence the name. The A3 approach focuses on identifying the root cause of the problem you are solving, eliminating it, and then following up with mutually agreed-upon measurements that validate elimination.

"There are other effective problem-solving tools out there, and they can be used to augment A3s, but, again, we felt it important to get everyone on the same page with one primary tool. This has been a powerful approach; other companies have developed a culture of alignment and teamwork aided by this common language. We'll put together an implementation plan and identify the needed resources."

Edward had a question: "Cooper, earlier you said your team would not begin introducing tools until the cultural transformation had taken hold, but it looks like your first two tactics are both tools. Can you explain that?"

"Fair question," Cooper replied. "Yes, these are both tools. However, there are different tools for different applications. These first two—strategy deployment and A3s—are both business support tools that aren't used to change an operation but rather to help us run the business more effectively. They'll help us align, work better as a team, and give us a common language. The ones we're delaying until the culture has taken hold are ones that change or improve an existing process and directly impact employee work patterns. That may sound like we're splitting hairs, but we see a difference between these first two and the tools for process improvement."

"Hmm, I think I get it. I see the difference, and you make a good point."

Cooper nodded. "Thanks, Edward. I know we'll be discussing the timing for implementing the twenty-one tactics in the next meeting. However, whenever we begin our continuous improvement journey, we want these to be the first two tactics we implement. Make sense to everyone?"

Everyone nodded, and Cooper continued.

"It was difficult to choose between two viable options for our third tactic. The two are either conducting a rattlesnake hunt—three hunts, actually—or implementing the principles behind the book *2 Second Lean*.

"We opted to go with the rattlesnake hunts initially as they will help us all begin learning how to see—that is, see our work areas through a different lens and open our eyes to improvement opportunities. *2 Second Lean* will be a great follow-up down the road when we begin teaching and equipping our employees with the tools of continuous improvement.

"Back to the rattlesnake hunts. We will hold three of them: one in manufacturing, one in the office areas, and one in the support areas. We have located an outside resource that has experience running these. The kinds of rattlesnakes we will be trained to find are safety issues, maintenance issues, bottlenecks, identified nonnegotiables, and waste.

"Each of the three rattlesnake hunts will be separated by a month. Within each area, we'll divide up into teams of three to five people and equip them with a digital camera, rattlesnake tags, and a conference room with three accessible walls to post their finds. We'll also have some inexpensive prizes on hand, such as candy bars. The first day will be a competition between the teams to see which of them can identify the most rattlesnakes.

"In the following three days, there'll be a second competition to see who can kill off the most rattlesnakes. Those that aren't killed off will be documented, and follow-up dates will be established to ensure they're addressed. We've heard positive feedback from companies that have run these, and again, it's a fun way to help everyone begin seeing their work areas from a new perspective. And yes, we will ask the remote workers to participate as well. Any questions on this?"

"It sounds fun, Cooper," said Edward. "How much advance training is involved?"

"It really doesn't take much to get going. There will be a fifteen-minute training session before the hunt begins, describing the eight wastes in the plant and office environments. It is straightforward and all part of the first day's agenda. Make sense, Edward?"

"Yes. Thanks for explaining."

Cooper looked around the room. "Other questions or comments?"

No other hands raised, so Cooper wrapped up his team's part of the day.

"To summarize, our three tactics are as follows:

1. Develop and implement a companywide strategy deployment process.
2. Use the A3 process as our companywide problem-solving tool; train all employees.
3. Conduct three separate rattlesnake hunts: in manufacturing, office, and the support areas.

"Any questions?"

Abby took this in before commenting, "All three of these are big ones. They'll require an investment in trainers and of course the time to train everyone. In fact, when we get to the sequencing stage, we'll need to consider the costs and the resources required to make all twenty-one happen. But these continuous improvement tactics are excellent. Kudos to you and your team."

Jason echoed, "I agree with Abby. These three look like a great start for our continuous improvement journey, without getting right into the nitty-gritty tools. If the culture shift is the trigger point for continuous improvement, we will have to figure out how we'll know when we're there."

Victor chimed in, "Since we're doing the Gallup Q12 survey, perhaps once we receive our baseline results we can agree on an improvement goal that becomes the trigger point you alluded to. Then it's a matter of monitoring our progress through the biannual surveys. We also should all be seeing and feeling the changes within."

"Great suggestion, Victor," Cooper responded. "Anything else on these three?"

Seeing none, Cooper gestured towards Jason. "Back to you, chief."

Jason said, "Thanks, Cooper and team. Another excellent job. Last but not least is the seventh element of transparent communications. Abby, go ahead and bring your team in and introduce them."

## ELEMENT #7: TRANSPARENT COMMUNICATIONS

"Thanks, Jason," Abby said before introducing her team members and getting started.

"We also want to briefly share information we found related to transparent communications. Like many of the other teams reported, there is so much information out there to draw upon. One piece connected the dots for us. On the *Glassdoor for Employers Blog*, it says, 'Organizations that are transparent with their employees experience increased employee engagement and a stronger company culture.'

"Glassdoor also reported that 'a transparent work environment helps people feel valued and encourages creativity.' Finally, the piece states that 'transparency creates trust between leadership and employees, helps improve morale, and lowers job-related stress—while increasing happiness and boosting performance.' These statements reinforced what we have witnessed today through these presentations: that these seven elements are both interrelated and dependent upon each other."

"Well said," Edward agreed. "It is important for our teams to understand those dependencies and the impact each element's success will ultimately have on our organizational outcomes."

"Indeed," Abby replied. "We have a lot to consider as we move forward. In terms of our strategy, we developed the following statement: 'Use transparent communications as a tool to inform our employees, to motivate us all to higher levels of achievement, and to hold each other accountable.' It's getting late, so I'm going to jump right in.

"Our first tactic is to conduct quarterly all-employee updates. We recognize the logistics in bringing everyone together can be a bit daunting, but with video communications available, we can minimize the travel expense associated with remote employees, unless there are other reasons to bring them in.

"This quarterly meeting would give us the opportunity to share the current progress of the company with everyone who works here. The agenda would include an update on our financials against budget, progress on our key result areas, updates on key projects, highlights of individual and team accomplishments, recognition of key work anniversaries and promotions, and the introduction of new employees. We could also have an open Q&A time. Again, the focus is on being transparent with employees and sharing pertinent company information.

"Jason, we expect you'll be presenting a good chunk of the information, but it'll be a good chance for many different people to come forward and share. That'll be healthy for the organization. Any questions or comments on this first tactic?"

"Long overdue," Mike and Victor said almost simultaneously.

"Excellent!" laughed Abby. "Let's move on to our second tactic, which is monthly functional area updates. By functional areas, we mean the functions represented by the senior leadership team.

"These would be conducted in each of the eight months in which a quarterly all-employee update is not scheduled—and would include a performance review of their area, significant company updates, and a time for open Q&As. This way, employees will be receiving monthly updates, either through the functional area review or the all-employee update.

"I am going to keep going right into the third tactic as it is similar. We're also requesting that department heads conduct weekly check-ins with their teams to review current needs, opportunities for improvement, safety, open projects, work scheduling, and so on. After asking around, we did find a few functional and departmental areas currently having some type of an update meeting, so we already have a start there.

"Going back to one of Edward's earlier statements, we're planning to develop a standardized agenda for all three meeting types we've presented: all-employee, functional, and departmental. To accomplish that, we recommend pulling together a group of departmental and functional leaders to help develop the standard formats and communication plans for all three. The remote workers will be able to participate in each of these communications via video.

"That's our initial set of three tactics. Are there any questions or comments?"

Jason was first to comment.

"I like the thought of routine meetings occurring virtually at every level. Our employees will be informed and connected to everything going on," he said. "I also applaud the caveat of having standard agendas for all three levels of communication. Thanks, Abby and team."

Victor chimed in, "I agree. I think this is a great starting point for transparent communications, and you've covered it on a broad scale and at an individual level. Good job!"

Abby moved to conclude, adding, "Thanks, everyone. Summarizing, the three tactics for transparent communications are as follows:

1. Quarterly all-employee company updates
2. Monthly functional reviews in the off months
3. Weekly departmental check-ins

"We also plan to develop a standardized agenda for all three."

Jason stepped back into the conversation: "Excellent job by Team Transparent Communications. Thanks for joining us."

After Abby's team exited the conference room, Jason continued, "We have our initial twenty-one tactics for consideration. I've been logging the overlaps between the elements and had thought initially that we'd work through those at the end of this meeting. However, you already managed through the overlaps and went on to your backup ideas. I don't see any conflicts to be resolved.

"Thinking back over the day, how do you all think it went?" Jason said.

Abby spoke first: "I have to say how impressed I am with every team and how everyone tackled their elements. For only having a month to do this, it was well thought out. And I thought the goal statements for each of the elements were right on."

Edward, smiling and looking in Cooper's direction, added, "I want to give kudos to Cooper and team for identifying tactics to help us see through continuous improvement eyes strategically without jumping into the tactical side right away. The more I reflect on that, the more impressed I am with your team's output."

"Thanks, Edward," Cooper responded, albeit with a look of surprise on his face.

Victor commented, "One of my concerns is how the budget comes out for next year and whether we'll have the funding to launch all twenty-one tactics."

"I share that concern as well," said Abby.

"Well," Jason said, "we'll have time to get started on some of these while lobbying Thompson Holdings through Adam and in my quarterly update trips. I'll be pushing for budget flexibility to get all twenty-one going."

Mike mentioned, "I think everything presented today was outstanding. But I have to say, my favorite aspect of the day was having our teams join the discussion. I could tell they enjoyed participating and they'll be sharing their experience with their colleagues."

"Great point, Mike," Cooper agreed.

"So this is what it feels like," Hannah said. "We've been in departmental silos for so long that I didn't have any idea what it could be like to work as a team—as one KCI team. It was fun to be cheering on all seven groups today."

"I agree, Hannah," Jason remarked. "It feels good, doesn't it?"

He continued, "OK, thanks again for putting this plan together. I think you all did outstanding work and should be proud of your teams today, and proud to be a part of the senior leadership team of this organization.

"We have more to focus on before launching the tactics. Our next step will be to set up the associated time frames. To do that, please begin working with your teams to develop estimates of the resources required to implement your three tactics, both people and expenses, as well as the time frame for implementation. Abby will be sending out guidelines or ranges to help you code them. We're borrowing from Yelp, which places dollar signs next to restaurants to indicate how expensive their meals are. We'll use something similar to denote the anticipated expense, the number of resources required, and the time frame to complete implementation.

"Send me your prioritized three tactics with this coding by noon the day before our next meeting so I can set up a table with all the tactics and their associated estimates. This scheduling meeting will help establish a tempo for the organization and balance the resources and expenses. Thanks, everyone. And again, great work in your teams this last month and as a team today."

After the meeting, Abby followed Jason back to his office.

"This was an amazing meeting," she said. "It feels like we're building something special here. And what's with Edward? And I mean that in a good way. Talk about an about-face. I thought we had the makings of a great team here, but now with him fully engaging, I'm even more optimistic. He does have an interesting way of speaking, though, doesn't he?"

"I agree, the team has made big strides, and Edward really shone in there today."

"He really did. Well, thanks again for what we are doing here. I'm excited to be a part of this."

"Ditto."

At the same time, Edward caught up with Cooper and Hannah and asked if they would join him in his office.

"Listen, I just want to quickly share something with both of you. Being on the respect team has helped me see things differently. I know I still have a long way to go, but I want to apologize to you both for the disrespectful comments I made during the first elements meeting when I referred to your areas as 'party central' and being full of back-slapping.

"The fact that you both do things to develop camaraderie in your teams just shows you are well ahead of me in all we are trying to do here. I am learning, and I hope you will have patience with me."

"Wow, Edward," Hannah said. "That's awesome that you'd even take the time to say this."

"No worries here," Cooper said.

"Thanks, both of you. I know it has already been a long day, so I will not keep you. Thank you for listening."

"You got it," they said in unison.

On the way out, Hannah and Cooper both looked at each other with raised eyebrows.

"That was surprising! But I sure like the change," Hannah said.

"Me too. People never cease to amaze me," Cooper replied.

# 14
## TIMING IS EVERYTHING

Jason reflected on the progress the senior leadership team had made so far. They'd come a long way since the opening meeting when they'd first discussed the seven elements.

He was pleased to see them beginning to gel as a team and that the notion of working collaboratively was starting to percolate down through the departments. This team's willingness to take on so much at one time was impressive; they were tackling the cultural transformation, a major new product development project, and potentially a new operating system, simultaneously. Any one of those would be a major undertaking for any company, let alone one that was just learning how to leverage all the resources from within.

Today they would establish the timetable for implementing the tactical aspect of the cultural transformation—the last step before formally launching their plan throughout the organization.

Jason opened the meeting: "Good morning, everyone. We've covered a lot of ground since we began working on this, and we have one more step today before launching our plan. We've identified seven key elements, proposed twenty-one tactics for implementation, and today we'll sequence those tactics so we can follow a coordinated implementation plan. Before we begin, I want to touch on a few other topics.

"First, there was a meeting to discuss the state of our systems. Many of you attended. Abby, I'd appreciate it if you'd give us a quick recap so we're all up to speed."

Abby leaned forward. "Sure, Jason, happy to share. Wow, where to begin?

"As we all know, a lot of our systems are spreadsheet driven and were developed on the fly by whomever needed or controlled the information. Most are standalone systems, so they don't interact with each other. One thing on which we all agreed is the need for a fully integrated system. Instead of spending time airing everyone's grievances, we went right to the solution and began discussing our needs for the future.

"To start, we need an enterprise resource planning—or ERP—system that includes integrated modules across the organization and, preferably, a package developed for medical device applications. We'd also like to see if the packages conduct business in a lean environment, which is the direction we're headed with our continuous improvement plans. That'd be a bonus.

"Our recommendation is to put together a cross-functional team of key users to develop the system specs and begin shopping. Jason, we also appreciate the operating systems recommendations you brought to us from our sister companies. They'll be included in our search process. That's a quick summary. Anyone else who was there have anything to add? Or are there any questions we can answer?"

Those who participated in the meeting echoed each other, saying everything had been covered.

There weren't any questions, so Jason said, "I recognize this is a huge undertaking, and it'll have to be considered with the work we're doing on Surthrival to develop our culture and leadership approach and, of course, along with the product development project. Thanks for the update, Abby."

Jason continued, "The other topics we need to be mindful of are the ones which surfaced at the quarterly update meeting I attended at Thompson Holdings. We need to tackle our product margins, leverage our overhead structure, and figure out how to bring our inventories down to an acceptable level. I suggest we incorporate those topics as active KRAs within the strategy deployment work we'll be completing. I was about to say 'completing soon,' but that'll be determined later today when we sequence the implementation of our tactics.

"OK, moving on."

Before he could continue, Victor interrupted, "Jason, I don't want to derail what we're planning to accomplish today, but when you put it all on the table, all that we're working on, I must share my concern for how we'll get it done with our limited resources. I'm already feeling overwhelmed. Anyone else feeling like that?"

Jason noticed everyone nodding while staring intently at the tabletop.

He responded, "That's a valid concern, Victor—one I was going over in my mind just before this meeting began. Listen, I wish I had a magic wand that could clone everyone here. If we're smart about how we tackle these challenges, I believe we can make it happen.

"We'll need to be careful not to overbook any one person or group. It'll be tricky, but I also think you'll be surprised when you see who steps up—just like Mike shared before with Bryan O'Conner. We'll make resource allocations a topic for each of our staff meetings as we go through this so it doesn't get away from us.

"Remember, as senior leaders, our job is to choose what we work on and where we place our resources. Going back to the arrows diagram, that means focusing on work that moves the needle towards achieving our goals. Right now, we need the new product to survive, and we need to build the culture and the operating systems to develop, manufacture, and deliver that product. Anything not related to those priorities is off our radar screen for now. We'll have to maximize every resource we have, but I firmly believe we can and will do that."

"And maybe we'll realize some of that 'two plus two equals five' teamwork effect along the way," Abby added.

"I do believe we'll see exactly that, Abby," Jason replied. "Thanks for bringing this up, Victor. Let's keep it as an active topic on the table until we agree it's no longer a concern. Does that work for you—and for everyone here?"

Victor nodded as the rest serenaded Jason with a chorus of "We're ready."

"OK, let's get to work sequencing these twenty-one tactics. To begin with, I want to show you a table I developed with the information you submitted [Figure 18]. Abby, thanks for putting together the coding guidelines. Please pass these around."

| Element | Tactic | Expense | Resources | Time | Sequence | Launch |
|---|---|---|---|---|---|---|
| **R**espect | Guidelines for respect | $ | 👤👤 | ⊙ | | |
| | Recognition and celebration program | $$ | 👤👤 | ⊙⊙ | | |
| | Exercise facility | $$ | 👤👤 | ⊙⊙ | | |
| **E**very Leader Buys In | Review elements and tactics with leaders | $ | 👤 | ⊙ | | |
| | Leader develop dept implementation plan and post | $ | 👤 | ⊙ | | |
| | Track progress through Gallup Q12 survey twice/year | $$ | 👤👤 | ⊙ | | |
| **S**trong Relationships | The Five Languages of Appreciation in the Workplace | $$ | 👤👤 | ⊙⊙ | | |
| | Company-organized outside activities | $ | 👤 | ⊙ | | |
| | Companywide communications training | $$$$ | 👤👤 | ⊙⊙ | | |
| **P**urposeful Teams | Each employee clarifies teams/roles | $ | 👤 | ⊙ | | |
| | Develop guidelines for setting up and operating teams | $ | 👤 | ⊙ | | |
| | Each dept conducts two interdepartmental meetings | $$ | 👤 | ⊙⊙⊙ | | |
| **E**mployee Engagement | Develop an individual daily plan and scorecard | $ | 👤👤 | ⊙⊙ | | |
| | Organized internal activities | $$$ | 👤👤 | ⊙⊙ | | |
| | Leaders touch base with every employee daily | $ | 👤👤 | ⊙ | | |
| **C**ontinuous Improvement | Develop and implement strategy deployment process | $$ | 👤👤👤 | ⊙⊙⊙ | | |
| | Implement A3 problem-solving tool | $$ | 👤👤👤 | ⊙⊙⊙ | | |
| | Conduct a rattlesnake hunt | $$ | 👤👤👤 | ⊙⊙ | | |
| **T**ransparent Communications | Quarterly all-employee update | $ | 👤👤 | ⊙ | | |
| | Monthly functional reviews in off months | $ | 👤👤 | ⊙ | | |
| | Weekly departmental check-ins | $ | 👤👤 | ⊙ | | |

Figure 18

After allowing the team a few minutes to look through the table, Jason explained, "This table includes the information each of you estimated for expenses, resources, and time to complete implementation of the tactics. I've also added a column for sequencing and launch time frame, which we'll fill in today. With the information we have, how would you like to approach prioritizing and sequencing these tactics today?"

Edward was first to speak up. "The foundation of our model is respect, so I would prioritize the tactics promoting respect for each other."

Everyone nodded in agreement.

Hannah chimed in, "Any tactic marked with one dollar sign, one resource, and one clock are no-brainers and should also be at the top of the list. They are low cost, low resources, and quick to do."

"Makes sense," Cooper added.

"I'll probably surprise you all with this comment," Abby said. "Let's not overlook the expensive, high-resource, long-term ideas just because they are that. They may have significant payback and/or be highly impactful. And the longer we delay starting them, the longer we wait for the benefits they'll generate."

"You're right," Jason said. "I'm surprised to hear you say it, and you make a good point."

Victor asked, "Shouldn't we start off with the back-to-back steps of reviewing the elements and tactics with the leaders and the subsequent development of their departmental plans? Once we have this overall plan completed, it's critical for each functional leader to develop and communicate the plans to their teams. While I'm at it, I'll also lobby for establishing our employee engagement baseline measurement before we start any activities. That means doing the Gallup Q12 as soon as possible."

"Good points, Victor," said Jason.

"Should we lay out a calendar so we can see the launch date for each tactic?" asked Mike. "Also, what happens if a team has implemented their first three tactics and we haven't implemented all twenty-one? Does that team have to wait until the initial twenty-one are all implemented before moving to the next one on their list?"

Jason responded, "Mike, I thought about that too. I agree with your first point and suggest we keep a master list of tactics, calendared with their planned start and end dates. We can update our progress monthly and consider additional tactics from teams who have completed implementation of a tactic. This master list would then be a rolling list of tactics to implement.

"You've all shared some great insights. Let's use those and begin working on this. We can start with the tactics we want to implement immediately, followed by ones we plan to implement sometime in the third quarter of this year, and go on from there. Since we're on a calendar year fiscally, Q3 will be July through September and so on. When we get to next year, let's simply designate those quarters with the quarter number followed by NY. So the first quarter of next year would be Q1-NY. Simple enough?"

There were positive nods all around.

"Great," said Jason. "OK, I know I sometimes resort to the ready-fire-aim approach, so how about we work together today to develop a well-thought-out rough draft of the sequencing. Then, let's appoint a project manager to put this all together into a formal plan using their project management software. They can follow up with everyone to fill in any additional details they'll need to tweak, finalize, and maintain the plan. Everyone good with that?"

Heads were nodding again around the table.

Jason continued, "First, I agree with Victor on establishing our employee engagement baseline and the communication of our plan. Both are paramount. I propose the following priority and launch timing:

1. Gallup Q12 survey completed twice yearly (initial survey immediately)
2. Review elements and tactics with the leaders (immediately).

3. Leaders develop departmental implementation plan, communicate, and post (immediately following review).

"Second, it's important we begin implementing our three-step communication plans. They will turn everyone's attention towards what we're trying to accomplish. Those would be as follows:

4. Quarterly all-employee update (immediately)
5. Monthly functional reviews in off months (immediately)
6. Weekly departmental check-ins (immediately)

"And next, I agree with Edward: we should prioritize any tactic related to respect, as it is the foundation of everything we'll be doing. I propose the following:

7. Develop the guideline for respect (immediately).
8. Recognition and celebration program (Q3)

"I propose it's safe to move forward with any of the tactics with one dollar, one resource, or a short time frame—thanks, Hannah. Those are as follows:

9. Develop guideline for setting up and operating teams (Q3).
10. Each employee clarifies teams/roles (Q3).
11. Company-organized outside activities (Q3)

"How's everyone so far with these priorities and timing?"

In unison came a resounding "I'm good" around the table.

"OK, we have ten tactics left to figure out their priority and timing. Recommendations?"

Hannah spoke. "I'd lobby for the individual plan and scorecard and leaders touching base daily to be included in the Q3 activities. They're straightforward and important to get going early in terms of developing engagement and showing respect."

"Agree, I will show them as the next two:

12. Develop an individual plan and scorecard (Q3).
13. Leaders touch base with employees daily (Q3).

"Sound good?"

Cooper then added, "I would also propose our team begins working on the strategy deployment process in Q3, with a goal of having it developed and in place for the new year. That will give us about six months to accomplish the task."

Jason nodded his agreement and looked to the group. Everyone likewise nodded.

"Adding that to the list:

14. Strategy deployment process (Q3)

"The third quarter appears full to me. Let's look at tactics to launch in Q4."

Hannah spoke up again. "I think Q4 is the perfect time to launch the team for organized internal activities with a goal of having next year's calendar set by this year-end."

"Makes sense, Hannah. Everyone else good with that?"

Abby interjected, "It needs to be early in Q4 to be included in next year's budget."

"We'll help make that happen," Hannah replied. "You mean even though we've identified it as one of our twenty-one tactics, there's a chance we won't be able to implement it?"

"Absolutely," Abby replied. "Anything we discuss here that involves additional expenses has to be in the approved operating budget for next year."

"Abby's correct," Jason said. "However, when we present the budget, we'll be sure to identify those and do our best to ensure they're included. That'll be part of the negotiation process. Just be sure you have the plan ready to be included in the overall budget plan we present."

"OK, got it," Hannah replied.

"We all good with this tactic in Q4?"

Jason got all thumbs-up and wrote:

15. Organized internal activities (Q4)

Mike and Edward raised their hands at the same time. Mike said, "Go ahead, Edward."

Edward said, "I would like to use the next couple of months to research the exercise facility with a goal of having a fully vetted proposal to this team by the end of Q3. If approved, we could begin work in Q4 and have it operational in Q1-NY. I think this will be a solid contributor towards establishing a culture of respect and showing employees we value them."

Abby, who had been writing all this down, looked up. "This is another one we'd need to get approval for within next year's budget—both for the capital and ongoing expenses. I'm in favor of giving it the priority and then seeing if it makes it through budget approval."

Jason agreed. "You got it, Edward."

He wrote:

16. Exercise facility (Q4)

Mike went next: "I propose we start interdepartmental meetings in Q4. This will likely go on through Q3 of next year."

"I don't see any harm in placing those there," said Jason. "The departments can set them up at their own pace. However, we do need to track their progress as there are bound to be those who procrastinate on this one."

Everyone agreed, so Jason wrote:

17. Interdepartmental meeting (Q4)

"That's about all we should try to do in Q4 as we'll have folks on holiday and vacation then. Let's move to next year," Jason said. "I'd like to target doing the Five Languages of Appreciation in the Workplace training in Q1 of next year. I'd also like to follow Edward's path and begin planning the launch of communications training and present a plan and budget to this group by the end of Q1-NY, with a goal of beginning training in Q3-NY. How do these work for everyone?" He pointed at what he'd added to the list:

18. The Five Languages of Appreciation in the Workplace training (Q1-NY)
19. Communications training plan and budget (Q1-NY), begin implementation (Q3-NY)

"Sounds reasonable," Cooper said. "And I'd like to place my rattlesnake hunt early in Q2-NY and the A3 training later in Q2-NY."

"OK, that completes all twenty-one tactics," Jason said as he wrote:

20. Rattlesnake hunt (Q2-NY)
21. A3 training (Q2-NY)

Jason continued, "I recommend we go with this for now. For our next step, let's add these to our shared calendar and look for any overlaps or resource bottlenecks, then identify concerns we have for expenses mounting up. I'll draw this up on my laptop now and then show it on the screen so we can review the plan. Go grab a quick drink or snack while I crank this out."

Jason's fingers raced across the keyboard, and a few minutes later he called the group back.

"All right, here's what it looks like [Figure 19].

| TACTICS | PRIORITY | IMMED | Q3 | Q4 | Q1-NY | Q2-NY |
|---|---|---|---|---|---|---|
| Track progress through Gallup Q12 survey twice/year | 1 | X | | | | |
| Review elements and tactics with leaders | 2 | X | | | | |
| Leader develop dept implementation plan and post | 3 | X | | | | |
| Quarterly all-employee update | 4 | X | | | | |
| Monthly functional reviews in off months | 5 | X | | | | |
| Weekly departmental check-ins | 6 | X | | | | |
| Guidelines for respect | 7 | X | | | | |
| Recognition and celebration program | 8 | | X | | | |
| Develop guidelines for setting up and operating teams | 9 | | X | | | |
| Each employee clarifies teams/roles | 10 | | X | | | |
| Company-organized outside activities | 11 | | X | | | |
| Develop an individual daily plan and scorecard | 12 | | X | | | |
| Leaders touch base with every employee daily | 13 | | X | | | |
| Develop and implement strategy deployment process | 14 | | X | | | |
| Organized internal activities | 15 | | | X | | |
| Exercise facility | 16 | | | X | | |
| Each dept conducts two interdepartmental meetings | 17 | | | X | | |
| The Five Languages of Appreciation in the Workplace | 18 | | | | X | |
| Companywide communications training | 19 | | | | X | |
| Conduct a rattlesnake hunt | 20 | | | | | X |
| Implement A3 problem-solving tool | 21 | | | | | X |

Figure 19

"And just so we have it available for reference, here's the original chart with the sequence and timing filled in [Figure 20]," he added.

| Element | Tactic | Expense | Resources | Time | Sequence | Launch |
|---|---|---|---|---|---|---|
| Respect | Guidelines for respect | $ | 👥👥 | ☺ | 7 | Immed |
| | Recognition and celebration program | $$ | 👥👥👥 | ☺☺ | 8 | Q3 |
| | Exercise facility | $$ | 👥👥 | ☺☺ | 16 | Q4 |
| Every Leader Buys In | Review elements and tactics with leaders | $ | 👥 | ☺ | 2 | Immed |
| | Leader develop dept implementation plan and post | $ | 👥 | ☺ | 3 | Immed |
| | Track progress through Gallup Q12 survey twice/year | $$ | 👥👥 | ☺ | 1 | Immed |
| Strong Relationships | The Five Languages of Appreciation in the Workplace | $$ | 👥👥 | ☺☺ | 18 | Q1-NY |
| | Company-organized outside activities | $ | 👥👥 | ☺ | 11 | Q3 |
| | Companywide communications training | $$$$ | 👥👥 | ☺☺ | 19 | Q1-NY |
| Purposeful Teams | Each employee clarifies teams/roles | $ | 👥 | ☺ | 10 | Q3 |
| | Develop guidelines for setting up and operating teams | $ | 👥 | ☺ | 9 | Q3 |
| | Each dept conducts two interdepartmental meetings | $$ | 👥 | ☺☺☺ | 17 | Q4 |
| Employee Engagement | Develop an individual daily plan and scorecard | $ | 👥👥 | ☺☺ | 12 | Q3 |
| | Organized internal activities | $$$ | 👥👥 | ☺☺ | 15 | Q4 |
| | Leaders touch base with every employee daily | $ | 👥👥 | ☺ | 13 | Q3 |
| Continuous Improvement | Develop and implement strategy deployment process | $$ | 👥👥👥 | ☺☺☺ | 14 | Q3 |
| | Implement A3 problem-solving tool | $$ | 👥👥👥 | ☺☺☺ | 21 | Q2-NY |
| | Conduct a rattlesnake hunt | $$ | 👥👥👥 | ☺☺ | 20 | Q2-NY |
| Transparent Communications | Quarterly all-employee update | $ | 👥👥 | ☺ | 4 | Immed |
| | Monthly functional reviews in off months | $ | 👥👥 | ☺ | 5 | Immed |
| | Weekly departmental check-ins | $ | 👥👥 | ☺ | 6 | Immed |

Figure 20

"OK, let's review them within their time groupings. The first group is the seven tactics in the 'immediate' time block. Do you have any concerns with overlap, resource constraints, or expenses?"

Victor responded, "I don't see any overlap issues. In terms of resource constraints, we've all developed our estimates per Abby's guidelines, but, like we talked about earlier, I don't think we have the skill set to figure out resource allocation on a companywide basis today. That's best left to the project manager, who does have the experience and tools to appropriately assess.

"However, from a leadership perspective, we're asking the leaders to participate in three of the first seven: the review meeting, developing their plan, and connecting with their direct reports. I don't think the ask is too much for them. I'd recommend for now that we continue eyeballing resources at the leadership level and then ask the project manager to dig deeper into our estimates and propose any scheduling tweaks from there."

Jason nodded his agreement.

Abby added, "In terms of the expenses, these seven are low. The only real cost is the Gallup Q12 survey, and I think it's merited given we need to establish a baseline measurement for employee engagement."

"Great, thanks, Abby," Jason said. "Is everyone in agreement to move forward on this first grouping then?"

With all in agreement, he moved on to the second grouping of seven tactics in the Q3 time frame.

Again, Victor spoke up first. "Like the first grouping, the leaders have a primary role in three of the seven. I'm concerned with overtaxing them between these first two groupings. I'll commit to developing and holding a training session for them on both the employee clarification of teams/roles and the development of individual employee plans and scorecards. Then I'll better understand how heavy a load this is. After the training sessions, if I think it's too much, I may come back to one or both teams and recommend moving out those tactics. Let's see how this shapes up, and we can respond once we explore a little deeper."

Again, Jason nodded in agreement.

Taking the lead again on financials, Abby said, "The recognition and celebration program and the company-organized outside activities are the two tactics with any associated out-of-pocket expenses. Even though these are unbudgeted expenses, we can absorb both without impacting the budget significantly. I think we're OK so far."

Jason looked to her. "We'll keep moving forward then, Abby. The next grouping contains three tactics in the Q4 time frame. Thoughts on these?"

Abby replied, "We're talking moderate expense on the exercise facility. With the state of our current financials, my recommendation is to put the launch team together and begin the planning. If it's green-lighted in the annual budgeting process, they can put it all together and open it in January. Our Q4 results will factor in there. Edward, are you good with that?"

"Yes," he replied. "It makes sense to get to a ready point and then see how it fares in the budgeting process. If for some reason it does not make it this pass, is the tactic dead for the year?"

Abby shook her head. "Not necessarily," she said. "If we get ahead on budget, we can take a second look at this during one of our quarterly updates."

"OK, I will advise the team, and we will calibrate our expectations accordingly."

"How about resource constraints on these three?" Jason asked.

"Once again, responsibility will go to the departmental leaders for one of these: holding two interdepartmental meetings. If we give them leeway on timing, they should be OK," Victor said.

"Yeah. I'm concerned with all we're asking of my production supervisors," Cooper added. "They have a lot of people to cover and a lot of these tactics to implement. Victor, I'd like to sit in on your meetings, and perhaps you and I can meet afterwards. I'd like to have input on whether or not to delay."

Victor nodded as Abby spoke up again.

"The only other expense concern is the organized internal activities," she said. "But the plan and its associated expenses will be part of the budget for next year—just like the exercise facility. If the budget is approved, then those expenses are also approved. If we must make cuts, they could be candidates. We'll cross that bridge when we get there."

Jason took all of this in before adding, "All right, it looks like we can move on to the second-to-last group, the Q1-NY time frame, which has the Five Languages of Appreciation training and the plan and budget for communications training."

He paused, looking at Abby. "I see a doubtful look on your face, Abby. What are you thinking?"

"My biggest concern is the communications training," she admitted. "We don't know what the training cost will be, and we're going to have the whole company off work for one week—assuming everyone signs up for it at some point. The good thing is the team estimated this to occur over a two-year time frame. We already have the Five Languages of Appreciation training in the first quarter, which will have its own out-of-pocket expenses and productivity losses to consider.

"Having given this more thought, I'd recommend delaying the communications training start at least one quarter. And we have A3 training and rattlesnake hunts right behind that. I'd back those both up a quarter too, at least for now. Jason, you said we would be reviewing this monthly, so we can adjust if we're doing better or slow down if we're behind schedule or budget, but I would push these out right now. Let's see how these first sets go. I know this is not what you want to hear, but my role is more than just scorekeeping. I'm the company lookout, and I'm looking out for us."

Cooper was quick to reply, "I get that, Abby, but I'd rather not push these out. It's a lot of work, and we need to get going on them as soon as we can."

Jason countered, "Abby, the Q1-NY start on communications training is just the planning and budgeting phase. According to this plan, we don't actually start the training until Q3-NY—although we could have some expenses prior for training the trainers, I suppose, so that cost could come into play. But I wouldn't want to delay the start. It's already about a year from now as it is."

Abby looked through her notes. "I missed the part about the actual training beginning in Q3-NY, Jason. Like Victor said, all of this can be overwhelming. I'll forego the soapbox speech then."

She continued, "So, from a spending perspective, we only have new expenses for the Five Languages of Appreciation in Q1-NY and then the rattlesnake hunts and A3 training in Q2-NY, with the expenses for communications training beginning in Q3-NY, unless you have some advance training costs for the instructors."

Abby concluded, "OK, I'm good for now. Let's get through the budgeting process, and we'll see how it looks within the overall operating plan."

"Fair enough," Jason said. "Cooper, have you caught your breath?"

"Yep, I'm good. You had me worried for a moment there, Abby. But like you said, we all have a lot rattling around up here," he said, tapping his head.

"From the leadership perspective," Victor commented, "I am concerned about the A3s and rattlesnake hunts being in the same quarter. I would recommend splitting those up. Could we consider moving up the beginning of A3 training to mid Q1-NY and holding off on the rattlesnake hunts until the latter part of Q2-NY? That would smooth out some of that load as both hit the entire company—meaning all those in leadership."

"That's a good point, Victor," Cooper said.

Jason thought for a moment before adding: "Likewise, we could hold off beginning communications training until later in Q3-NY to continue smoothing the load. Everybody good with this? Cooper,

Abby, Victor?"

"Yep, good to go," they said together.

Jason made the adjustments on his laptop and then said, "Here's the updated and final version for today [Figure 21].

| TACTICS | PRIORITY | IMMED | Q3 | Q4 | Q1-NY | Q2-NY |
|---|---|---|---|---|---|---|
| Track progress through Gallup Q12 survey twice/year | 1 | X | | | | |
| Review elements and tactics with leaders | 2 | X | | | | |
| Leader develop dept implementation plan and post | 3 | X | | | | |
| Quarterly all-employee update | 4 | X | | | | |
| Monthly functional reviews in off months | 5 | X | | | | |
| Weekly departmental check-ins | 6 | X | | | | |
| Guidelines for respect | 7 | X | | | | |
| Recognition and celebration program | 8 | | X | | | |
| Develop guidelines for setting up and operating teams | 9 | | X | | | |
| Each employee clarifies teams/roles | 10 | | X | | | |
| Company-organized outside activities | 11 | | X | | | |
| Develop an individual daily plan and scorecard | 12 | | X | | | |
| Leaders touch base with every employee daily | 13 | | X | | | |
| Develop and implement strategy deployment process | 14 | | | X | | |
| Organized internal activities | 15 | | | X | | |
| Exercise facility | 16 | | | X | | |
| Each dept conducts two interdepartmental meetings | 17 | | | | X | |
| The Five Languages of Appreciation in the Workplace | 18 | | | | X | |
| Companywide communications training | 19 | | | | X | |
| Implement A3 problem-solving tool | 20 | | | | | X |
| Conduct a rattlesnake hunt | 21 | | | | | X |

Figure 21

"OK, this is the plan we're starting with, pending review by the project manager. Once we share this with everyone, it's critical we do everything we can to meet these deadlines. Remember those three statements of 'Leadership is a test,' 'Leadership is a trust,' 'Leadership is a temporary assignment.' All eyes will be on us to see if we're going to walk the talk. At the same time, we have a new product release date we must hit, and I expect we'll have a proposal to upgrade our operating system.

"Folks, we're going to be tested as a company, as a team, and as individuals. We need the new product for our survival, and it is mission critical that we implement the culture and systems to successfully commercialize, sustain, and build out this new platform.

"We talked about being on the KCI burning platform together. Well, the fire is officially lit!"

# 15

## "THE ONLY PERSON WHO LIKES CHANGE IS A WET BABY"—PRICE PRITCHETT

Jason grabbed a soda and headed to his office, closing the door behind him so he could prep for his monthly check-in call with Adam.

Surthrival was off and running—or was it?

So far since the launch, he and the leadership team had participated in two monthly updates with the project manager appointed to track the project progress and manage resource allocations, and the company had already fallen behind schedule. To Jason, it seemed like the teams were struggling to launch the first set of tactics. Although everyone appeared to buy into the plan, they had—so far at least—not been able to establish a rhythm.

Jason kept going over the steps in his mind, wondering what he had missed. He was leading this transformation, and it wasn't starting out well. He needed to figure it out, quickly. Perhaps Adam would be able to steer him in the right direction.

His phone lit up as the call came in.

"Hi, Adam. I've been looking forward to our call."

"Hey, Jason. How's everything at KCI?"

"OK. Well, sort of mixed results right now. Listen, I know we have a few business updates to go over on this call, including the status of both the new product development project and our progress on selecting a new operating system. But I really want to bend your ear about our cultural transformation."

"These calls are your time to discuss anything you want. What's going on?"

"Thanks, I appreciate that. Hmm. Where to start?

"Well, it's been a little over two months since we formally launched the seven elements of the cultural transformation and the associated twenty-one tactics, and we're still struggling to get traction across the business.

"I'm confident we have a solid plan, and from my discussions with employees and feedback from the leadership team, everyone buys into where we're headed. However, there's a disconnect somewhere between the plan and execution. I'm leading this charge, but I feel like I'm missing something. I know you have experience in this area. I'm hoping you can share some insights or at least steer me in the right direction."

Adam listened carefully, paused, and then said, "Sure, happy to help. Actually, I think I have a very recent situation at home that may be applicable to what you're experiencing. I might have shared with you that about a year ago we got a new puppy."

"I do remember you saying something about that. A mini goldendoodle, if I recall."

"Yes, exactly. She's sure cute—and a lot of work! Don't get me wrong: it's been fun, but much more than we expected. Back to the story. She just turned a year old about two weeks ago, and it was time to switch her from puppy food to adult dog food. I did a little research on this and made some interesting finds. I found out dogs have a very strong digestive track. They can process raw meat and even bone—although we do have memories of her trying to eat our slippers; those probably would've been tougher for her to digest! But anyways, whenever you change their food, you must do it gradually. So, the change process begins with mixing a quarter of the new food with three-quarters of the old for a couple of days.

"Next you mix it half and half for a couple of days. Then you mix three-quarters new with one-quarter old for a couple of days.

Finally, you can fully change them over to all new food, as long as they're doing well. So, even though they have a strong constitution and can digest all kinds of food items, if you don't transition them slowly through the change and allow their bodies time to process it, they can have all kinds of bad reactions.

"Well, people aren't a whole lot different when it comes to change."

Jason took it all in.

"I think I see where you're going with this," he said. "We all agreed on where we're going, but we didn't necessarily consider how we'd make the transition or the obstacles we might encounter along the way."

"Exactly. Well put," said Adam. "There's a whole body of work surrounding change management, and I think it would be good for you to spend time researching it. I'll give you a couple of names to get you started, and then let's discuss your findings in a few days. The names are Harry Levinson and John Kotter. They'll get you going in the right direction, and you can spread out your research from there."

"Great. It sounds like an interesting challenge. OK, onto the other projects."

Jason spent nearly all his waking hours for three days researching change management. Excitedly, he punched in Adam's number for their follow-up call.

"Jason, tell me what you've discovered!"

"You were right, Adam. There's a lot of information out there on change management. Both guys you steered me towards had great insights on the subject. Then, I found a lot of good thinking that was either spawned by their publications or from others who researched change management. Through that information, I was able to put together some additional insights we can use."

"That's excellent, Jason. What resonated with you?"

"Well, I won't bore you with all the details of what you already know. But I'd say the first thing that struck me was the eye-opening statistic that 'over 70 percent of all organizational change initiatives fail.'[12] That's daunting and merits taking this step back to dig deeper into this topic. Thanks for your guidance."

"My pleasure. That's what I'm here for."

Jason continued, "One other thread that rang true throughout my research was understanding that resistance to change is a normal reaction for *all of us*, and it's not something to be ignored, avoided, or underestimated. In fact, if we don't address it, there's a good chance we'll end up in the 70 percent that fails. I'm summarizing my research and will share it with my team so we can develop our plan for change management. If we get good at it, it'll also pave the way for future changes we'll want to bring about beyond this cultural transformation."

Adam agreed: "Looks like you did your homework and are on the right track. I'm confident you and your team will find your way from here. You know, this is much like what you've said all along about the seven elements, in that they were the right ones for KCI today. Similarly, there are a lot of approaches to change management. I encourage you to figure out what approach or combination of approaches will work best for your team. Then, I believe you'll be able to establish the positive momentum you're looking for.

"One last hint: just remind your leadership team that leading change is less about their title and more about their role as coach and mentor. If they stay focused on that, it'll serve them well."

"Makes sense," said Jason. "I'll share that with them and keep it in mind myself. Thanks again, Adam."

"You got it. I look forward to hearing your plans. Keep me posted on your progress."

---

12   Higgs and Rowland, 2005, Pg 121–151

"Yep, will do."

A couple of days later, Jason pulled his senior leadership team together to go through his research on change management and to begin developing their plan.

"Good morning," he said. "Thanks for coming together on short notice. Today, I want to talk about the cultural transformation—Surthrival. We've been in two monthly update meetings, and according to the project manager, we've already fallen behind on the scheduled launch dates and a couple of the planned early completions. I had been struggling to figure out what's going on; however, I believe I have a better understanding now. I'd like to share that with you, but before I do, let me start by asking you all a question, and I want you to be open with your feedback. What's *your* read on the launch?"

Mike was the first to respond. "It feels like we're stuck in the mud, Jason. I meet with the purposeful teams team, and we're all excited, but there seems to be something going on when we talk about implementation within the organization. I can't describe it other than maybe a . . . hesitancy. Everyone nods yes when we talk about our plans, but it feels like they're not ready to move forward."

Hannah nodded, adding, "I agree. Everyone appears to be waiting for someone else to make the first move. We're all crowded around the pool, but no one's jumping in."

Victor surmised, "I think everyone was generally dissatisfied with how things were run in the past, but that's all they knew. I don't want to say they were comfortable with it, but they seem to be afraid of the unknown and are struggling to envision what the future will look like outside of status quo. Does that make sense?"

Jason took in their feedback and replied, "Yes, it does make sense. I think I can shed some light on this, and hopefully we can begin working our way towards the future vision we all share.

"I believe we have an excellent plan of what we want our culture to look like. What we're missing—and I take full responsibility for this—is a plan of how to go about the process of change. Would it surprise you to hear that more than 70 percent of all organizational change initiatives fail? It sure surprised me! Staggering, isn't it?"

"Staggering indeed," Cooper commented. "Why is that?"

"Great question," said Jason. "Based on guidance from Adam, I spent three days—literally—researching and learning about the topic of change management. I found a publication by a group of academics who dug into everything they could find on change management and boiled it down to the essentials. Their publication, *Using Teams to Facilitate Organizational Development*,[13] identified three primary reasons for the failure rate I quoted:

1. The first reason is we fail to understand the systemic nature of change. It's not change just at an individual department level or of a particular group; it's change across the entire organization.

    We touched on this systemic approach here at KCI when we discussed team participation and ownership versus a representative approach; it touches all parts of the company. When we look at change, we need to see the entire organization and provide organization-wide solutions and support.

2. The second reason is that change takes time, which organizations typically don't have.

    Generally, the more substantial the change, the longer the transition process. We're feeling the pressure to see progress here because we're facing a deadline; the clock is ticking towards our scheduled new product release, and we

---

[13] Boyle M, Goodwin K, Higgs M, 2021

know we must be ready. However, we can't stop the business to change. We have to fix the bus while we're driving it.

3. The third reason is that too often we see the case for change as logical or rational, based on a well-thought-out plan, like ours. We fail to realize change is an emotional event in that it challenges many of our deep-seated human fears.

Ignoring people's need to process change is disrespectful—something we clearly wouldn't want to be.

"There's also a great quote by renowned psychologist Harry Levinson, who focused on the topic of organizational change. He said, 'All change is loss, and all loss must be mourned.' We need to acknowledge what is being lost through the changes we're advocating and help employees balance their outlook with consideration of the possibilities ahead. Finally, we should be mindful that everyone won't progress through the adjustment period at the same speed. We must allow for that—within reason.

"I saw that, statistically speaking, about 25 percent of our employees will embrace most changes rather quickly, while 25 percent will resist with all their power.[14] Initially, we'll need to focus on the middle 50 percent who are neutral to change and help them come along as quickly as we can. We won't give up easily on those who do resist, but we can create a lot of momentum with the other 75 percent."

Abby spoke up: "Based on the 70 percent failure rate, it looks like we could be doomed if we don't tackle this head-on. I imagine addressing this situation is going to incur additional training expense at the least, but failure isn't an option, is it? So, how do we help our employees through this?"

Jason nodded. "Good segue, Abby. I want to share two pieces of information from my research which I believe will expose the gaps in our plans. However, when we examine these, it's also clear that there

---

14   Maxwell J, 2019

are many areas where we're well prepared for change, so we weren't completely off base. I'll show them one at a time through animation and ultimately side by side on the screen so we can see them at the same time [Figure 22]."

"The first one is from the book I just mentioned, *Using Teams to Facilitate Organizational Development*, in which the authors discuss an organization's capacity for change, or OCC, focusing on eight dimensions critical to success. The second one is from change management thought leader John Kotter. In his book *Leading Change*,[15] he introduced his eight-step change model.

| Organizational Capacity for Change (OCC) | John Kotter's Eight Step Change Model |
|---|---|
| *People:* | |
| 1. Trustworthy Leaders | 1. Create a sense of urgency |
| 2. Trustworthy Followers | 2. Build a guiding coalition |
| 3. Capable Champions | 3. Form a strategic vision and initiatives |
| 4. Involved Middle Management | 4. Enlist a voluntary army |
| *Structural:* | 5. Enable action by removing barriers |
| 5. Systems Thinking | 6. Generate short-term wins |
| 6. Communications Systems | 7. Sustain acceleration |
| 7. Accountable Culture | 8. Insitute change |
| 8. Innovative Culture | |

Figure 22

"I've color-coded where I believe we are on each dimension or step. On OCC, shown on the left column, I coded number 1,

---

15   Kotter J, 2012

trustworthy leaders, as yellow: a work in progress. We are working to establish that, but we aren't there until it is evidenced by number 2: trusting followers, which I have coded red. We also don't have capable champions or involved middle management—numbers 3 and 4—coaching and mentoring our employees, so those are also coded red. I do believe we have effective plans underway for numbers 5, 6, 7, and 8 within the structural group, which are coded green.

"On Kotter's eight-step change model, I believe we've established a strong sense of urgency—step number 1, which is coded green—and formed and communicated a strategic vision and initiatives: step 3, also coded green. However, we haven't done any work on building a guiding coalition or enlisting a volunteer army of folks who would be coaching and mentoring our employees through the change process and enabling action by removing barriers—step numbers 2, 4, and 5, which are all coded red. I coded the last three steps, number 6, 7, and 8, as gray, as they cannot begin until we establish forward progress in the first five steps.

"Team, I think we have a great plan for our future. But looking at it from both the OCC model and Kotter's eight-step change model, we've missed the important step of helping our employees process the information and get on board with all the proposed changes. Without those pieces, we stand a good chance of falling into the 70 percent who fail at implementing change."

Jason looked to Edward, who appeared ready to comment, and motioned for him to go ahead.

Edward spoke quickly. "I agree with you. We have not recognized all that is involved in the change process, nor have we developed or trained change agents who are equipped to help people through this transition. I am a great example of that exact need. I was stuck in my rut, and you may not know this, but early on, Victor came to me and offered to be a sounding board for my team's work on respect. That offer led to a series of discussions where he helped me see the benefits of where we were going and encouraged me to let go of the past.

"In the same way, the 50 percent of the employees you talked about focusing on are going to need our help getting through this process. We need to educate everyone on the change management process and be open about the hurdles we will each have to overcome. Then we will need to coach everyone through those changes. It will also be important to equip and train change leaders to be their guides throughout the transition period. This will demonstrate respect for our employees by showing them that we understand their need to process the changes we will be going through, and that we are right there with them—side by side."

Jason smiled. "Well said, Edward. I couldn't have put it better."

For several weeks, Jason and his team paired up and conducted small group listening sessions, being sure to include every employee. Jason himself paired up with Bryan O'Conner to even out the teams. Victor prepared an overview of the discussion for the teams, which also included talking points if they encountered employees who didn't buy in. After everyone had met with their groups at least once, Jason held a follow-up meeting with his staff and Bryan to discuss their progress.

He explained, "Bryan and I have had some interesting groups to work with so far. I thought it would be good to get together and share what we've each heard and make sure our responses are consistent. How has it been for each of you?"

Cooper responded first: "I think the most surprising thing to Mike and me is how candid everyone has been about their struggles with change. It's opened the door to sharing the dynamics of the change process and together developing ideas for next steps. As we discussed initially, we see how important it is for our teams to continue meeting with the same groups and ensure continuity of these discussions."

"Absolutely. Thanks, Cooper."

Victor shared, "I've been following up with each of the teams, and through their feedback, we've been able to identify leaders who we're coaching to become champions and mentors within their groups. That should accelerate the process and fill in the gaps between our follow-up discussions."

"Excellent," Jason replied.

Edward chimed in, "I want to compliment Abby and the transparent communications team for how they have shared our plans, our progress, and our successes through the visual boards and town hall meetings. I have heard feedback that employees are feeling more connected to us, to the company, and to each other through these communications. I think it is making a difference."

Abby replied, "Thanks, Edward. I appreciate your comments. What's important is that these meetings are helping employees make the transition and helping to develop trust in our leadership team. Taking the time to help folks process these changes is going to impact our organization for a long time.

"I think you said it before, Jason. The step-up in communications is only effective if employees trust us and believe the information we're sharing—and trust our motives for providing it. We started with respect, which is leading to trust, which establishes a solid foundation to build our future upon."

Jason nodded in agreement with Abby and asked, "Has any team encountered naysayers, either openly or passively?"

All the hands around the table raised.

Jason took note. "Hmm, yeah, so did we. How did you handle it, and how did it turn out?"

Hannah responded, "Thankfully, Victor's scenarios helped immensely. We did just like he instructed and shared that the new direction is the consensus of all the employees, and how it will benefit both the company and each employee.

"We emphasized that we're moving forward and offered to help them better understand the direction and the benefits, as well as the downside of remaining at status quo. We also offered to meet with them personally to discuss this further; however, no one has taken us up on that offer."

"How did it end up?" Jason asked.

"We agreed we'll continue monitoring their status with their supervisors and see how they progress," she replied. "We'll support their supervisor however we can. One positive benefit was that it gave us the opportunity to reinforce the positives to the rest of the group, which can only help."

Edward nodded and added, "Abby and I had pretty much the same scenario within our groups as well. It was not every group, but we saw it too. We also used Victor's recommendations, and some listened and opened up, and others just kept quiet."

"OK," said Jason. "We knew it wasn't going to be easy. Let's all follow these leads and monitor those within our groups and maintain contact with their supervisors. We want to do everything we can to help them work through this. We have opportunities to engage with them through the coaches and mentors who've been identified, as well as through the communications that Abby's team is providing. Once folks see the successes, they'll be more inclined to join in.

"By the way, Cooper, what ultimately happened with the production supervisor and assistant who said they didn't need the seven elements and wanted to continue just doing their own thing?"

Cooper explained, "We met with them the day after our meeting when it was brought up, and they were firm in their position and showed no inclination towards supporting the team. We had a similar discussion with them about the benefits and direction of the company and set up follow-up meetings. About three weeks later, they both resigned. It turned out the supervisor got hired by a start-up company about a mile from here and hired his assistant to join him.

"And when they left," Cooper continued, "I wasn't too concerned. Had they stayed, they likely would've been toxic and damaging to our culture. Leaving was best for them and the company. Not every organizational culture will work for every person, and those who are unhappy should be supported if they want to leave."

"I agree with that, Cooper," Jason said. "Are there any more in leadership roles who have not bought in or are teetering?"

Victor answered, "None as blatant as those two, but there are a couple who are probably teetering, as you said. We are working with them, and I'm optimistic they're coming on board. They see the benefit of where we're going. They're just struggling with giving up their autonomy. They've been on their own for so long, it's an adjustment. Other than that, we have good buy-in with our leadership team."

Bryan spoke up: "From my perspective, since we started these meetings, it feels like we're beginning to get traction with the elements and the twenty-one tactics—certainly with our three tactics in purposeful teams."

Jason was encouraged by the comment and asked, "Are all of you seeing the same thing?"

Edward responded, "Yes, I can see it within my team, and I am hearing the same from others."

Jason could see them all nodding.

"I think we may have dodged a bullet on this one," he said. "It would have been tough to take if we put in all that work on the elements and tactics just to lose it on change management. However, we've learned a valuable lesson and are learning a new tool that we can use in the future. That's what good teams do when they encounter an obstacle. Together, they find a way to succeed.

"But we're not out of the woods yet. So, keep focused, and let's continue meeting every two weeks to update each other on our progress. In fact, if something is working or not working in your teams, it's OK to send out a quick blurb and let everyone know. We don't have to wait for the update meeting. We should also remain open to any other countermeasures that could help.

"I believe we are at a tipping point in this journey. Let's help everyone work through these changes and continue supporting each other each step of the way. I'm really proud of our team and the way we're handling this.

"Let's keep learning together and keep getting better every day."

# 16

## TIME FLIES BY FAST: PART ONE

Jason was in his office prepping for the day's tour: KCI was to host a group of CEOs and senior executives from a national best-practice association. They had come to hear, to see, and to learn about the turnaround this team had achieved. Jason had planned to begin the day by giving an overview of their journey, followed by an open Q&A session. Afterwards, the group would go on a facility tour, ending back in the training room for lunch.

In the afternoon, there would be a panel discussion with a range of employees who had participated in the turnaround. The tour group would then board the bus for the ride back to their hotel and end the event with a dinner hosted by many of the employees involved in the day's proceedings.

Jason had enjoyed giving back to these groups, recalling how much he'd learned from the site visits he went on before joining KCI. This was the fourth tour of the year, and so far, based on the surveys, each one had been a great learning experience for the attendees. They'd been equally beneficial for Jason and the KCI team.

Jason welcomed the group and began, "Four years ago, I would've needed a vivid imagination to picture myself standing before you today. We were a broken company then, without much of a future. I'm not saying we're fixed now, but we're headed in the right direction.

I have the privilege of sharing our story, but it doesn't belong to me; it belongs to the entire KCI team.

"For years, our company was in survival mode, but we were ambitious and passionate about being a thriving company again. Based on a team member's suggestion, we named our transformation effort 'Surthrival.' We agreed to make Surthrival an unending journey—one we'd take together. We're happy to share what we've learned so far, but come back in a few years, and I know we'll have even more to share.

"This diagram depicts accurately where we started and where we're headed [Figure 23].

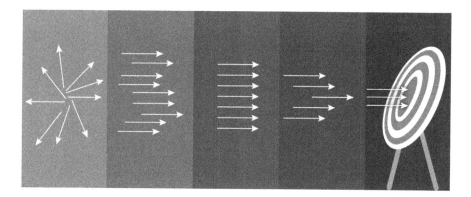

Figure 23

"I'll bet you can guess which box we started in. Like many other companies, there were well-meaning people here with good intentions, but there were disconnects everywhere, so, unfortunately, their combined efforts didn't move the needle. There was no strategic direction in place to align the work of the organization. The arrows in the far-left box represent independent and autonomous groups who just happened to work at the same company. Everyone was busy, but we were going nowhere fast.

"We began revitalizing our business by identifying four major components needing immediate attention:

1. The *people* within our business
2. The foundational *culture and leadership model* for our business
3. The *product portfolio* we offered our customers
4. The internal *operating systems* supporting our daily activities

"We began with people, and the first step was to put together a senior leadership team that could—and *would*—lead. The team we assembled was comprised of members of the existing leadership team, an internal promotion, and an outside hire. Soon after we made those moves, our R&D team pulled off a major product breakthrough, which then became our catalyst for change. This happened much sooner than expected, which was a good thing—or was it?

"We needed this breakthrough technology to be a relevant player in the market as our company and products had stagnated. However, as much as we needed this new technology, we were in no position to commercialize it successfully. The product development cycle was estimated at two years. That meant we had two years to transform our business approach, and ourselves, into a commercialization-ready team. Not that we needed more pressure, but the corporate eyes of Thompson Holdings were watching closely.

"Back to the four components. We agreed the grouping was sequenced and prioritized correctly: people, culture and leadership, product portfolio, and operating systems. The first of those four steps was people.

"Our newly formed leadership team embraced a quote by the late Robert Pritzker, who co-founded the Marmon Group in Chicago and said, 'People are not the greatest asset of your business; they are your business.'

"We intended to examine who was doing what and how well, but we quickly recognized our employees were held back, by us—by the lack of an intentional plan for both the company culture and our approach to leadership. I can almost guarantee that if those two are left to evolve on their own, you'll end up with forty different cultures and leadership models operating within your business—which was exactly where we were. However, we believed that if we developed the right model for us and applied it consistently throughout the organization, our employees would have the opportunity to reach their full potential. Then, we could determine more accurately if the right people were in the right seats.

"With that in mind, we moved to the second step, which was developing a plan for our culture and leadership model. After researching and benchmarking best practices, we came to realize an important insight. Each of our organizations—yours and ours—is comprised of a unique set of individuals, in a unique setting, with unique requirements. You probably noticed I used 'unique' three times there. That's because I want to encourage you to develop your own culture and leadership model—not one based on what you've learned from another company's culture or one taken from a past employer. The most effective solution is to develop a culture that best fits the needs of your *unique* organization.

"How do you find that out? Just ask your employees—all of them.

"Yes, there are a lot of commonalities within our organizations; however, there are also specific areas and needs on which your organization will have to focus to become the best it can be. The optimal way to find that out is not by assuming you know what's important, or by designating a small group of people to decide for everyone, but by involving the entire organization in some way. You will hear some surprising things, but, in the end, you will achieve a much higher level of employee buy-in to whatever you decide to establish. For us, listening was the first step towards showing respect for our employees and developing trust across our organization."

At this point, one of the attendees raised her hand and asked, "Can you share an example of a surprising thing you heard when you asked your employees what they desired in a culture?"

Jason thought quickly.

"Sure," he said. "Here's one. We had evolved into those forty different cultures I mentioned. In the feedback we received, one employee shared how he was reprimanded in front of his peers for helping another department solve a problem they were stuck on. He was told to 'let them figure that out for themselves.' So, there we were, actively working against ourselves and against our best interests. It probably won't surprise you to hear that purposeful teams is one of our seven cultural elements. I'll be sharing more about those later in the discussion."

"Thanks," she said. "I'm sure that wasn't something you were expecting to hear."

"Indeed," replied Jason. "But it's the kind of thing that can happen when you don't establish an intentional culture or leadership model. The void will be filled by something, and you don't control whether that something is good for the organization or not. Thanks for your question.

"Again, the starting point on our journey towards establishing a winning culture and turning from survival mode towards thriving was when we began to listen to our employees and then acted on their feedback.

"As I shared, this showed them respect, and we began to develop trust. We then synthesized their—or our—feedback into seven elements on which to focus. The seven spell out the acronym RESPECT, and in order are respect, every leader buys in, strong relationships, purposeful teams, employee engagement, continuous improvement, and transparent communications.

"While there are seven elements and they're all interrelated, one is truly the most critical—the hub of the wheel and the starting point: respect. Let me bring up a slide of a poster we developed [Figure 24]."

Figure 24

"The word 'respect' comes from the Greek word '*timēsate*,' which means to honor and value." Jason wrote the words on a flip chart with the words "to honor and value" below them. "We believe, as a team, that if we center our culture on honoring and valuing each other, we open the doors to achieving a higher level of success in the other six elements," he said.

"You might ask why we chose to center our culture on respect. Well, we all felt that respecting each other was the right thing to do, the most responsible action we could take, and ultimately the most profitable approach for our business. There's more, and I could keep going, but I am sure you get the gist of our passion for this topic. Respect is essential, the core of everything we do here.

"It also holds true for us that, as leaders, we're entrusted with the awesome and important responsibility for our employees' lives while they're under our duty of care. We've charged each of our leaders to become the person they'd want to work for—one who'd motivate them to become the best version of themselves. Work is such a significant and important part of every person's life; it should be fulfilling every day. And fulfillment is another way we can honor and value our employees."

Jason then presented the seven elements, the steps the team had gone through to develop and establish them, and the initial twenty-one tactics that were identified and implemented.

He shared, "We also wanted to be sure that within each element, we blended the business- and people-centric viewpoints into our solutions."

A hand went up immediately.

"Yes," Jason said. "Question?"

"I'd like to understand the statement you just shared, in context," he said. "Can you give us an example of being both business- and people-centric?"

"Absolutely," Jason replied. "We can use employee engagement as an example. We recognized that there were at least two perspectives on employee engagement, the business and the people perspective, and our goal was to create a win-win solution. Generally, the business-centric viewpoint on employee engagement is that a higher level of engagement will result in improved productivity.

"If we only considered the business-centric viewpoint, we'd likely employ tactics targeting productivity improvement masquerading as attempts at improving employee engagement. The employees would see through this veil and be discouraged, feeling like the company just wanted them to do more work for the same pay.

"On the other hand, we felt the benefit to being an engaged employee—the people-centric viewpoint—was ending each workday with this sense of fulfillment, which I referred to a moment ago.

"We examined how these goals interacted and decided it'd be optimal if we focused our tactics towards helping employees achieve daily fulfillment. In turn, that would create more engagement, which, ultimately, would result in higher productivity numbers. So, through the implementation of our employee engagement ideas and tactics, employees can achieve a sense of fulfillment in their jobs, and the company realizes increased productivity—a blend or optimization of the business- and people-centric viewpoints.

"OK, I see how you got there," said the visiting executive. "How has it worked out?"

Jason smiled. "We measure both engagement and productivity, and both have risen in tandem year over year for the last four years. It's truly been a win-win for our company.

"But I would like to expound further on this concept of blending business- and people-centric mindsets. I believe that the key is not how they're different but how they relate to each other.

"I've seen in the past where companies are so focused on the business results that they forget how they're obtained, which is through people. What we advocate here is that we go after high-level business results through our employees—beginning with respect.

"As in the example I just shared, respect leads to trust, and trust leads to engaged employees. Statistics have shown that business results are highly impacted by employee engagement. Gallup, who is internationally respected for their expertise in this area, published statistics comparing companies who are in the upper quartile of Gallup's employee engagement surveys to those companies in the lower quartile. The upper-quartile companies had the following statistics:

- 81% less absenteeism
- 28% less shrinkage or theft
- 18% higher productivity
- 64% less safety incidents
- 41% less quality defects
- 10% higher in customer loyalty or engagement

- 18–43% less employee turnover, depending on the type of organization
- And, importantly, 23% higher profitability

"So, if you are interested in achieving outstanding business results, focus on people, and we advocate that you do that by starting with respect. You can have both: engaged and fulfilled employees and business results. They are not mutually exclusive; rather, engaged people lead to better business results—much better than if you only focused on the business aspect. My advice is to keep people central to all your business equations."

Jason added, "In one of our work sessions, Hannah Parker, a team member who will be facilitating our afternoon Q&A, suggested a goal statement for our work in Surthrival—one that we all agreed accurately encompasses our work and has become our central focus. Our goal, which you can now see on the screen, is 'to develop a connected culture based on respect that is engaging and fulfilling, creates alignment and accountability, and maximizes the potential of every employee and the company.'"

Jason, thinking it was a good time to open it up for Q&A, summarized for the group, "In the end—and I can't stress this enough and will repeat it again—if you start with respect, and you listen and act upon what you hear, I'm confident you'll find the right path for your organization."

He paused for a moment as he remembered one final addition. "There is much more to this, but for us, I'll share a very powerful second key, and that's alignment. Whether you lead a group of ten employees, three hundred, or one thousand or more, remember there's power in aligning the arrows!

"At this time, I'd like to open it up to any questions you have relative to what I've presented. And remember, after your facility tour and luncheon, we'll have a panel of employees from all departments up here so you can ask more detailed questions about our journey."

Jason saw many hands go up and called on one.

"What were some of the biggest obstacles this team had to overcome?"

"Yes, good question," Jason said. "There were a lot of obstacles, and I'll name a few.

"Let's see. One of the most difficult obstacles was to earn the trust of the employees. They'd been through a lot and were weary of anyone wearing a management hat. It took time, and it took each leader walking the talk. Earlier I spoke of having forty different cultures within our walls. Well, there were some leaders who wanted to keep doing it their way and didn't embrace the element of every leader buys in. That slowed our efforts to earn our employees' trust. We persevered until we were confident there was 100 percent leadership buy-in.

"I'll share a quick story about earning the trust of our employees. At our first all-employee meeting when we rolled out the seven elements, I noticed a machine shop operator sitting in a very defensive position about halfway back. He was clearly not buying what we were selling, if you know what I mean. At lunch that day, I sat down at the same table with him and his team and talked with them. He made it clear that he hadn't trusted my predecessors and didn't trust me either. We talked more about trust, and in the end, I pledged to meet with him and his team every week to evaluate and discuss our progress as a company.

"We did that for one full year. We had many candid conversations, and this group really kept me on my toes. But once we got everyone in leadership walking the talk, the team said that while they appreciated my time, they were on board with where we were going, and I probably had more serious issues to be working on with my time. It was a great experience for all of us, and I'll never forget it.

"Before I leave this obstacle, there's another aspect I want to share with you. Part of getting all of our leadership on board was teaching them how to be leaders. We realized that, like many companies, we promoted folks into leadership roles and assumed they knew how to lead. For many, it was their first time. For others, perhaps it was an increase in their leadership responsibilities. Our HR team developed a leadership curriculum that helps new and/or growing leaders assimilate into their new roles. In fact, we continue to expand the curriculum based on the changes we continue to see in business—like the increase in remote working employees. This additional training has been a significant contributor towards building an effective and consistent leadership team here at KCI.

"So, moving on. Another major obstacle for us was something we overlooked initially: the change management process. We thought we had an excellent plan of where we were going, a plan that was logical and sound. Intellectually, we all bought into it. However, we failed to recognize that change is an emotionally charged event, and one that had to be addressed if we were genuinely committed to our value of *respect* for our associates.

"It is said that 70 percent of all change initiatives fail in organizations, and change management can be a determining factor as to which side of that statistic your organization will fall on. Applying the 'educating both sides of the equation' approach, we shared this information with our employees through small group listening sessions. From there we were able to identify and train leaders throughout the organization—both the formal and informal leaders—on how to coach and mentor their colleagues through the change process. Additionally, we communicated with our employees, probably to a fault, each step of the way through this change process.

"I will say again, much like the seven elements, there are many ways to approach this, so be sure to do your homework and develop a plan that fits your organization. But whatever you do, don't overlook or underestimate the importance of this step.

"The consulting firm McKinsey & Company took a look at this by studying the change programs at forty companies. These companies recognized the importance of change management to their success and invested in developing their competency level. Still, 58 percent of the companies they studied failed to meet their targets; 20 percent capturing only a third or less of the value expected. The remaining 42 percent gained the expected returns or exceeded them—in some instances by as much as 200 to 300 percent. Not surprisingly, it was the companies with the stronger change management programs who netted the large returns.[16] Remember, this area is critical to achieving a successful transformation and meeting your company goals."

Jason paused and took a sip of water while he thought.

"OK, let's see," he continued. "More obstacles to share.

"Another challenge we faced was trusting the financial picture to turn around. It tested our patience and the patience of Thompson Holdings, as well as our very belief in what we were doing. In the earliest days of our transformation, we incurred up-front expenses which hit before any of the improvement activities began paying dividends. We expected and forecasted for this and, thankfully, it was short lived. As improvements began taking hold, the savings evened up against the costs. That led to seeing the productivity improvements outweighing the expenses. So, ultimately, our financial picture turned around, and we're doing well now; the trends are all in the right direction. You can ask Abby, our CFO, more about it in the afternoon panel discussion.

"We also had a major hiccup on the new product development path when a key raw material became scarce. We had to reengineer the product quickly and complete the full battery of product tests a second time. We accomplished this while still hitting the original product release date, proving what a powerful force teamwork can be.

"The final obstacle I'll share was engaging the remote workforce. Our remote and hybrid employees were used to being left out, and we had to make intentional efforts to include them in what we were doing to build a new culture. It wasn't insurmountable; it just took effort and creativity. Does that give you a feel for the obstacles we encountered?"

---

16   LaClair J, Rao R, 2002

The attendee nodded. "Yes, it does. Thank you for being so candid. It's helpful to have an idea of what to expect."

Jason called on the next person.

"Following up on your comment about leaders who wanted to keep doing it their way, were there any leaders—or for that matter, any employees—who didn't get on board?"

Again, Jason allowed himself another sip of water to gather his thoughts.

"That's fair," he said. "The simple answer is yes. We worked with every leader and did our best to help them see the benefits of the cultural transformation—both to them and their teams. For employees, we outlined the benefits to their lives, their careers, and to the company. But sometimes there just isn't a fit. It was rare, but a few people left on their own, and a couple who would probably be classified in Gallup's actively disengaged category just couldn't make the transition. After many efforts, we did part ways with those few.

"Fortunately, most of the employees embraced where we were going, and as we got into a rhythm, we found they began jealously protecting our newly developed culture, doing everything they could to sustain the changes. Then, it wasn't so much the case of leadership trying to make these changes. It was the employees demanding that leadership walk the talk, holding us accountable for our actions and then holding each other accountable to the same standards. I think that's a good sign you've changed the culture."

Jason called on the next person.

"Once you established the seven elements and the initial twenty-one tactics, how close were you to keeping to the timing for your implementation plan?"

"Great question." Jason smiled, this time ready to answer quickly. "First off, up front, we had our most experienced project manager assigned to the implementation plan and specifically managing the resource allocations. I wish I could say we kept perfectly to plan, but like most plans, it became obsolete the moment we published it. We worked our way through the obstacles one by one, but our monthly progress review meetings tended to focus more on what tactic got which resource.

"I believe this is where most organizations get tangled up when trying to accomplish this much change in a relatively short time frame. We were around one or two quarters later than planned, and we only got that close because of significant pivoting and a healthy amount of scrambling. My recommendation is to invest fully in the resource-planning part before you launch an effort like this.

"Thanks for the question. Yes, in the back corner there."

"How did your corporate group respond to your plans?"

Jason hesitated for a moment.

"Well, initially it ranged from skeptical to supportive," he chuckled. "I can share we have a real champion and supporter in the medical group president at Thompson Holdings. Without his support and advocacy, I'm not sure we would've had the space to get this done. It's *never* a straight path to success, and you need support and belief along the way.

"I'll share one interesting sidelight. After our team came up with the product breakthrough, we considered how Thompson Holdings might respond. One of the responses we considered was the possibility of them moving our new idea to a sister division who had demonstrated success in commercializing new products. That didn't happen, of course, but I can share with you that now *we* are the company to which they're moving products; in fact, two will begin transferring to us next quarter. We never imagined that happening!"

The next question came in.

"You talked about accountability a few moments ago. What does it look like here?"

"First and foremost, it's our line-of-sight plan. It keeps the arrows aligned throughout the organization," said Jason before describing the process briefly from end to end.

"To tie our line-of-sight plans together, we have quarterly report-outs for everyone in leadership roles. Those report-outs are a time to shine but also a time where we hold each other accountable for doing what we said we'd do. I'd also say the actions developed by our transparent communications team play a large role in accountability. We share all the pertinent company information quarterly in an all-employee meeting format. Those meetings present another opportunity for us to be accountable as an organization. We also have monthly, weekly, and daily follow-ups at the functional, departmental, and individual levels. These aren't opportunities to beat up on each other but rather a time to identify who needs help—and to make use of an opportunity to support and prop up one another."

Another hand raised, and Jason called on her.

"We couldn't help but notice several awards in the lobby. Has that been a focus for your team?" she asked.

"While it's gratifying to earn the recognition, it's not about winning awards per se," Jason explained. "It's about using the opportunities for outside experts to come in and evaluate how we do things. Sometimes you can't see the forest for the trees, so we enjoy getting constructive feedback on how we can get better. We believe the award process has accelerated our growth and rate of improvement. We've been strategic in which awards we apply for by examining different aspects of our business and graduating in intensity and scope."

"Thanks, Jason."

"You're welcome. Yes, next question."

"How involved were you personally in the transformation process?"

Jason beamed. "Great question. Listen, a transformation of this magnitude must be led from the top. The leadership team has to be committed and fully involved. Personally, I love doing this, so it was easy for me. An example I can give is I too am doing my *2 Second Lean* improvements in my office every morning to start my day. It's amazing what you can improve if you are looking for it. The employees see my improvement videos—like the ones you were shown on the tour—and know we're in this together. I'll say that whether you're attempting to transform an entire company, a department, or a small team, it will take the senior leader's involvement and commitment to effectively change the culture. I appreciate your question. Thanks. Next question."

"One of the seven elements you shared was strong relationships. Can you give examples of what you've done to build and sustain relationships between employees here at KCI?"

Jason answered, "That's an important aspect of our success here, and there's been a lot of work in this area. Some of what we've done are one-time exercises, and other activities have become part of what we do every day.

"Let me see. I can give you two examples of what we have done—one a specific exercise to develop relationships and the second an ongoing exercise we do to build on and sustain those relationships."

"That would be great," replied the executive.

Jason began, "The first one is called the lifeline exercise. Essentially, it's an opportunity to reflect on your life and identify the stories that shaped who you are today. The first to do this exercise was the senior leadership team. I'll explain it briefly.

"We began with a large blank sheet of paper and drew a horizontal line across it from one end to the other. We then used three different-colored sticky notes and filled one out for each significant event in our lives. One color was for significant events that were positive, one color for significant events that were negative, and one for events that were neither positive nor negative.

"We began at our earliest memory point in our lives on the left side of the sheet and worked our way to the right over time. Positive events are stuck above the line, negative events below, and non-events stay on the line. The next step was to group them by significant time periods in our lives, and some just used decades. After we completed them individually, we had a report-out and explained our lifelines to the other team members in attendance.

"It was quite eye opening. Some people shared very candidly, and some weren't comfortable saying too much, but we got to know a lot about each other, and that drew us closer as a team. We also understood each other better and could be more supportive and respectful as a result. This exercise was so effective that all the departments began doing them, and now all our employees have gone through the lifeline exercise with their respective teams.

"The second exercise is ongoing, simple, and yet very powerful. We start each of our team meetings with the question 'What's new in your life?' Folks were hesitant to share much when we first adopted this, but now they share openly. Again, by understanding what's going on in someone's life, we are given opportunities to celebrate together or in some cases to support each other through difficult times.

"Both exercises have contributed to improving relationships throughout the company."

"That sounds very powerful. Thanks for sharing that."

"You're welcome," Jason replied.

He asked for one more question as time was getting short.

An attendee asked, "Which one of those boxes in your arrows diagram would you place your company in today?"

"Ha, that's a tough one," said Jason, again taking the opportunity to have a sip of water while he gathered his thoughts. "We're always harder on ourselves than outsiders are. But I'd place us in the middle box. We have good alignment now, but there's still a lot of work ahead in tightening up how we move as one team on a daily basis.

"Thanks for the questions this morning. I hope I was able to provide you with a good sense of where we started and how we approached the work of transforming our culture and leadership model. As I shared earlier, you can ask more detailed questions of the panel in the afternoon session. Right now, we're going to break you up into groups for the facility tour."

He advised them, "As you go throughout our facility, please talk to as many people as you can. No one's off limits. They all look forward to these tours. If there's anything you would like to take a deeper look at, just ask your tour guide or the tour-stop host."

The group took off for their facility tour and returned a couple of hours later for lunch. After eating, Jason prepared to introduce the panel for the afternoon session.

# 17

## TIME FLIES BY FAST: PART TWO

After the tour and lunch with the attendees, Jason opened the afternoon session: "I hope you enjoyed your tour of our company and got to spend some quality time with our employees. During the Q&A this afternoon, we'd like to hear from you: please tell us what you observed on the tour and share your key takeaways.

"We've assembled a panel of folks who participated in the transformation and who are anxious to answer your questions. Let me introduce them to you now. In the center is Hannah Parker, VP of sales and marketing and your moderator for this discussion. Please direct your questions to her unless you have a question for a specific member of the panel.

"Starting at the left end is Abby Mills, our CFO. Next to Abby is Nelson Chow, director of continuous improvement. When we began our journey, Nelson was production manager, but he found that he had a real passion for process improvement and is now leading the charge there. Next to Nelson is Edward Eggleton, VP of RA/QA. To Edward's right is Bryan O'Connor. Four years ago, Bryan was Nelson's counterpart in operations as supply chain manager. With the early retirement of Cooper Collins six months ago, Bryan was promoted to VP operations. To Bryan's right is Latecia Johnson, distribution manager. Next to Latecia is Victor Delacruz, VP of HR. On the far right is Jimmy Marino, who works with Hannah in marketing as a product specialist. Back at the beginning, Jimmy was new to our company and working for Latecia as a distribution associate. That's your panel for this afternoon.

"We did plan for Mike Montgomery, our VP of product development, to sit on the panel, but he was called into a cadaver lab to evaluate a new product at the last minute with a couple of surgeons. With that, I'm handing it over to Hannah."

"Good afternoon, everyone. As Jason mentioned, I'm Hannah Parker, and I'm happy to be hosting the panel discussion for you. How's your day been so far?"

There were lots of positive comments and nods across the attendees.

Hannah smiled and continued, "I am sure you have a lot you'd like to cover, so let's get going with the first question."

She called on a gentleman in the back, who asked, "I'd like to ask Jimmy a question, especially since he's the only nonmanagement person on the panel. What was your role in this, and what sticks out in your mind that you saw or learned during the transformation?"

Jimmy replied, "As far as my role, I had the opportunity to be on Hannah's employee engagement team. When Jason first shared the team's goal statement of 'Engaged throughout the day and fulfilled when we end it,' it really resonated with me. So I asked Latecia, my leader at the time, if I could participate on the team. She spoke to Hannah, and the rest is history.

"As far as what sticks out for me, it's the change in attitude throughout our company. Before, it was pretty gloomy around here, and you rarely got a greeting when you passed someone in the hallway. Around the time our shifts ended, it'd get really quiet throughout the company. Many people were skipping out a few minutes early—or, at least, as early as they could get away with.

"In one of our employee engagement team meetings, someone brought up a crazy indicator we started monitoring, which was how many cars had backed into their parking spaces. They had read somewhere how it was an indicator of employees anxious to leave work as quickly as they could. It's amazing, but you almost never see it anymore. I'm not sure if it's tied to our cultural changes, but it's definitely decreased substantially."

"I've never heard that one. Thanks, Jimmy! Hey, can I ask you another question?"

"Sure," Jimmy said.

"You're an example of someone who's worked in multiple departments during this transformation. When you went from one department to the other, was it a difficult transition?"

Jimmy responded, "My transfer happened about nine months ago, after I completed my business degree. By then, we were more than three years into the cultural transformation, all the systems were synced up, and communications and policies had been standardized. As far as how the two departments operated, it was seamless. I had a lot to learn about marketing, but, again, the way the departments were run was very similar. That was the easy part of the transition for me.

"Also, a big positive for me is that in this role, I can participate in a flexible work schedule—working in the office two days a week and from home the other three days. Overall, I'm a pretty fortunate guy. I get to work for a company that cares about its employees while making products that help people improve their quality of life.

"Sorry for the tangents. Does that answer your question, sir?"

"It does, and thanks again, Jimmy," said the attendee with a broad smile.

Hannah said, "Next question. Yes ma'am, over here to the side."

"I have a question for Nelson," she said. "Can you tell us more about the implementation of continuous improvement? What was your approach? Were there any bumps along the way?"

"Sure, I'm happy to," Nelson said while adjusting his glasses. "Right from the outset, we made a conscious decision to develop our culture first and then begin introducing the tools of CI. We believed if we could establish trust in the organization, resistance to change would be significantly reduced. And by building on a foundation of respect, trust, transparency, and the elements Jason shared earlier, not only would the tools be embraced, but they'd be ingrained deeper into our mindsets, and the improvements made would be more sustainable over the long term.

"To determine when the cultural change took hold, we established a baseline measurement by completing Gallup's Q12 survey on employee engagement prior to launching the seven elements. Then we set a target improvement level as a trigger, a level we could validate through our six-month follow-up Q12 surveys.

"For our team, hitting the trigger point signaled we could begin launching the process improvement tools. However, we felt in the meantime it would be beneficial to start with a couple of business management tools—to initiate the process of thinking in a continuous improvement mindset.

"The first of those tools was our strategy deployment process, which addressed alignment and accountability. Jason shared those details with you earlier. You asked about bumps. One we encountered with this process was that we tended to procrastinate getting those quarterly tasks completed, so it was typically a mad dash at quarter end before the report-outs. No one wanted to face their peers and say they didn't meet their commitments. Of course, then everyone was competing for the same resources to complete their commitments.

"However, one group began using a rolling one-month plan to mitigate the quarter-end syndrome—at least bringing the fire-drill effect back to the end of each month instead of each quarter. They've had success there, and more are trying that approach, but procrastination remains a hurdle for us. However, overall, this process has achieved what we hoped for: alignment and accountability throughout our organization.

"The second business management tool was a standardized problem-solving approach—the A3 methodology. This tool gave us a common language throughout the company when we encountered a problem. It also got us all thinking about our problems in terms of root cause elimination."

A hand went up immediately and the attendee said, "Excuse me, I have a question about this. You mentioned 'standardized.' Do you mean every employee is expected to use A3s for problem-solving? And if so, how did you get them all on board, and how many are using this tool today?"

Nelson nodded. "Yes, to your first question: all employees were involved. We took a unique approach to this. From a training perspective, our goal was for every employee to be both competent and confident in using A3s. However, let me share an important insight we learned about training in general that we applied to this. Like many other companies, we learned this the hard way. Hopefully we can spare you that experience.

"The first step in our training, which is missed by many teams, including us at first, is training your leaders on how to use the tool and, importantly, how to coach their employees to the desired level of proficiency.

"The second step is the employee training, which has two parts to it. The first part is what we call book learning: teaching the employee how the tool works. The second part we call practical training, and this is where their supervisor comes in. We provide time for each employee to demonstrate their ability to use the tool in actual work situations, guided and coached by their supervisor. They don't graduate from this step until their supervisor is satisfied that they're both competent and confident. We also recommend a fourth step of having either peer groups, accountability partners, or huddle groups to support the behavioral changes they're working to establish.

"We used this approach to provide A3 training to every employee in the company, including our direct sales force. In some areas, they immediately grasped what we were trying to achieve and got on board. Some groups were slower and needed some prods, but we all got there. We followed up continuously and required all supervisors to report their area's A3 progress in the line-of-sight quarterly report-outs. That kept peer pressure on all of us. Now, anecdotally, in meetings we routinely hear someone asking, 'What's the problem we're trying to solve?' We're focused as a company on this 'root cause elimination' way of thinking, and combined with the line-of-sight tool, these two provided an excellent start to our continuous improvement journey.

"I hope that answers your questions on A3s."

"Yes, that was even more helpful than I expected. Thanks!"

"You're welcome," said Nelson. "Continuing on about our journey—at about the two-year mark, we hit the trigger point on our employee engagement surveys and began launching process improvement tools. We now have a fifteen-minute period at the start of each shift for all employees to complete an improvement, following the insights from a book we all read called *2 Second Lean*. We've also implemented continuous improvement tools such as 6S processes, one-piece flow, and a pull system with electronic Kanbans, which we showed you on the stops during your facility tour. There is much more going on, but to share everything would be a meeting in itself.

"One bump in the road—or in this case, a step we took to avoid a bump. We recognized the need to establish a cross-functional team of advisors whose job it is to determine the pace for introducing new tools. They essentially review the status of each tool or countermeasure that's been launched and advise when we're positioned to sustain the gains and take on the next one. We have a graduation ceremony to celebrate our accomplishment and to launch the next tool officially. Pacing the organization has kept us from going too fast or too slow—or losing what we've established."

Nelson summarized, "We believe we've developed a culture of respect and trust throughout, the arrows are aligned, and now we're going as fast as we can. I hope that answers your question over here about continuous improvement."

"Yes, thank you," she said.

Hannah gestured to the next person for a question.

"I have a question for Abby. I realize you may not be able to share specific details, but how has this transformation impacted the company financials? Any surprises? Are there key insights you can pass along?"

Abby replied, "I'm happy to share what I can. First, we made a pivotal decision early on to bring our corporate group into the mix. We started with the group president of medical device companies, who's been a strong advocate for us, and then, together with him, we met with key executives at Thompson Holdings to share our plans. At the time, our financials weren't great; we were profitable, but we weren't meeting Thompson Holdings' expectations. We believed the work on which we were embarking was the right thing to do for the long-term health of the company, but in the short term, our financials would likely take a hit.

"They agreed to support us if we kept them well informed on our progress. So, we stepped up our corporate reporting frequency and included more details than previously. We also developed plans to improve the three areas they'd expressed concerns with: inventory levels, product margins, and overhead rates. Through our line-of-sight planning, we targeted those and saw steady improvement across the board.

"I guess I can share a little more of the details on those. Specifically, we analyzed our inventory and immediately saw the imbalances and began working those off. We also implemented a pull system and electronic Kanbans, as Nelson explained. In fact, our new product line was completely set up with a 'one-piece flow' approach from the start. As part of that system, suppliers make deliveries to the production line weekly and even daily on some parts.

"So now, between the two years of active continuous improvement activities and the early start on inventory reduction through attacking the imbalances, inventory turns have increased from a little under one turn per year to over four turns and improving. This freed up a lot of cash for investment.

"Also, through employee engagement and daily improvement,

we've realized significant increases in productivity. This has allowed us to grow the business and take on new lines without much in the way of employee additions. In turn, the productivity improvements and leveraging of our overhead has resulted in steady margin improvement across all product lines. It was also a bonus that our product development project team hit the timeline for the new product release and, early on in that process, the R&D team discovered what would become the proprietary technology of the second-generation product. Importantly, since that initial product release, sales and profitability have both been enjoying double-digit growth year over year.

"As Thompson Holdings saw us meeting our commitments, the executive leaders gave us more latitude to invest in our culture and leadership development efforts.

"Going forward, we have every reason to expect we'll continue reaping the benefits of those investments. Our employee engagement results have improved with each survey we've taken every six months. As we believed, respect led to trust, which led to engagement and fulfillment, which in turn led to improvements in every important business metric we track—including productivity, which I already shared, as well as quality, safety, and attendance. I hope this gives you a feel for how the work in this area has impacted the financial picture over the last four years.

"As far as surprises or insights, I think the whole teamwork idea Jason sold us on—that with teamwork, two plus two could equal five—was both of those: surprising and insightful. I can't put a number to it, but you feel it all around here; work happens faster and better than before. Yes, it was a commitment to make the investments we made, including allocating time each day for improvement, but it's paid off tremendously for our organization."

"OK, thanks, Abby. Next question," Hannah said.

"What does employee engagement look like here? Is there an example you can share with us?"

Victor raised his hand and said, "Hannah, if you don't mind, I'd like to answer this question. Hannah's the team leader for employee engagement, but I think I can summarize it well, and I have a recent example that I'd like to share."

"Absolutely, Victor. Go right ahead," Hannah replied.

"As with many of the elements, we looked for solutions that were both business- and people-centric, addressing both sides of the equation. Abby shared the sequence of events we were targeting, but it started first with a realization that if we put people first, the business would reap the benefits. You've heard our goal statement: 'Engaged throughout the day and fulfilled when we end it.' We believed if we showed our employees we cared about them, they would care about each other and about how the company does. And that's exactly what we've seen: improving engagement numbers and improving business metrics.

"The example I'd like to share with you depicts how much they care about each other. We had an employee who had a major illness and was going to be off work for three months. This person was the family breadwinner, so three months off work would've hit them hard financially. I had twelve people come to my office and donate their vacation days to cover the time off this employee needed for surgery and recovery. We had more than the three months donated, so our employee didn't have to worry about paying their bills and taking care of their family. We had to make some adjustments in payroll to account for any differences in pay level, but it really impressed me how much we care as an organization."

"That's awesome. Thanks for sharing that with us."

"Next question. Yes, in the back?"

"What percentage of your workforce is remote? Did they take part in the cultural transformation? And are they engaged with the changes, and how can you tell? Sorry, I guess that's a lot of questions."

Hannah replied, "I'll take these questions, and no worries—happy to answer them all.

"We've settled right at 20 percent of our employees working

remotely. About 5 percent of those are our field sales team, so they've always been remote. As far as the cultural transformation, absolutely; they were a part of it all. Right from the beginning, we made a conscious effort to include them in everything we did. When we first asked the employees what they desired in a company culture, we polled the remote employees, captured their input, and developed a separate affinity diagram to illustrate their feedback.

"When we took the first Q12 survey to establish our employee engagement baseline, we included the remote employees in the overall results and their departmental tallies, but also as an independent group. We continue to monitor them on all three counts.

"When we began working in teams on the seven elements, we had at least one remote working employee on each team. And for each tactic suggested, we asked the team to examine it from the perspective of our remote working employees and figure out how to make it inclusive.

"The results show that employee engagement for remote working employees has tracked right along with the other groups, steadily improving on the surveys we've taken every six months."

"Thanks, Hannah. That's encouraging to hear."

"My pleasure. Next question. Yes?"

"From Jason's presentation and from what I observed on the tour, it looks like respect is at the center of the transformation. Can someone from the panel elaborate on that?"

Hannah looked to Edward. "I think this one goes to you."

Edward replied, "You hit the nail on the head. Respect is the hub of the wheel everything turns on here; it is the glue that keeps it together. I can see that Jason already discussed the origin of the word 'respect' and its definition: 'to honor or value.' That is exactly what we want to do here—honor and value each other. Jason said early on that our goal was to create a culture that was a blend of business- and people-centric. And I loved the definition he shared with us for the word 'blend,' which was 'to combine into an integrated whole.'

"So, when we say respect is the center of our business model, it drives all the relationships here. That includes honoring and valuing each other, our supplier partners, our stakeholders—every relationship related to our business. Our desire in all of this is to achieve commitment, to each other and to KCI, and to combine all our talent into an integrated whole. When that happens, well, you can imagine the rate of improvement and growth we are able to achieve. Can you tell I am a little passionate about this topic?"

"Great answer. Thanks, Edward."

Hannah solicited the next question from a gentleman up front.

He said, "Did anyone on the panel resist getting into what many would call the relational side of business? Perhaps it wasn't your cup of tea, or you didn't feel comfortable?"

Latecia took this one.

"I resisted initially," she admitted. "I'm the distribution manager here, and we push out a lot of orders each day. We don't have time to be all chummy, and we absolutely cannot afford to lose focus and make any mistakes. There are doctors and patients depending on us every day."

"What changed for you?" he asked.

"I'm getting to that," she replied.

"It wasn't like I saw a bright light in the sky or anything," she said. "The first step was Jimmy, right over here. I saw him get all excited about being on Hannah's employee engagement team. At the time, he hadn't been with our company long, but he'd already become one of the most productive workers in distribution. It seemed like each week he participated on her team, he got even better—and it was somehow contagious within our group. It really opened my eyes. I thought to myself, *Latecia, there just might be something to this, and you best get yourself going.*"

She glanced over and saw Jimmy grinning.

"It all made sense," Latecia continued. "There's nothing radical about the seven elements—just treating people the way you'd want to be treated. I asked Jimmy to share what was happening in employee engagement each week in our distribution team meetings, and that was fun. It really brought our team together. Productivity and accuracy improved. Everyone began helping each other, they were polite, and they were on time every day. I run a tight ship, but this was more fun, and we had better results. Hard to go against that. So, yeah, I jumped on board, and I'm glad I did."

Latecia decided to share a little more. "I do know there were other leaders who didn't necessarily get on board right away. Some of those leaders liked doing things their own way and had gotten to do that for many years. But I have to say that Victor and his team did a great job of explaining what we were doing and why it was so important to the company and to our employees. They gave us very practical examples to which we could all relate."

The man interjected, "Sorry to interrupt, Latecia, but could you maybe share one of those examples?"

"Sure," she responded. "I remember one that hit home with me. Victor asked us how our household would run if each parent in the home had a completely different set of rules for the family to live by. I have four children, and I know that would be chaos. He said that it was the same thing here at work.

"It took a while for all the leaders to get on board; however, everyone was given time and support all the way through the transition. Now that we are on the other side of that and have 100 percent buy-in, it's made a huge difference in how we operate daily, and the trust of the employees has grown dramatically."

"Thanks, Latecia. I'm already coming up with loads of ideas for our organization just from listening to you!"

"Another question?" Hannah asked.

"Was there a pivotal moment that helped you establish the team environment that's so apparent here?"

Bryan took the floor this time. "Hi again. I'm Bryan and am a member of the purposeful teams team. There's a lot that's impacted working in teams. The first step was senior leadership learning that they were indeed a team and not an assembled group of representatives for their respective areas. Until the walls were torn down in the executive conference room, figuratively speaking, the barriers between the departments throughout the building would never be removed. However, they learned how to function as a senior leadership team, and from there, it spread throughout the organization. That was crucial. I applaud what they did and am proud to now be a member of that team.

"But I also think one of the tactics we developed really tipped the scales towards employees operating in teams across our organization. We asked every department to conduct two department-to-department meetings. One with a department that's a supplier to them—that could be materials, or subassemblies, or information; and then one with a department to which they're the supplier. We received more feedback on what was learned in those meetings than anything else we did.

"First off, each department realized the other departments aren't their enemies; they're teammates. And once they got a glimpse of what others were trying to accomplish and the obstacles they faced, they had more compassion and understanding for them. There were some real 'aha' moments when colleagues began to understand how they could help each other and make their own jobs much easier. And these meetings opened new lines of communication, which are now in place for the future obstacles they'll encounter. It was a huge win-win for everyone. Many departments didn't stop at the original ask of two meetings; they set up additional meetings with other customer and supplier departments. I hope I answered your question."

"You did, and thank you for those insights, Bryan."

Hannah addressed the group: "We have about twenty minutes remaining, and I need to save five of those for Jason to give the final wrap-up. We'd like to hear from you. What are some of your key takeaways, and what did you learn? Also, if you have suggestions for improvement, we'd all enjoy receiving your feedback.

"Yes, right here in the front."

A man in the front began speaking. "A comment rather than a question. Thank you for allowing us to participate in this today. It's refreshing to see your approach towards culture and leadership. From what I saw and learned, it's clear you've achieved a blend of business- and people-centric ideologies, and it makes sense for both the company and employees."

"Thanks. We agree," Hannah replied. "Yes, right over here on the side."

"What I saw and felt today was a pervasive feeling of joy, team, support, and care. I'm not sure I would want to go home if I worked here every day! Is there any way I can bottle some of this up and take it back to my business?"

"Wow, thank you for those kind words," laughed Hannah. "That could be our next new product! Yes, right here in the middle."

"Well, if this was a public company, I would buy stock in it. I would also like to see if I can bring some of my teams through here. But I do have an improvement suggestion."

The panel leaned forward as Hannah replied, "Yes, by all means. We'd love to hear it."

"I've seen where companies add blue lights to the front and back of their forklifts; it helps everyone see them coming sooner. It's an excellent and inexpensive safety measure."

Bryan responded, "Yes, we heard that from the previous group who visited and have the lights on order. They're scheduled to be installed this weekend. Thanks for sharing that."

Hannah said, "Another question or comment? Over here."

"I have to say I was wowed by the on-site exercise facility. Is there someone I could hook up with after this meeting to get more information? I would like to better understand how you went about it, and how you were able to financially justify the investment."

"Edward or Victor, do one of you want to help this gentleman out?" asked Hannah.

Edward replied, "I will be happy to, and I am sure Victor will join in too. My team was responsible for planning it out, and now Victor's HR group manages it. So, between the two of us, we can provide you with the details. I will share that we started out much smaller than what you saw today. The employee demand kept growing, so we kept adding more equipment and different types of exercise programs. The equipment is now available Monday through Friday, we have three aerobic classes each week, a weight-loss program, volunteer exercise coaches, and some of our outside activities include various kinds of exercise groups. Just contact either Victor or myself, and we will be glad to help you in any way we can."

"Thanks. That would be wonderful."

"We have time for one more question or comment. Yes sir."

"When did you feel like you were on top of this and everything was moving in the right direction?"

Hannah looked around, and Victor raised his hand to take this last question.

"The first big feeling of movement was when we addressed the change management process," he said. "We began to literally see employees helping other employees let go of the past and embrace our future. Then employees began driving the cultural changes and became protective over what we established. That's when we felt like the culture was transforming right before our eyes."

"Fair enough. Thanks for your answer."

Hannah moved to wrap it up. "Well, we enjoyed your visit today, and on behalf of the panel, thank you," she said. "Our contact information is on the screen now, and we'll send you all a follow-up email with our details. If we can be of any help to you in the future, please don't hesitate to reach out. With that, I am handing it back to Jason."

Jason addressed the group once more. "Thanks for allowing us to share our journey with you. When we tell our story, especially the highlight version, it sounds straightforward and easy. Our recipe for success started by showing respect for each other and developing trust throughout our organization, which resulted in employee engagement and fulfillment, and the product of those two are outstanding business results. That's the straightforward part.

"But the process was and is anything but straightforward and easy; to get to where we are today, we came up with a lot of ideas, developed action plans, and implemented them. It's challenging each and every day, but it has been worth all the hard work. Engaged and committed employees produce better results, and it makes for a much richer and more fulfilling experience for them—a win-win for all.

He paused to reflect once more before adding a final thought, "Together we've produced the results we targeted but also enjoy an environment of the 'joy, team, support, and care' this gentleman over here said he felt today. It doesn't get any better than that.

"We aren't accepting status quo. We're striving to improve every day. Surthrival is not a destination; it's an unending journey we're taking together."

# EPILOGUE

I hope you enjoyed the journey of Jason and his team. Are you in a leadership role, or do you aspire to be? If so, I encourage you to thoughtfully consider the path you choose to take.

We've explored many concepts within this story, and I recommend that, like Jason, you research these topics in more depth and develop an intentional plan for how you'll lead and the culture you'd like to establish. That plan should be developed jointly with your team.

Keep in mind that you're their role model, and you have responsibility for the lives entrusted to you, whether that's one or one thousand, and you don't know for how long—perhaps just a short while or long term.

I encourage you to be the leader you've always wanted to work for.

In the book, we also learned how blending both business- and people-centric approaches maximizes the results and benefits to all stakeholders. Strive to include people in all your business equations. You can make a difference for good in their lives, their families' lives, and the communities in which you operate—while achieving outstanding business results.

After all, people *are* the company.

And finally, respect for and between people is at the heart of all of this. It can be the cornerstone of your culture and the glue that holds it all together. Start there, and you can't go wrong.

All the best to you—wherever you are in your journey.

## ACKNOWLEDGMENTS

I would like to thank all those who mentored me along in my career and the leaders who taught me what to do—and what not to do—in a leadership role.

Thanks to my friends and colleagues who participated as readers of this manuscript and whose feedback helped make this a much better book than I imagined.

I also want to thank my dear friend Kim Rutherford for all the countless readings and feedback he provided.

Finally, thanks to my wife, Suzette, for always being my first-pass reader and for her support throughout the process.

# REFLECTIONS

## CHAPTER 1:

1. What do you think are the essential foundational systems or building blocks of a company? How would you assess each of those systems within your organization?
2. Do you think it's wise to blend different mindsets into the makeup of a team or, in this case, the senior leadership staff; or should you focus on hiring the most qualified person for each role?
3. Jason signals that he thinks building the foundation of the company is a higher priority than short-term financial results. What do you think his priority should be at the start of his tenure?

## CHAPTER 2:

1. Jason defines culture as "the connector between our beliefs and behaviors that determines how we interact with each other and with people outside the organization." How would you define your organizational culture?
2. How would you describe the current state of your team, department, or organization?
3. Do employees generally like working at your company? Would they encourage their friends or family to come to work there? Do you have a method to measure that?
4. Has there been an investment in an intentional plan for the company culture or leadership model in your organization?
5. Do you think it is wise of Jason to discuss the three possible options he thinks Thompsons Holdings has, relative to the new product opportunity, with the whole team?

6. Jason instructs the team to "focus on what we can control, like determining how we'll operate as a team and as a company." As an operating company of a holding group, what does KCI likely have control over, and what do they likely not have control over? Describe the landscape they are probably dealing with.

## CHAPTER 3:

1. How does someone like Jimmy find their way in your organization? Is guidance available to help someone develop their career path? How might you help those whom you supervise find the right path for their career?
2. What do you think of Jimmy's vision for a company culture? Is it realistic? What might it look like in practice?
3. How would you describe the state of the operating systems at your organization? Could the systems support a potential growth spurt of the organization?
4. Is there an "over the wall" mentality at your organization? How do departments interact with each other? Are they cooperative and supportive of each other's needs?
5. When things go wrong at your organization, how does management respond?

## CHAPTER 4:

1. How could you use the concept of "the perspective chair" in your organization?
2. How did you relate to the staff's list of what is important in a company culture? Did any element(s) resonate with you? Describe why.
3. Where would you place your organization today within the boxes in figure 3—described as the arrows diagram—and why? What would have to happen to move your organization to the right?

4. How would you characterize your organization's approach to leadership: business-centric, people-centric, a mix of those two, or no real plan in place?
5. Did it surprise you to learn that companies that embrace the relational side of business have generally outperformed those that didn't? What would you attribute this to?
6. How would you define respect in the workplace? What role should it play in a company culture and why?
7. How important is it to show respect in all directions in the workplace?
8. How does training take place in your organization? Does it include "both sides of the equation," as Jason describes it?
9. How important is the supervisor–direct report relationship? Describe the best supervisor you've had and your least favorite supervisor. How did their actions impact your life?
10. Can you identify with Edward's reluctance to share within a group of employees with whom he is not familiar? How would you react in that situation?
11. What do you think of Edward's statement about not getting too close personally with any of his direct reports? Discuss the pros and cons of that approach.
12. Do you think Jason handles Edward's concerns appropriately? Discuss.

## CHAPTER 5:

1. How important is full leadership buy-in to a company's success? What happens when a leader or leaders do not buy-in? How consistent is the buy-in at your company?
2. How can you achieve buy-in effectively? Is it an ultimatum, as Victor cautioned against, or are there certain methods you can employ? Discuss your view.
3. Describe the best and worst performing teams you've been on or associated with. What are the key characteristics

that contributed to each type? Compare and contrast those characteristics.
4. Which circle position, facing in or facing out, best describes teamwork at your organization?
5. How do teams operate at your organization? Do team members participate only as representatives, or are they fully engaged and accountable owners of the team deliverables and results? Discuss Jason's take on teamwork.
6. Do you think the employee engagement percentages at your organization are higher or lower than the Gallup averages? Why?
7. Do you agree with Jason's notion of trading engagement for fulfillment? Share why.

## CHAPTER 6:

1. Does your organization embrace continuous improvement? Is there commitment all the way to the top? Is it deployed organization-wide, or is it an operations-only initiative? What is the overall continuous improvement strategy?
2. What are the potential benefits to any organization that invests in continuous improvement? Are they any downsides?
3. What is the relationship between culture and continuous improvement? How has your organization approached it?
4. How do you address the trade-offs between up-front investment and the ROI for continuous improvement?
5. How does your organization control the pace of deploying continuous improvement tools and countermeasures?
6. What are the benefits of adding the caveats of "competent" and "confident" to equipping your employees with the tools of continuous improvement?
7. How important do you think transparency is within an organization, and how does your organization approach sharing information at all levels?

8. How would the seven elements resonate with your organization? Are there any you would delete or others you would add? Describe why for each.

## CHAPTER 7:

1. How would you describe the role of a leader? Discuss how leadership is a test, a trust, and a temporary assignment.
2. Do you agree with the company's decision to use in-person interviews with the employees versus a survey to capture their thoughts on the company culture? Discuss your view on each method.
3. Is Jason too overbearing with the senior leadership team or providing the right amount of leadership? Discuss.
4. Do any of the themes emanating from the rest of leadership and the employees surprise you? Why?
5. Do any of Victor's highlights resonate with what's happening at your company?
6. Is your company actively addressing the engagement of remote working employees? How so?
7. Is the process KCI uses to develop its seven elements appropriate for this size of company? Would you add or subtract to its approach?

## CHAPTER 8:

1. Do you agree with Jason's statement "We can have great products and great systems, but without great people in a winning culture, we'll never realize our full potential"? Why or why not?
2. Jason asks his leadership team to spread out during the luncheon and sit at tables where no managers are present. Does your leadership team take the opportunity to mix with employees at functions like this?

## CHAPTER 9:

1. Have you experienced what Jason describes as "two steps forward and one step backward"? What does he mean by this, and can it be overcome?
2. Jason describes his sales projection numbers as "a little science and a lot of hope." Is that true in your experience?

## CHAPTER 10:

1. Do you think Hannah gives sound career advice to Jimmy? Discuss.
2. Edward uses the word "enforce" regarding respect. What is your initial reaction when reading that? How would you respond to Edward?

## CHAPTER 11:

1. Take a moment to review Hannah's suggested goal statement for Surthrival. How does this resonate with you? Discuss.
2. Do you agree with Edward's statement that respect is the hub of the wheel and at the core of each one of the elements? Why or why not?
3. Does your organization have a recognition and celebration program? Do you agree with Cooper's concern about the involvement of money? How would you respond?
4. Jason begins his team's report-out with the role relationships have in the workplace. How does your company develop relationships within departments and cross-functionally?
5. How important are the three areas of appreciation, outside activities, and communications to building good relationships within the workplace?
6. Do you agree with the team's recommendation to offer the communications training as optional to employees? What would you recommend and why?

## CHAPTER 12:

1. In your opinion, how critical is Victor's first step of communicating the rationale of the seven elements to leaders in achieving the goal of "Every leader buys in"?
2. How do you identify leaders who haven't bought into your organizational culture? What percentage do you think are bought in? What steps does your company take to help engage them?
3. How would you respond to the supervisor and his assistant who claim they don't need the seven elements?
4. According to Patrick Lencioni, teamwork is "both so powerful and so rare." Do you agree? If so, how is it so powerful, and why is it so rare?
5. Are your teams clear on their charter and the individual deliverables? If yes, how do you accomplish that? If no, how could you improve that situation?
6. Do you have team operating guidelines in place? Discuss.
7. How have you gone about breaking down the walls between departments? Discuss.
8. How important is it for Victor to challenge Jason, even in this small way?
9. The Gallup statistics (performance results) relating to employee engagement are impressive. Take a look at each one and comment on why employee engagement would make such a difference.
10. Looking at Jimmy's tactic, how do you show (versus tell) your subordinates that their work contributes to attainment of the company goals?
11. How often do leaders connect with their direct reports at your organization? How is this achieved?

## CHAPTER 13:

1. Does your organization have a strategy deployment process in place? Does it align and engage the entire organization? Describe the process.
2. How do you solve problems at your company? Is there a structured approach? What are the pros and cons of focusing on a singular problem-solving tool?
3. Cooper says the rattlesnake hunts will help everyone see their work through a different lens. What do you think he means by that? Discuss.
4. Do you agree that transparent communications could increase employee engagement, create a stronger culture, help employees feel valued, encourage creativity, create trust between leadership and employees, improve morale, lower job-related stress, increase happiness, and boost performance? How does transparent communication impact each one of those?
5. What type of communications plan does your organization have? Does it touch every employee in the organization? How could it be improved?
6. Mike says it is important to have the element teams attend the report-outs. How pivotal do you think that is and why?

## CHAPTER 14:

1. How would your organization respond to the challenge of taking on these three major initiatives simultaneously? Any advice for Jason and team?
2. How would you approach sequencing the twenty-one tactics? Contrast your approach to the way this team chooses to establish the priorities.

## CHAPTER 15:

1. How does your organization handle change management? Is there a formal or organized approach? How could it be improved?
2. Were you aware that 70 percent of all organizational change initiatives fail? Is that surprising to you? Why or why not?
3. What do you think Adam means by his advice to the leadership team that leading change is less about their title and more about their roles as coach and mentor?
4. Have you experienced reluctance or resistance to change? How did you address it?
5. Discuss Harry Levinson's quote "All change is loss, and all loss must be mourned." Why is change loss, and how should it be mourned?
6. Jason shows statistics that say 25 percent of employees will embrace most changes rather quickly, and 25 percent will resist with all their power. He decides to focus on the middle 50 percent who are undecided. What would your strategy be for the 25 percent who will resist change?

## CHAPTER 16:

1. Jason comments on both the commonalities and the uniqueness of organizations. Make a list of the commonalities and the unique qualities/needs of your organization.
2. How would you describe the level of trust between employees and management at your organization? How about between departments and between employees in general?
3. When someone at your organization is promoted into a leadership position or increased leadership role, is training provided to help them develop their leadership plan and style? How would you go about it?
4. Jason brings up the issue of resource allocations. Does your organization have a good method for balancing resources

against the needs of the organization?
5. Are senior leaders and the CEO of your company personally involved and committed to developing a vibrant culture at your company?

## CHAPTER 17:

1. Nelson brings up a point about training and the importance of supervisors being able to coach their employees to the desired level of proficiency on whatever the employees are learning. Why is that so important, and how do you approach this at your company?
2. What role do employees play in sustaining the culture at your company?

# APPENDIX

## SEVEN ELEMENTS:

1. **R**espect
2. **E**very leader buys in
3. **S**trong relationships
4. **P**urposeful teams
5. **E**mployee engagement
6. **C**ontinuous improvement
7. **T**ransparent communications

## FIGURES:

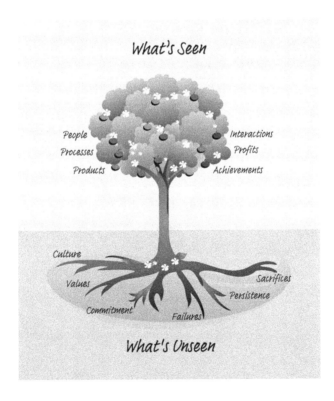

Figures 1 and 2 (Rootfulness as a foundation for fruitfulness)

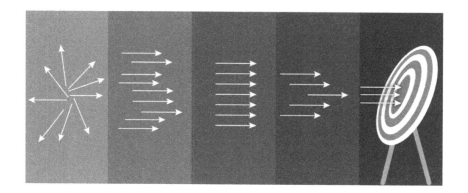

Figures 3 and 23 (Aligning the arrows)

## RETURN ON INVESTMENT

| Cumulative Performance | 15 Years | 10 Years | 5 Years |
|---|---|---|---|
| US FoE | 1681% | 410% | 151% |
| International FoE | 1180% | 512% | 154% |
| Good to Great Companies | 263% | 176% | 158% |
| S&P 500 | 118% | 107% | 61% |

Figure 4 (Return on Investment for Firms of Endearment)

Figure 5 (Gallup's survey results for employee engagement)

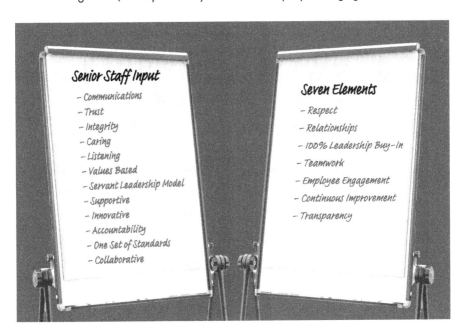

Figure 6 (Initial seven elements compared to senior leadership team input)

# CULTURAL ELEMENTS COMPARISON

| Seven Elements | Senior Staff Input | Employee Feedback Summary |
|---|---|---|
| Respect | Trust | |
| Relationships | Listening | |
| 100% Leadership Buy-In | One Set of Standards, Values Based, Integrity | Consistency |
| Teamwork | Collaborative | Teamwork |
| Employee Engagement | Caring, Supportive | Care |
| Transparency | Communication, Integrity, Accountability | Communication |
| | Servant Leadership Model | |

Figure 7 (Cultural Elements Comparison by input source)

| Seven Elements | Senior Staff Input | Employee Feedback Summary | FINAL SET OF ELEMENTS |
|---|---|---|---|
| Respect | Trust | | **Repect** |
| Relationships | Listening | | **Relationships** |
| 100% Leadership Buy-In | One Set of Standards, Values Based, Integrity | Consistency | **100% Leadership Buy-In** |
| Teamwork | Collaborative | Teamwork | **Teamwork** |
| Employee Engagement | Caring, Supportive | Care | **Employee Engagement** |
| Transparency | Communication, Integrity, Accountability | Communication | **Transparent Communications** |
| | Servant Leadership Model | | |

Figure 8 (Cultural Elements Comparison to final elements)

| Element | Leader |
|---|---|
| **R**espect | Edward Eggleton |
| **E**very Leader Buys In | Victor Delacruz |
| **S**trong Relationships | Jason Bailey |
| **P**urposeful Teams | Mike Montgomery |
| **E**mployee Engagement | Hannah Parker |
| **C**ontinuous Improvement | Cooper Collins |
| **T**ransparent Communications | Abby Mills |

Figures 9, 10, and 11 (Assigned leaders to seven elements)

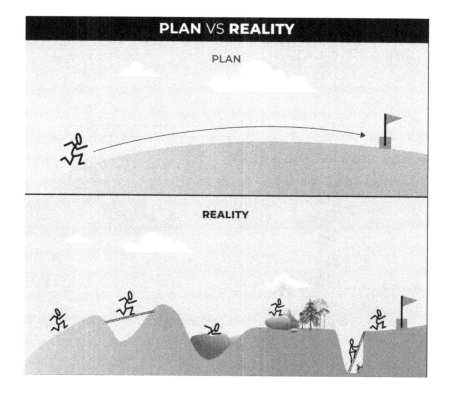

Figure 12 (Plan vs. Reality)

Figure 13 (Surthrival banner)

1. **Say something.** If you see disrespectful or unsafe behavior that undermines the work environment, speak up. Everyone deserves to be treated respectfully.
2. **Smile.** Empathize and be considerate of others. Make it a routine to smile and greet everyone as you arrive at work—it's a sign of courtesy and kindness.
3. **Say "thank you."** It may seem like common sense, but many people forget to say thank you or don't say it with sincerity. Show gratitude often by making sure people know you appreciate them and their actions. Give encouragement to show you value your team's contributions.
4. **Be considerate and discreet.** Be mindful of your surroundings. If you work in an open workspace and need to make a phone call, make sure to control your own volume and respect your neighbors.
5. **Apologize.** If you make a mistake, take responsibility and have a corrective action plan. Saying "I'm sorry" (without excuses) is courageous and proves your commitment to your colleagues and to your job.

6. **Participate constructively.** Make sure your contributions in meetings are on topic and respectful. Avoid interrupting others, and give others your full attention.
7. **Respond in a timely manner.** Answer emails and phone calls promptly—this shows people you value their time. Ensure that information is communicated and shared openly as appropriate. Sharing information signals trust and confidence.
8. **Go the extra mile.** Sometimes your team needs additional help to get the job done. Offer to pitch in and share the load. If a co-worker has helped you in the past, then returning the favor is a good way to show both your respect and gratitude.
9. **Be reliable.** Follow through on your commitments and responsibilities. Keep your word. Make task lists or reminders if needed and avoid distractions that make it easy to lose sight of deadlines. You'll earn your co-workers' respect when they know they can count on you.
10. **Feedback is a gift.** Praise much more often than you criticize. Share your expertise respectfully and be open to growth and learning. A collaborative workplace where everyone shares their ideas and offers creative solutions is one that thrives.

Figure 14 (Guidelines for respect from UTMB)

## CHECKLIST FOR TEAM START-UP

**How to use this tool:**

The following checklist contains questions that should be answered early in the start-up phase of a project team. Ideally, the project sponsors will discuss these matters with the team leader or team members <u>prior</u> to the actual team formation. That information, along with any relevant unanswered questions, should be part of the team's kick-off activities and discussions.

### A. Driving Issues
11. Why is this team being formed?
12. What are the critical issues the team should address?
13. What is the team's scope? (Has the scope been set by or approved by the team's sponsors?)

### B. Goals
1. What are the specific project (or process improvement) goals?
2. What constitutes success?
3. How can we make these goals measurable? If they are not quantifiable, how can we look for qualitative data about improvement?
4. How do these goals support the overall mission of our department, the project, the company?

### C. Roles and Responsibilities
1. Why has each member of this team been selected? What skills/expertise does each team member bring?
2. What is the role of the team leader?
3. What is the role of the facilitator?
4. What is the role of our sponsor?

### D. Deliverables/Timeline
1. What is the output/product for this team?
2. What is our timeline overall?
3. Are there mid-point milestones or approval processes?
4. What is the deadline for deliverables?

### E. Commitment
1. How much time are we expected to spend on this effort?
2. Do all team members need to be available for each meeting?

Figure 15 (Guideline for setting up a team, from MIT)

## OUR ATTITUDE & CULTURE

- We treat each other with respect.
- We intend to develop personal relationships to enhance trust and open communication.
- We value constructive feedback. We will avoid being defensive and give feedback in a constructive manner.
- We strive to recognize and celebrate individual and team accomplishments.
- As team members, we will pitch in to help where necessary to help solve problems and catch up on behind schedule work.

## TEAM MEETINGS

- We will hold a regular weekly meeting on _____.
- Additional meetings can be scheduled to discuss critical issues or tabled items upon discussion and agreement with the team leader.
- All team members are expected to attend team meetings in person or via video connection unless they are out of town, on vacation or sick. If a team member is unavailable, he or she should have a designated, empowered representative (another team member, a representative from their functional organization, etc.) attend in their place.
- The team leader can cancel or reschedule a team meeting if sufficient team members are unavailable or there is insufficient subject matter to meet about.

- The team leader will publish and distribute an agenda by email by 12 p.m. each Monday. Team members are responsible for contacting the team leader or leaving a voice message or email with any agenda items they want to include by _____. Agenda items can be added at the meeting with the concurrence of the team.
- Meetings will start promptly. All members are expected to be on-time. If, for extenuating circumstances a member is late, he/she will need to catch up on their own.
- An action-item list with responsibilities will be maintained, reviewed in meetings, and distributed with the meeting minutes.
- No responsibilities will be assigned unless the person to be assigned the responsibility accepts it. If a person to be given a responsibility is not able to attend the meeting, the team leader must review that assignment or action item with the person before the responsibility is designated.
- The responsibility for taking and distributing meeting minutes will rotate monthly among core team members.
- Meeting minutes will be distributed within __ hours after the meeting.
- We will emphasize full discussion and resolution of issues versus sticking to a timetable

Figure 16 (Operating guidelines for teams, from MIT)

Figure 17 (Line of Sight process)

| Element | Tactic | Expense | Resources | Time | Sequence | Launch |
|---|---|---|---|---|---|---|
| **R**espect | Guidelines for respect | $ | ♟ | ⏱ | 7 | Immed |
| | Recognition and celebration program | $$ | ♟♟ | ⏱⏱ | 8 | Q3 |
| | Exercise facility | $$ | ♟♟ | ⏱⏱ | 16 | Q4 |
| **E**very Leader Buys In | Review elements and tactics with leaders | $ | ♟ | ⏱ | 2 | Immed |
| | Leader develop dept implementation plan and post | $ | ♟ | ⏱ | 3 | Immed |
| | Track progress through Gallup Q12 survey twice/year | $$ | ♟♟ | ⏱ | 1 | Immed |
| **S**trong Relationships | The Five Languages of Appreciation in the Workplace | $$ | ♟♟ | ⏱⏱ | 18 | Q1-NY |
| | Company-organized outside activities | $ | ♟ | ⏱ | 11 | Q3 |
| | Companywide communications training | $$$$ | ♟♟ | ⏱⏱ | 19 | Q1-NY |
| **P**urposeful Teams | Each employee clarifies teams/roles | $ | ♟ | ⏱ | 10 | Q3 |
| | Develop guidelines for setting up and operating teams | $ | ♟ | ⏱ | 9 | Q3 |
| | Each dept conducts two interdepartmental meetings | $$ | ♟ | ⏱⏱⏱ | 17 | Q4 |
| **E**mployee Engagement | Develop an individual daily plan and scorecard | $ | ♟♟ | ⏱⏱ | 12 | Q3 |
| | Organized internal activities | $$$ | ♟♟ | ⏱⏱ | 15 | Q4 |
| | Leaders touch base with every employee daily | $ | ♟♟ | ⏱ | 13 | Q3 |
| **C**ontinuous Improvement | Develop and implement strategy deployment process | $$ | ♟♟♟ | ⏱⏱⏱ | 14 | Q3 |
| | Implement A3 problem-solving tool | $$ | ♟♟♟ | ⏱⏱⏱ | 21 | Q2-NY |
| | Conduct a rattlesnake hunt | $$ | ♟♟♟ | ⏱⏱ | 20 | Q2-NY |
| **T**ransparent Communications | Quarterly all-employee update | $ | ♟♟ | ⏱ | 4 | Immed |
| | Monthly functional reviews in off months | $ | ♟♟ | ⏱ | 5 | Immed |
| | Weekly departmental check-ins | $ | ♟♟ | ⏱ | 6 | Immed |

Figures 18 and 20 (Twenty-one tactics by element, measurements, sequence, and timing)

| TACTICS | PRIORITY | IMMED | Q3 | Q4 | Q1-NY | Q2-NY |
|---|---|---|---|---|---|---|
| Track progress through Gallup Q12 survey twice/year | 1 | X | | | | |
| Review elements and tactics with leaders | 2 | X | | | | |
| Leader develop dept implementation plan and post | 3 | X | | | | |
| Quarterly all-employee update | 4 | X | | | | |
| Monthly functional reviews in off months | 5 | X | | | | |
| Weekly departmental check-ins | 6 | X | | | | |
| Guidelines for respect | 7 | X | | | | |
| Recognition and celebration program | 8 | | X | | | |
| Develop guidelines for setting up and operating teams | 9 | | X | | | |
| Each employee clarifies teams/roles | 10 | | X | | | |
| Company-organized outside activities | 11 | | X | | | |
| Develop an individual daily plan and scorecard | 12 | | X | | | |
| Leaders touch base with every employee daily | 13 | | X | | | |
| Develop and implement strategy deployment process | 14 | | X | | | |
| Organized internal activities | 15 | | | X | | |
| Exercise facility | 16 | | | X | | |
| Each dept conducts two interdepartmental meetings | 17 | | | X | | |
| The Five Languages of Appreciation in the Workplace | 18 | | | | X | |
| Companywide communications training | 19 | | | | X | |
| Implement A3 problem-solving tool | 20 | | | | X | |
| Conduct a rattlesnake hunt | 21 | | | | | X |

Figures 19 and 21 (Twenty-one tactics by priority and implementation schedule)

| Organizational Capacity for Change (OCC) | John Kotter's Eight Step Change Model |
|---|---|
| *People:* | |
| 1. Trustworthy Leaders | 1. Create a sense of urgency |
| 2. Trustworthy Followers | 2. Build a guiding coalition |
| 3. Capable Champions | 3. Form a strategic vision and initiatives |
| 4. Involved Middle Management | 4. Enlist a voluntary army |
| *Structural:* | 5. Enable action by removing barriers |
| 5. Systems Thinking | 6. Generate short-term wins |
| 6. Communications Systems | 7. Sustain acceleration |
| 7. Accountable Culture | 8. Insitute change |
| 8. Innovative Culture | |

Figure 22 (Comparison of change management approaches)

Figure 24 (Seven elements)

# REFERENCES

Wolf DB, Sisodia R, Sheth J, 2007, *Firms of Endearment,* Second Edition, Wharton School Publishing

Collins J, 2001, *Good to Great,* First Edition, HarperCollins Publishers

Chapman B, Sisodia R, 2015, *Everybody Matters,* First Edition, Penguin Random House LLC

Gallup, 2015, *The State of the American Manager: Analytics and Advice for Leaders*

Chapman G, White P, 2019, *The Five Languages of Appreciation in the Workplace,* Third Edition, Northfield Publishing

Harter J, 2022, *U.S Employee Engagement Slump Continues,* Workplace

Akers P, 2016, *Two Second Lean: How to Grow People and Build a Fun Lean Culture,* Third Edition

Warren R, 2002, *The Purpose Driven Life: What on Earth am I Here For?,* Tenth Edition, Zondervan Publishing

Herrity J, 2021, *12 Reasons Why Teamwork Is Important in the Workplace,* Indeed

Lencioni P, 2002, *The Five Dysfunctions of a Team: A Leadership Fable,* First Edition, Jossey-Bass

Hamilton K, Sandhu R, Hamill L, 2019, *The Science of Care,* Limeade

Higgs M, Rowland D, 2005, *All Changes Great And Small: Exploring Approaches to Change And Its Leadership,* Journal of Change Management

Boyle M, Goodwin K, Higgs M, 2021, *Using Teams to Facilitate Organizational Development,* First Edition, Creative Commons Attribution – NonCommercial – ShareAlike 4.0 International License

Maxwell J, 2019, *The 25-50-25 Principle of Change*

Kotter J, 2012, *Leading Change,* 1R Edition, Harvard Business Review Press

LaClair J, Rao R, 2002, *Helping employees embrace change*, McKinsey Quarterly

**Credits:**
Illustrations and infographics: Meghna Kamboj

# ABOUT THE AUTHOR

As a coach, a writer, and a speaker, George Saiz actively promotes enterprise excellence through a people-centric culture to the next generation of leaders.

In this business novel, he shares from his executive experience in the medical device industry and the many best-practices sites he visited as president and CEO of the Association for Manufacturing Excellence. He is retired and currently resides with his wife in Carlsbad, California.

CPSIA information can be obtained
at www.ICGtesting.com
Printed in the USA
LVHW050545140623
749670LV00002B/5